GREENS FOR A BETTER EUROPE

TWENTY YEARS OF UK GREEN INFLUENCE IN THE EUROPEAN PARLIAMENT, 1999–2019

EDITED BY LIAM WARD WITH JAMES BRADY

LONDON PUBLISHING PARTNERSHIP

Published by London Publishing Partnership
www.londonpublishingpartnership.co.uk

ISBN: 978-1-907994-88-3 (paperback)

ISBN: 978-1-907994-89-0 (ePDF)

ISBN: 978-1-907994-90-6 (ePub)

A catalogue record for this book is available from the British Library

This book has been composed in Adobe Garamond Pro

Copy-edited and typeset by T&T Productions Ltd, London
www.tandtproductions.com

Cover design by Minute Works

CONTENTS

BIOGRAPHIES   vii

PREFACE BY TONY JUNIPER   xiii

Part I Setting the scene: history and context

1. Green parties and elections to the European Parliament, 1979–2019   3

Wolfgang Rüdig

2. Proportional representation and Britain's democratic deficit   49

Klina Jordan and Owen Winter

Part II The UK's Green MEPs: in their own words

3. London, Brussels and beyond: my work as a Green MEP   83

Jean Lambert

4. From Brussels to Westminster: how corporate power captured politics   115

Caroline Lucas

5. Changes   133

Keith Taylor

Part III The UK's Green MEPs: perspectives from friends

6. Greens and campaigners: a natural affinity   165

Natalie Bennett

7. Powerhouse parliamentarians: how Greens made
friends and influenced policy   183
Samir Jeraj

Part IV Brexit and beyond: solidarity for the future

8. Stronger In? The logic of pan-European co-operation in
the era of Trump and climate change   207
Molly Scott Cato

9. European Greens: a global vision?   227
Reinhard Bütikofer

INDEX   237
ACKNOWLEDGEMENTS   249

GREENS FOR A BETTER EUROPE

BIOGRAPHIES

About the authors

Natalie Bennett was born in Australia, where she began her working life as a journalist, after studying agriculture at the University of Sydney. She has lived on three continents, having spent four years in Bangkok, half of which saw her working as a volunteer for the National Commission on Women's Affairs. Natalie was also involved in UN consulting on women's and children's issues. However, she was always going to head back to the UK (having visited first as a backpacker in 1990). So, after settling in England, she fostered a career in British national newspapers, working for *The Telegraph*, *The Times*, the *Independent* and finally as editor of *The Guardian Weekly* for five years. Natalie joined the Green Party in 2006 and was leader of the Green Party of England and Wales from 2012 to 2016. After serving two terms as leader, she has continued in full-time politics as former leader, focusing particularly on the North and Midlands of England, on issues including universal basic income, fracking and making the UK a democracy. In 2017 she was the Green Party general election candidate for Sheffield Central, where she now lives.

Reinhard Bütikofer is an MEP (Greens/EFA) and the co-chair of the European Green Party (EGP). He sits on the Committee on Industry, Research and Energy (ITRE) as a full member, and on the Committee on Foreign Affairs (AFET) as a substitute member. He is the vice-chair of the European Parliament's Delegation for relations with the People's Republic of China as well as a member of the Delegation to the United States and a substitute member of the ASEAN delegation. Before being elected to the European Parliament in 2009, Mr Bütikofer was the co-chair of the German Green Party, *Bündnis 90/Die Grünen* (Alliance 90/The Greens), from 2002 until 2008. He was the party's secretary general from 1998 until 2002. Prior to that he served as the chair of the Greens in the Federal State of Baden-Württemberg. From 1988 until 1996 he served as a member of the Baden-Württemberg State Parliament. His engagement with the German Greens began when he was elected as a member of the city council in Heidelberg in 1984.

Samir Jeraj is a freelance journalist and author. From 2008 to 2012 he served as a Green Party councillor in Norwich. He has written extensively on housing issues and social affairs in the UK. In this capacity, he served as Keith Taylor's researcher on his reports on the growth of foodbanks and other types of emergency food aid in the South East of England. Samir co-authored *The Rent Trap: How We Fell Into It and How We Get Out of It* (Pluto Press, 2016), a book about private rented housing.

Klina Jordan co-founded and facilitates Make Votes Matter, the UK movement for proportional representation. A lifelong activist, Klina's dedication to environmental and social meliorism has led to a focus on systemic change to enable progress: working to get the basic building blocks of democracy into place. She has diverse expertise from a 20-year career including events, marketing, business development, management and sustainable enterprise. She uses that experience to lead a positive and practical movement for real democracy, including a growing alliance of parties, organisations and public figures, dozens of local campaign groups and tens of thousands of activists.

Tony Juniper CBE is a long-serving British environmentalist. He has worked with many environment and conservation organisations, including as executive director of Friends of the Earth and as president of the Royal Society of Wildlife Trusts. He has worked as an environment advisor to The Prince of Wales and as a fellow with the University of Cambridge Institute for Sustainability Leadership. He is the author of many ecologically themed books, including the multi-award-winning best seller *What Has Nature Ever Done for Us?* (Synergetic Press, 2013). Tony was the Green Party candidate for the Cambridge constituency in the 2010 general election.

Jean Lambert has been London's Green Party MEP since 1999 and a member of the Green Party since its early days. She has been a long-standing member of the European Parliament's Committees on Employment and Social Affairs, and Civil Liberties, Justice and Home Affairs; the chair of its official Delegation for relations with South Asia; and the co-president of its anti-racism intergroup, among others. She has participated in EU election observation missions in Africa and Asia. Jean is a winner of *The Parliament Magazine*'s award for human rights work, and she is a patron of human rights theatre company ice&fire. A passionate internationalist, Jean co-chaired the Green Party's *Greens for Europe* campaign during the EU referendum, and she is the party's national migration spokesperson. Jean was a teacher in East London before becoming a Green MEP.

Caroline Lucas was first elected as MP for Brighton Pavilion in 2010. She served as leader of the Green Party of England and Wales from 2008 to 2012, and co-leader from 2016 to 2018. From 1999 to 2010 she was one of the party's first MEPs and represented the South East region until becoming the UK's first Green MP. Caroline holds numerous senior positions in parliamentary groups, such as chair of the all-party parliamentary groups (APPGs) on climate change and limits to growth; deputy chair of the APPG on renewable and sustainable energy; and vice chair of the APPGs on better Brexit for young people, drug policy reform, European citizenship rights, proportional representation, refugees, and sixth form colleges, among others. She also sits on the UK parliament's influential Environmental Audit Committee and has sat on temporary committees set up to scrutinise British government legislation. Caroline's book, *Honourable Friends? Parliament and the Fight for Change* (Portobello Books, 2015) details her first parliamentary term as a fresh, Green voice before the House of Commons. She has also co-edited a book on cross-party working: *The Alternative: Towards a New Progressive Politics* (Biteback Publishing, 2016).

Wolfgang Rüdig is a Reader in Politics at the University of Strathclyde, Glasgow, Scotland. He has been researching green parties since the early 1980s, with a particular focus on green party members. His latest book is *Ecological Political Parties: The European Experience and the Greek Dimension* (The Green Institute, 2016: in Greek, co-edited with Iosif Botetzagias). Most recently, he has been organising a new wave of the European Green Party Membership Survey: www.egpm.eu.

Molly Scott Cato was elected as Green MEP for South West England and Gibraltar in 2014. She is a member of the European Parliament's economics and monetary policy and agricultural and rural affairs committees. She has played a leading role in the Green Group's work on tax justice and was the parliament's rapporteur for sustainable finance. After the EU referendum in June 2016, Molly became the Brexit speaker for the Green Party of England and Wales, and continued to be the party's speaker on finance. Before being elected as an MEP, Molly was professor of green economics at Roehampton University. She has published widely on issues concerned with co-operatives and socially managed firms as well as environmental, financial and bioregional economics. She has been a Green Party member since 1988 and led the Green Group on Stroud District Council from 2011 to 2014.

Keith Taylor is the Green Party's former principal spokesperson, the former leader of the Brighton & Hove Green Group, and now the party's MEP for the South East of England and its spokesperson on animal rights issues. Keith entered politics in his mid-40s and has never conformed to the (somewhat unfair) green party 'bookish academic' stereotype. From the council chambers to the European Parliament, Keith has prided himself on being down-to-earth and always focused on the changes for the better he can make for his constituents. He has served voters and the Green Party for more than 20 years as an elected representative. Keith is also a big fan of David Bowie.

Owen Winter became involved with the electoral reform movement at age 16, when he started a petition for a fairer voting system around the time of the 2015 general election. This petition has received almost 300,000 signatures and was handed to Prime Minister David Cameron as part of the half-a-million-strong collection of signatures after the election. Since then, Owen has co-founded Make Votes Matter and is the group's official spokesperson. In 2016 he was named by Nesta and *The Observer* as one to watch in their list of 'New Radicals' for innovative campaigns. When he's not making votes matter, Owen is usually revising for exams. Since starting his petition, Owen has sat his GCSEs, AS Levels and A-levels. He now studies History and Politics at Jesus College, Oxford.

About the editors

James Brady is an interdisciplinary artist and publisher, whose creative practice embraces a synergy of art, ecology and activism. In 2014 he founded Gaia Project, an independent publishing and curatorial initiative. James is an associate of both the CIWEM Arts & Environment Network and the international ecoartnetwork. Over the years, his diverse project partners have included the Green Party, Environment Agency, Liverpool Biennial, Manchester University and the Society for Ecological Restoration. James is the editor and publisher of *Elemental: An Arts and Ecology Reader* (Gaia Project, 2016). He has been an active member of the Green Party for over a decade, and in 2013 he was guest editor of the arts and ecology special issue of *Green World* magazine (GW79).

Liam Ward has worked in communications and marketing for almost a decade, having started his career as a band and gig promoter. After graduating from the University of Leeds with a degree in broadcast journalism, Liam worked as a digital and investigative journalist with the BBC in Yorkshire. A keen political and environmental activist, he has worked with Keith Taylor as his press officer since 2016.

PREFACE

Collective action for our common future
Tony Juniper CBE

Of all our senses, it is smell that most powerfully jogs memory: a single whiff connecting distant times to the present day. For me, there is one particular aroma that conjures vivid recollections of the faraway summer of 1973, when, aged 12, I went on a family holiday to Cornwall. I have many memories from that trip, including from a day when I bobbed about in the surf by the mouth of a little river on Porth Beach near Newquay. A pungent smell came from the water, and although I didn't know what it was, my grandmother, who was collecting mussels from the rocks nearby, soon found out. That evening, back at our holiday home, she cooked her newly harvested shellfish and became violently sick after eating them. That smell was raw sewage: she'd been poisoned.

Back then, it was perfectly legal to discharge minimally treated human waste into the sea, a practice which only stopped after the 1975 referendum that confirmed British membership of the European Economic Community (EEC). Today, we regard clean bathing water as the norm and tend to take for granted the many other environmental benefits that accompanied our membership of the EEC, and later the European Union (EU).

As a result of rules negotiated with European partners, we have enjoyed elevated standards in relation to pollution control, waste disposal and recycling; there is stronger regulation of chemicals and dangerous substances; wildlife protection is tighter; and, more recently, there has been European-level action on climate change. The tangible changes that have followed these European policies and laws are quite striking.

For example, back in 1995 around 83% of municipal waste generated in the UK was still being landfilled, but because of the rules we chose to adopt with European partners, by 2011 this had fallen to 49%. Despite continuing air quality challenges, EU legislation was the principal driver of improvements made between 1990 and 2001 that led to the avoidance of 4,200 premature UK deaths per year.

When the UK joined the EU, so-called acid rain was a huge environmental problem. This was largely addressed in the UK through EU rules that by 2011 had resulted in a 94% reduction in sulphur dioxide emissions and a cut of 61% in emissions of nitrogen oxides. For wildlife, too, the EU has been very good news. For example, a review of the effects of the Birds Directive shows that on average the more land that is protected with EU rules, the more likely it is that bird populations will increase.

National targets adopted under the Renewable Energy Directive have led to a dramatic increase in renewable energy capacity throughout the EU. Between 2000 and 2012 more than half of the EU's new power capacity was renewable, with a growth of nearly 97 GW in wind power and 69 GW in solar photovoltaics.[1]

These and many other specific achievements in EU member states have also contributed to wider positive outcomes. The latter may be seen in the extent to which some environmental challenges can only be solved by collective action, eg the air pollution that drifts over national borders; the ocean pollution that travels to distant beaches; and the migratory wildlife that knows no national affiliation, and which can only be conserved by countries acting together.

Of course, some environmental challenges can only be addressed through actions that reach far beyond even the borders of the EU. Climate change, for example, requires global action and the agreement of co-ordinated steps. During the last two decades, the political breakthroughs needed to deal with this complex challenge have been rendered more achievable as a result of EU leadership, and via European countries negotiating international treaties as a powerful unified block rather than individually.

The EU's collective influence has also spread via markets, including as a result of the standards established for consumer goods, which require manufacturers across the world to raise their environmental performance in order to export to the EU: the world's biggest single market area. This is one reason why the EU's environmental regime is not only the most developed in the world, but also the most influential.

By creating a common sense of direction, the EU has also made it possible for European countries to share technical resources, thereby avoiding duplication, cutting costs, harnessing economies of scale and generally making it more efficient to do things better. And while some critics of Europe's unified approach have claimed the 'dead hand of regulation' has held back competitiveness and opportunity, there is a powerful body of evidence that shows the exact opposite.

For example, regulations on air quality and carbon emissions have driven innovation, including in the automotive industry, giving the UK a competitive edge and creating jobs. On top of this, member states have ensured such regulations include considerable flexibility so that national circumstances might shape implementation in different countries, enabling the adaptation of approaches to suit particular cultures, politics and practices.

Politicians across the spectrum have made all of this possible, from those in national assemblies and governments to the Members of the European Parliament (MEPs). In the vanguard working on policies to protect people and the planet were Greens, including British ones. Britain's Green MEPs – Caroline Lucas, Jean Lambert, Keith Taylor and Molly Scott-Cato – all played important roles in promoting and maintaining the EU's commitments to the environment as well as in addressing the social and economic questions that are so deeply entwined with and inseparable from environmental ones.

This book documents and celebrates these MEPs' contributions and achievements during a period that saw progress across a wide range of environmental and related policy agendas, from trade and energy to agriculture, and from public health to the conservation of tropical rainforests. They also had positive impacts on a variety of animal welfare and social justice questions, lobbied for the rights of asylum seekers and refugees, and championed civil liberties and the interests of LGBT people. Everyone living in modern Britain will have been touched by the causes they campaigned for and will now, of course, be affected by the consequences of the vote to leave the EU.

When it comes to that momentous decision, the only thing that can be said with certainty is that no-one really knows what is going to happen. The vast body of EU law pertaining to environmental and social questions will be brought across into UK statutes, but whether these laws will stay in place or keep up with new EU-level standards and objectives remains to be seen, as does the extent to which they will be upheld given the withdrawal from European institutions that hitherto enforced such codes in Britain.

One thing that is more clear, however, is that the issues our Green MEPs campaigned for in the EU are not going away. Climate change, ecosystem damage, resource depletion, pollution and the fundamentally related social and ethical issues that come with these are, if anything, becoming more prominent.

The big question is how our society and its political institutions are going to deal with them. Will we set aside these pressing subjects for later, focusing instead on short-term growth and competitiveness and leaving our children and grandchildren to deal with the consequences? Or will we show the vision, foresight and leadership that befit the times in which we find ourselves? The answer to this will in part be written in the continuing story of the Greens and the extent to which Green political ideas inspire and influence the kinds of discussions in the UK that over the last four decades have made the EU such a leading voice on the global stage.

As a former candidate for the Green Party in the Cambridge constituency during the 2010 UK general election, I can say with confidence that the power of Greens and their ideas in politics have never been more essential in shaping debates and policies even where

Greens are not directly elected. It will be that continuing influence, presence and trusted voice that help to determine whether Britain steps up to that leadership challenge or steps down into the kind of low-standards, free-trade zone advocated by some of those who said we should leave the EU. Which way policy heads in future is yet to be seen, and will no doubt be the subject of future books.

In the meantime, read on, take stock of the inspiration, determination and passion that shaped our recent past, and from this draw the energy needed to direct our common future.

Endnotes

1   All figures relating to the benefits arising from UK membership of the EU can be found in 'Report on the influence of EU policies on the environment', produced by the Institute of European Environmental Policy (IEEP) on behalf of the World Wide Fund for Nature (WWF), the Royal Society for the Protection of Birds (RSPB), the Wildlife Trusts and Friends of the Earth. URL: https://bit.ly/2Qj1TXm.

Part I

Setting the scene: history and context

Chapter 1

Green parties and elections to the European Parliament, 1979–2019

Wolfgang Rüdig

Introduction

The history of green parties in Europe is closely intertwined with the history of elections to the European Parliament. When the first direct elections to the European Parliament took place in June 1979, the development of green parties in Europe was still in its infancy. Only in Belgium and the UK had green parties been formed that took part in these elections; but ecological lists, which were the predecessors of green parties, competed in other countries. Despite not winning representation, the German Greens were particularly influenced by the 1979 European elections. Five years later, most participating countries had seen the formation of national green parties, and the first Green MEPs from Belgium and Germany were elected.

Green parties have been represented continuously in the European Parliament since 1984. Subsequent years saw Greens from many other countries joining their Belgian and German colleagues in the European Parliament. European elections continued to be important for party formation in new EU member countries. In the 1980s it was the South European countries (Greece, Portugal and Spain), following their successful transition to democracies, that became members. Green parties did not have a strong role in their national party systems, and European elections became an important focus for party development. In the 1990s it was the turn of Austria, Finland and Sweden to join; green parties were already well established in all three nations and provided ongoing support for Greens in the European Parliament. The third major addition came in the 2000s, when East-Central European countries (as well as Malta and Cyprus) took part in European elections for the first time. This provided more of a challenge for the European Greens, who were keen to establish a strong presence in these new member countries. Despite the strong role played by Greens in the transition to democracy of the late 1980s and early 1990s, green parties had faded away in most countries, with the European focus becoming a major element in efforts to revive green politics.

European elections were also of major importance for well-established parties in Western Europe. Green parties have tended to do better in European than in national elections, in many cases benefitting from the unpopularity of national government parties. Thus, European elections often provided a welcome spur to the standing of green parties in national politics. Such a boost was particularly important in countries where the electoral system used in European elections provided Greens with a better opportunity to win representation than in national elections. This, at first, applied especially to France, where a proportional representation system was used from the start (as opposed to the majority voting system used at national elections). France was joined by the UK when the first-past-the-post system employed from 1979 to 1994 was replaced by a proportional representation system in 1999. However, there are also cases of opportunities in European elections being worse than in national elections. This applies to small European countries, who are only allocated a small number of MEPs, meaning that the electoral thresholds for winning representation are higher in European than in national elections. The Netherlands – a country in which European elections majorly influenced the formation of its green parties – is one such case.

Finally, the co-operation of green parties in Europe has also been greatly influenced by European elections and the presence of Green

MEPs. Starting with the first informal attempts to coordinate green efforts in 1979, this partnership eventually led to the formation of the European Green Party (EGP) in 2004. Membership of the EGP became a major aspiration in many countries, particularly new EU member states.

With a five-year cycle of European elections, the last 40 years have seen eight parliamentary sessions, with Greens represented in seven of them. Each election and each parliament has its own distinctive features. The first decade was perhaps the most important for European green politics, with major progress in green party formation being made between the 1979 and 1984 elections. Environmental and peace issues were very high on the political agenda in that decade and provided a strong basis for party growth. The second decade of European Parliaments (1989–99) may be seen as a period of further consolidation. By 1989 the formation of green parties had essentially been completed in most countries throughout Western Europe, although there were some important exceptions (eg France). Most of the green parties that competed in the 1989 European elections still represent green politics in their home countries today. The late 1990s also saw the first entries of green parties into government at a national level (in Belgium, Finland, France, Germany and Italy), which resulted in the 1999 elections being fought by these parties as government rather than opposition parties for the first time, with some but not all experiencing losses. The third decade (1999–2009) saw the entry of new member countries from East-Central Europe. Efforts to boost green parties in these new member states proved difficult, and it was 2014 before the first MEPs from Eastern Europe (from Hungary and Croatia) were elected. The fourth decade (2009–19) brought with it new challenges in the form of a major economic crisis, with several countries facing extremely harsh austerity policies, as well as the rise of right-wing parties with euro-sceptic and anti-immigration policies. Green parties did particularly well in 2009 but less so in 2014. The unpopularity of national governments was a major factor bolstering green votes, particularly in 2009, while green parties that were part of national coalition governments faced more difficult elections.

The overall results of green parties in European elections are documented in the appendix at the end of this chapter. The figures show the strength of green parties in Northern Europe, in the low countries (Belgium, the Netherlands and Luxembourg), and in Germany and Austria. In addition, the UK has shown consistent support for the Greens since 1989. The picture is more patchy in Ireland and particularly unstable in France. Southern European countries are also a mixed bag in this respect. The Italian Greens started quite well but have struggled in recent years; Greens in Greece and Portugal have been represented in some parliaments, and consistently in Spain since 2004, but their share of the vote is generally well below that achieved in Northern Europe. Even more difficult is the situation for green parties in East-Central Europe, with only Croatia and Hungary sending Green MEPs to Brussels.

There is a fairly large body of literature on green parties in Europe,[1] which also includes analyses of their performance in European elections.[2] What are the key contributions that elections to the European Parliament have made to these parties' development? In the rest of this chapter, I will try to highlight some key aspects that have helped, or hindered, the development of green parties in Europe.

Helping the establishment of green parties, 1979–89

The introduction of direct elections to the European Parliament in 1979 could not have come at a better time for green parties. The 1970s had seen the emergence of strong environmental and anti-nuclear (energy) movements through much of Western Europe. Limited opportunities to influence governments, particularly on the nuclear issue, had been a major impetus for these movements to enter the electoral arena. In countries where the anti-nuclear movement had provided the main focus, such as France and Germany, there was a strong reluctance to embrace what was seen as joining the establishment by forming a political party. In France, ad hoc electoral lists had formed to take part in parliamentary and presidential elections beginning in 1974. In

Germany, electoral and party law made the formation of a political party a virtual necessity. With various parties and lists having taken part in local and regional elections since 1977, the 1979 European elections provided an opportunity to take a step towards an intermediate form of organisation: unlike in federal elections, so-called other political organisations not constituted as parties were allowed to participate at a national level. This provided Petra Kelly and others with the chance to bring together a wide range of groups to join the 'Other Political Organisation: The Greens' and participate in the European elections of June 1979. This predecessor of the modern-day Greens, which was formally constituted as a party in January 1980, failed to win any seats in the European Parliament but gained an unexpected bonus via the generous German system of funding political parties based on electoral results. Polling 3.2% of the vote qualified this new political force to receive public funding of 4.8 million Deutschmarks. This financial windfall allowed the new party to be set up very quickly, with a national office and permanent staff. Two-thirds of the funds were passed on to regional parties, which further boosted the party's fortunes with a series of successes in land (state) elections.[3] These initial election successes at regional level were quickly followed by a breakthrough in the 1983 federal elections.

Objections to the idea of a green 'party' were much stronger in France, which meant the formation process took significantly longer there. The electoral system introduced for European elections in France was a proportional representation system with a national 5% threshold. This provided small parties with a much better chance of gaining representation than the system for national and subnational elections. The 1979 European elections followed the pattern of previous elections, with a list called Europe Ecology – which was set up specifically for the elections – taking part. Garnering 4.4.% of the vote, Europe Ecology narrowly missed the 5% threshold, but the potential for a successful green party had been established. The candidacy of Brice Lalonde in the 1981 presidential elections gave the Greens a further boost. Disappointment over what was seen by many as a betrayal of the Greens by new socialist president François Mitterrand led to a greater effort to organise electoral participation.

The 1984 European elections provided yet another major incentive. Various ecological groups agreed to form a party called The Greens in January 1984 to present a united front in the European elections. However, unity was not achieved: former presidential candidate Brice Lalonde failed to join The Greens and decided to field his own list. The green vote in the 1984 elections was thus split. A united green list would have passed the 5% threshold comfortably with 6.7%, but each separate party fell short. This lack of unity and splits between different groups plagued the French Greens for many years afterwards.

In Belgium, the Flemish Greens – known as Agalev – had emerged mainly from a left–Catholic movement with counter-cultural elements, which had been campaigning on environmental, peace and social justice issues since 1970. It started taking part in elections in 1977. Polling 2.3% in Flanders in 1979 established Agalev as the main green group in the Flemish-speaking part of Belgium. Greens in the French-speaking part of the country – Ecolo – initially struggled with competing groups, but the 1979 European elections provided an opportunity to unite all ecologist groups in Wallonia under the Ecolo heading, with the party polling 5.1%.[4] Following their participation in the 1979 elections, both parties entered the Belgian Federal Parliament in 1981 and grew steadily in the 1980s and 1990s.

In the UK, questions of party unity and links to social movements were not a major issue. The party had been formally set up as People in 1973: the first green party in Europe. After changing its name to The Ecology Party in 1975, it made its first major breakthrough in the 1979 general election, which took place just before the European elections in May. Having managed to field more than 50 candidates in order to qualify for the right to a 'party political broadcast', The Ecology Party succeeded in drawing wider public attention to its existence in the election campaign, and membership rose dramatically from fewer than 1,000 in 1978 to more than 5,000 in 1980. Unlike in Germany and France, the European elections did not provide a special opportunity to win representation. The financial cost of taking part in the elections was very high, with deposits to be paid by each candidate and no system of public funding for political parties in place, and the electoral system was extremely unfavourable. Contrary to the French model, the British system for European elections mirrored the system used for national elections, and MEPs in the UK were elected via the first-past-the-post system in single-member constituencies. This rendered the possibility of winning any seats a fairly remote one. The Ecology Party made barely a token effort to take part and contested just three out of 87 constituencies, winning the support of an average of 1% of voters. By 1984 the party was contesting 26 constituencies and achieving an average share of 2.6% of the vote: a small but significant improvement.

While there were relatively minor problems with recognising the ecological and green lists and parties in the UK, Belgium, France and Germany as genuine members of what was emerging as a new 'green party' family, such consolidation was more difficult for other parties in Europe. Even within these parties, there were different concepts as to what constituted a 'green' party. Some emphasised a strictly ecological identity, as was the dominant view in Belgium, France and the UK. Others, particularly the German Greens, favoured what might be called a left–libertarian view of green politics,[5] representing the broader new social movements and New Left politics that had emerged with the rise of the student movement in the 1960s.

Various New Left parties had managed to establish themselves in countries such as the Netherlands, Italy and Denmark well before the Greens had appeared on the scene and embraced an environmental and anti-nuclear agenda. When the fledgling green movement looked for possible partners for the 1979 European elections, the Dutch and Italian parties expressed their interest and became part of the first attempt to set up a European organisation to coordinate the development of green and 'alternative'/radical parties in Europe.[6]

In Italy, the Radical Party (originally formed in 1955) had in the 1970s campaigned on various left–libertarian issues, but it had also taken an active role in opposition to nuclear power. Under the charismatic leadership of Marco Pannella, the Radical Party had its best electoral result in the Italian general election of 1979, held just one week before the European elections, when it polled 3.5% and won 18 seats in the Chamber of Deputies. The party did slightly better in the European elections, polling 3.7% to elect three MEPs.

In the Netherlands, the Radical Party (or Political Party of Radicals, PPR) was formed in 1968 by a group of activists with a left-wing Catholic background. The party campaigned on left–libertarian, environmental and peace issues. As the Dutch electoral system makes it fairly easy for small parties to gain representation, with an effective threshold of just 0.67%, the PPR had no serious problems being elected to the Dutch Parliament: by the 1970s it had joined a centre–left government as a coalition partner. European elections provided more of a challenge. With only 25 seats in the European Parliament, parties had to win at least 4% of the vote to have a chance of gaining representation. The PPR only polled 1.7% in the 1979 European elections and thus fell far short of that target, as did other small left-wing parties such as the Pacifist Socialist Party (PSP).

Both the Italian and Dutch Radicals joined the Coordination of European Green and Radical Parties that was set up after the 1979 elections. However, the involvement of radical parties proved difficult. The Italian Radicals displayed little interest in building up any formal structure, preferring instead to concentrate on campaigns for individual issues. Their involvement proved to be short lived, and the party did not become a predecessor of green parties in Italy. In the Dutch case, the development was somewhat different. The idea of several left-wing parties co-operating had been discussed already in the 1970s, and the conditions for contesting European elections provided a further incentive. The political project that took shape in the run-up to the 1984 European elections was an electoral alliance between the PPR and two other small left-wing parties – the PSP mentioned above and the Communist Party of the Netherlands (CPN) – called the Green Progressive Accord (GPA). This was highly controversial; a rival party called The Greens was set up to compete with the GPA in the 1984 European elections (as the European Greens). Internationally, while the German Greens supported the GPA, other green parties favoured The Greens. However, The Greens only polled 1.3% and failed to win any seats, while the GPA won 5.6% of the vote, electing two MEPs. The split between the two parties was never resolved; the GPA became the predecessor of the GreenLeft party that was eventually founded in 1990 and accepted as a genuine Dutch green party.

Another case in which the presence of left–libertarian parties provided an obstacle to the development of green parties was Denmark. Here, several established parties – in particular the Left Socialists (VS), who had led the Danish anti-nuclear movement, and the Socialist People's Party (SP) – competed for green votes. A separate green party was formed in 1983 but failed to win enough support even to appear on the ballot paper.[7] The Greens never managed to take part in any European elections. Eventually, following a path similar to that of GreenLeft, the SP became part of the European green party family in the late 2000s. A number of other green parties had formed in the early 1980s in Sweden, the Republic of Ireland, Portugal and Spain. The 1984 European elections (including the 1987 elections taking place in the new member states of Portugal and Spain) saw green parties competing in eight out of 11 member states as well as the election of the first Green MEPs in Belgium and Germany, plus two MEPs from the GPA in the Netherlands.

Given the failure to integrate radical parties and the strong controversy regarding the situation in the Netherlands, the majority of green parties originally wanted to move ahead with a European organisation limited to green parties on a more exclusive basis. The founding members of the European Green Coordination in 1983 came from Belgium, France, the UK, the Republic of Ireland and Sweden: the German Greens were not included. However, the relative weakness of these parties, and the wish to include the German Greens – who continued to support the idea of including alternative and radical parties – eventually led to the need to form technical alliances. Within the European Parliament, green party MEPs became part of the Rainbow Group that includes MEPs from regional parties and anti-EU Danish MEPs. The Green–Alternative Europe Link (GRAEL) was set up as a subgroup: this included Belgian and German Green MEPs as well as MEPs from the Dutch GPA. As the 1980s progressed, the intensity of the conflict surrounding the

GPA finally receded, and the German Greens were admitted into the Coordination in 1987.

Growth and consolidation, 1989–99

The political conditions for green parties in the 1980s continued to be favourable. Following the boost that the peace movement of the early 1980s had provided to many green parties, the nuclear accident at Chernobyl in 1986 led to a revival of anti-nuclear protests in many Western European countries. The rise of global environmental issues – the threat of a hole in the ozone layer, detected in 1985, followed by increasing concerns about climate change – created a political agenda on which the environment was placed very highly, often for the first time. The 1989 European elections in many countries were thus predominantly fought on environmental issues, and green parties made further strides forward.

Green parties contested elections in ten out of 11 member states, with Denmark being the only country with no green party on the ballot paper. Among the three countries with green representation in the European Parliament in 1984, the Greens did particularly well in Belgium. The German Greens only narrowly improved on their result. In the Netherlands, the electoral alliance of left-wing parties again competed, this time under the label 'Rainbow', and marginally increased its support.

The big success stories were the UK and France. In the UK, the Green Party had the resources to use the European elections as an opportunity to raise its profile. For the first time, it was competing in all constituencies in the hope that a strong showing would help in national elections. The situation was extremely favourable for the Greens. Environmental issues had for the first time become very important, not least due to Prime Minister Margaret Thatcher's efforts to highlight the threat of climate change in 1988. Saturation media coverage of environmental issues, also the result of a series of environmental scandals following the privatisation of the water industry in England and Wales, contributed to this heightened public attention.

The Greens also benefitted from the crisis of the Liberal party, which had traditionally been the main establishment party campaigning on environmental issues. After the merger of the Liberals with the less environmentally friendly Social Democratic Party in 1988, the new Liberal Democrats party had not succeeded in establishing its identity. The Greens managed to win support from across the political spectrum, including from former Conservative supporters, and polled 14.5% in the UK. At the time, this was the highest share of the vote ever achieved by a green party in an election at the national level. However, despite this unprecedented electoral success, the first-past-the-post system meant that not a single Green MEP was elected. And while the party experienced a major surge in membership, it was unable to translate that into a breakthrough in the UK general election.[8]

In France, the Greens had finally overcome their divisions – at least temporarily – and presented only one green list in the European elections. With 10.6% of the vote and nine MEPs elected, the French Greens also had high hopes of translating their result into success at the national level. As concerns over nuclear power and climate change were less salient in France, it was increased disillusionment with the Socialist government that provided the major spur for the Greens. With Socialist voters seeking to send a message to President Mitterrand but reluctant to vote for a party on the right, the Greens were in a perfect position to win over Socialist protest voters. However, as in the UK, hopes of a European success being the starting point for a breakthrough at the national level were disappointed. With all green groups joining forces in the legislative elections of 1993, the opinion polls were at first extremely promising, raising Greens' hopes of winning representation in the National Assembly and potentially exerting influence on government formation. However, the bipolar French system provided a major obstacle to this. By presenting itself as neither a left- nor a right-wing party, the Greens suffered the same fate as many other efforts to overcome the left–right divide in the Fifth Republic; despite polling a record 7% in the first round, the Greens did not win a single seat.

The issue of competition from rival green parties and lists also plagued green politics in several other countries. In Italy, a number of local and regional green parties had been emerging since the early 1980s. The formation of a national party proved to be rather difficult. The Federation of Greens Lists was formed in 1986 and won seats in the Italian Chamber of Deputies in 1987. Shortly before the 1989 European elections, the Rainbow Greens was formed, mainly by former members of the Radicals and other left-wing parties. Both the Federation and the Rainbow Greens competed with each other. Given the Italian proportional representation system's very low effective threshold, both parties managed to elect MEPs with 3.8% and 2.4% of the vote, respectively. They soon afterwards merged to form the Federation of the Greens in 1990. However, any hopes for a major boost to the party have since been dashed, as the 1989 result (in terms of vote share) remains to this day the best achieved by Italian green parties in any national election.

Green parties also competed in the elections of other South European countries. In Greece, several small parties took part but did not come close to winning representation. The situation in Spain continued to be particularly complex, with a number of regional and national formations competing against one other. In Portugal, the Green Party continued to compete in elections as part of an electoral alliance with the Communist Party, and in 1989 had one MEP elected. This would prove to be the first and only occasion on which the Portuguese Greens were represented in the European Parliament.

While the potential green vote that could be mobilised in poorer South European countries was fairly low, the situation was completely different in the EU's most affluent member state: Luxembourg. Here, an alternative list had competed in the 1979 election and that contributed to the formation of the Green Alternative Party (GAP) in 1983, which almost immediately won two seats in the national parliament and also competed in the European elections, winning a creditable 6.1% of the votes. As Luxembourg (being a small country) only sent six MEPs to Brussels, this was not sufficient to win representation. Also, fractures emerged within the party, similar to those experienced in the Dutch case, between a left-wing faction and a rival group committed to a more ecological identity. This led to the formation of a new green party, the Green List Ecological

Initiative (GLEI), and both parties competed with each other in the 1989 European elections. While both had enough support to win representation in that year's national parliamentary election, neither party had an MEP elected. It was only once this split was overcome in the 1990s that the Luxembourg Greens started to be represented in the European Parliament as well.[9]

The 1989 elections were a major breakthrough for the Greens, who saw 28 MEPs elected that year. At a European level, the Greens were now strong enough to form their own parliamentary group, The Green Group, in the European Parliament; this had 31 members after two MEPs from small Italian parties and one Basque MEP were also admitted. In 1993, the European Federation of Green Parties was formed to improve the co-operation of green parties in Europe. Being admitted as a member of the Federation in subsequent years became an important stepping stone for aspiring green parties wanting to be recognised as genuine members of the green party family.

Based on a strong performance in the 1989 elections, there were high hopes that further progress would be made in the 1990s. The 1994 elections saw some successes, but these were marred by serious setbacks. The general context was slightly less favourable. Economic conditions had worsened in many countries in the early 1990s, and the saliency of environmental issues had faded somewhat since 1989. Also, setbacks at the national level had knock-on effects for European results. These particularly affected results in the UK and France, the big winners of 1989. The disappointed ambition of making a breakthrough in the national elections of 1992 and 1993, respectively, had deflated green enthusiasm. The French Greens were again facing the problem of rival lists competing. In a repeat of ten years earlier, the Greens were being challenged by a rival green party led by Brice Lalonde. Together, the parties managed to get 5%, but separately they ended up with no seats. The German Greens had their own national disaster in the first election of a newly unified Germany in 1990, when they failed to win any seats in West Germany. An all-German green party, called Alliance '90/The Greens, was formed in 1993, and the 1994 European elections constituted its first national electoral test. The Greens did very well, gaining 10.1%

of the vote: a clear sign that German voters were willing to support the new party, which a few months later entered the *Bundestag* again.

Other countries previously plagued by rivalries that showed signs of recovery were the Netherlands and Luxembourg. The Dutch left-wing parties that had formed electoral alliances in 1984 and 1989 finally agreed to merge into a new party, GreenLeft, in 1990. They comfortably won representation again, despite continued competition from the Greens, who again failed to make an impact. In Luxembourg, the split that emerged in 1984 had been healed, with both parties forming a joint list and electing their first Green MEP. Otherwise, the Irish Greens were the main newcomer, electing two MEPs for the first time.

A further boost to the Greens' fortunes was expected from green parties in Northern Europe, where Sweden and Finland had joined the EU together with Austria. Sweden and Finland had well-established green parties, and there had not been the divisions and splits experienced in other countries here. The Austrian Greens had gone through a period of rival lists in the 1980s, but this had been overcome. In elections taking place between 1995 and 1996, all three parties were successful in electing Green MEPs, with the Swedish result standing out as a new record: 17.2%. The Swedish Greens had mainly campaigned on an anti-EU platform and had attracted many anti-establishment voters protesting against the main parties of both the left and right that had brought Sweden into the EU. The Swedes' success was welcome, but it injected a stronger euro-sceptic note into the European Greens, opening up a major divide between enthusiastic pro-EU parties and those more sceptical about further European integration, such as the Danish and, to a lesser extent, the British Greens.[10]

The overall aim of the 1994 elections, despite taking place under more difficult circumstances, was to confirm the advances made in 1989. This was undoubtedly achieved. Greens by the mid-1990s had successfully established themselves in many party systems. As a result, green parties were soon increasingly considered as coalition partners in government. Starting with the Finnish Greens in 1995, green parties were to enter government in several major Western European countries, and the 1999 European elections were to be the first in which many green parties would fight as government rather than opposition parties.

Facing new challenges: government and East-Central Europe, 1999–2009

One explanation for the success green parties have been enjoying in European elections is the theory of 'second-order' elections.[11] As no government is elected in European elections and most voters do not expect the outcome to affect their lives, the elections could be viewed as a popularity contest. This would make it more likely that government parties would suffer losses, and voters might be more willing than in national parliamentary elections to cast their votes for smaller parties. As turnout is generally lower in European than in national elections, dedicated supporters of small parties might make more of an impact in this forum. The Greens could be seen as having benefitted from these conditions, attracting many voters who might otherwise have shunned giving their support to new and small parties in national elections.

With green parties becoming established and joining government coalitions at a national level in Finland, Italy, France, Germany and Belgium in the late 1990s,[12] the conditions for some green parties changed, making it more difficult for them to benefit from the second-order nature of European elections. The first test under these new conditions was faced by the Finnish Greens, who had entered national government in 1995 after polling 6.5% in the national election; the party improved on this result in the next European elections in Finland (1996), garnering 7.6% of the vote. The Finnish Greens continued their role in government after 1999 and, again, the party improved on its national parliamentary election result of 7.3%, achieved in March 1999, with a record result of 13.4% in the European election of June 1999. At least for the Finnish Greens, the theory of second-order elections does not seem to apply. Here, the Greens appear to have benefitted from the popularity of their lead candidate as well as misgivings about the record of the Greens' coalition partners.[13] In 2002, the Finnish Greens decided to leave the government after losing a parliamentary vote on the construction of a new nuclear power station. The 2004 European elections thus provided a test of whether the electorate approved of that decision – with 10.4% of the vote, the Greens did creditably well.

The second party to enter a national coalition government was the Italian Greens in 1996, as part of the left-wing Olive Tree coalition. Following a change in the electoral system in the early 1990s that limited the role of proportional representation, the Italian party system saw a right- and a left-wing bloc compete for power: the Greens became part of the latter. Their participation in government was, however, quite controversial. In particular, the party's support of North Atlantic Treaty Organization (NATO) action in Kosovo proved unpopular and led to the Greens only polling 1.3% in the 1999 European elections. The Greens' role in government came to an end in 2001, and their performance as an opposition party in the 2004 European elections did not constitute a major improvement, earning them just 2.5% of the vote.

The third green party to join the government was the French Greens. After a disappointing result in the 1993 legislative elections, there was a debate in the party over whether to abandon the policy of not becoming involved with either the right- or left-wing blocs that were competing for power. In 1995, the majority of members opted to seek an electoral alliance with the Socialist Party. Weakened by the legacy of the Mitterrand presidency, the Socialists agreed to form the so-called Plural Left, a partial electoral alliance of centre–left parties. The Plural Left won the legislative elections of 1997, and the Greens found themselves with not only representation in the National Assembly for the first time, but also an invitation straight into government. With the proportional electoral system used for European elections, the Greens could run on their own in 1999; they found the electorate appreciative of their decision, winning 9.7% of the vote and electing seven MEPs. After the Socialists lost the 2002 presidential and legislative elections, the Greens returned to opposition and polled 7.2% in the 2004 European elections.

So far, we have seen two cases in which green parties did quite well after entering government, and one in which the Greens fared less well. The two cases to which we now turn, Germany and Belgium, provide further contrasting experiences. The German Greens entered a coalition government with the Social Democrats in 1998. The party was caught in strong conflicts with its coalition partner; in particular, plans to phase out nuclear power and the decision for Germany to become involved in NATO action against Serbia were very controversial, causing severe frictions within the party. As a result, the German Greens lost voters in every election they stood for between 1998 and 2002. The 1999 result was a case in point, which saw them polling their worst result since 1979 (6.4%). After being re-elected in 2002, the Greens' fortunes improved. All major controversies had been resolved by then, and the green electorate appeared to support this less adversarial approach. The German Greens recovered to achieve a new record result, 11.9%, in 2004.

The Belgian Greens had the reverse experience. In the 1999 European elections they still fought as an opposition party, benefitting from various environmental scandals and cases of government incompetence to poll a record 16%. The federal elections were held on the same day, and with Agalev polling 11% and Ecolo 18.2%, the two green parties formed a coalition with the liberal and socialist parties. The experience of government was, however, less than positive. A combination of ministerial incompetence and divisions between the two green parties led to electoral disaster in 2003, with both parties suffering major losses and Agalev failing to win representation for the first time since 1981. The 2004 elections thus provided an indication of the extent to which both parties had recovered: the Greens had lost almost half of their voters from 1999 but still returned two MEPs with 8.7%.

Green parties without a background in government also had some mixed experiences. The GreenLeft in the Netherlands achieved its best ever result (11.9%), credited in part to the charistmatic leadership of Paul Rosenmöller. The Austrian Greens improved their result, while the Greens in Luxembourg maintained their position. The Swedish Greens could not repeat their sensational performance of 1994, but they still achieved a creditable result of just below 10%.

There was one important change in the UK that added to the number of Green MEPs elected. Following the election of a Labour government in 1997, the electoral law for European elections was changed to bring in a form of proportional representation. The country was divided into 12 regions, nine in England plus Scotland, Wales and Northern Ireland. The change did not affect Northern Ireland, which continued to elect MEPs by single transferable vote (STV). Proportionality was applied within each region, rather than nationally. The size of the constituencies – particularly in Southern England, where Greens could expect to do particularly well (with 11 and 10 seats available in the South East and London, respectively) – gave Greens the chance to have their first MEPs elected. Polling 7.7% in London and 7.4% in the South East was sufficient to elect the first two MEPs from the UK: Caroline Lucas and Jean Lambert.[14] The Green Party of England and Wales was represented continuously between 1999 and 2019.

Overall, 1999 was a good year for the Greens, with 38 MEPs elected: a new record. In the European Parliament, there was a change of organisation; this saw the Greens joining forces with the European Free Alliance (EFA), which consisted mainly of regional parties. The Greens–EFA mustered 48 MEPs and thus became the fourth largest group in the European Parliament. At the party level, the European Federation was replaced by the EGP in 2004.

Such a shift was timely and helped prepare the Greens for a major change to the shape of European politics: this came in the form of 12 new countries joining the EU, who took part in European elections for the first time in 2004 (2007 for Bulgaria and Romania). This proved to be a significant challenge for the Greens. The record of green parties in East-Central Europe had been quite promising during the transition phase from communism to liberal democracy. Green parties had been formed in several countries and in many had played an important role in their first democratically elected governments.[15] After these transitions were completed, however, most green parties disappeared rapidly from the political scene. The severe economic hardship experienced by Eastern Europe in the 1990s was a large contributor to this, changing the agenda completely and pushing environmental concerns into the background. In most countries, green parties had vanished as serious political contenders by the time of the EU accession in the early 2000s.

For Western green parties, who had welcomed the EU's enlargement with open arms, the prospect of finding partners in Eastern Europe in the early 2000s proved a daunting prospect. What remained of the green movements and parties of the transition phase was generally very weak but still sometimes regarded as politically problematical. Green activists of the 1980s often had backgrounds in the natural sciences and engineering, and their expertise in environmental matters was an important element of their success; however, this profile led them to appear as mere 'environmentalists' and unpolitical in Western eyes. Also, the green parties of Eastern Europe often did not share the libertarian–left agenda of Western green parties. Many were strongly in favour of the free market and embraced a neoliberal economic agenda. In some countries, environmental politics had become closely linked with nationalist movements and agendas. This jarred with the multicultural approach of Western Greens, in which the protection of minority rights plays a very important role. In other cases, green parties teamed up with communist successor parties, or were deemed to have become vehicles for the interests of 'oligarchs' or other established interests.

One of the green survivors of the transition phase were the Latvian Greens.[16] Their record was quite impressive, having maintained a role in government for many years (1993–8 and 2002–11). They were also the first green party to hold the post of prime minister: Indulis Emsis was head of an interim government from March to December 2004. In 1998 the Greens joined with the Latvian Farmers' Union to form the Union of Greens and Farmers (ZZS). After the ZZS had polled 9.5% in the 2002 national parliamentary elections, receiving a share of 4.3% in the European elections at the time of Emsis's premiership was rather disappointing. The ZZS failed to win representation. Other green parties that were founded during the transition phase still existed in Bulgaria and Romania, but with support below 1%, their role in European elections (held in 2007) remained very marginal.

The European Greens were more hopeful about green parties in Poland and the Czech Republic.[17] In Poland, a number of parties claiming to be green had existed in the early 1990s, but they had long since faded away. Environmental activists associated with the Solidarity movement became involved with the Freedom Union, which was in government in the 1990s before losing representation. With the support of the European Greens, a new party called Greens 2004 was formed in September 2003 to take part in the 2004 European elections. Greens 2004 also involved feminist activists; it was thus not narrowly environmental in its views, but displayed features akin to those found in post-materialist Western European green parties. The 2004 European elections proved to be a difficult beginning for the new party: it only managed to field candidates in three of the 13 European constituencies (Warsaw, Silesia and Lower Silesia), and its national result of just 0.27% was an obvious disappointment. The Greens persevered but ultimately failed to make an impact at local or parliamentary elections.

A green party existed in the Czech Republic in the early 1990s but had become discredited by claims of having links with the old communist regime. The Greens were revived just in time for the 2004 European elections by a range of environmental nongovernmental organisation (NGO) activists and intellectuals. While this relaunch brought the Greens back from complete obscurity, their 2004 European election result of 3.2% was disappointing. However, the party entered the national parliament in 2006 to join the Czech government as a coalition partner.

In other new member states, green parties participated in the elections as part of electoral alliances in Slovakia and Slovenia but failed to make a major impact. Greens in the Mediterranean states of Cyprus and Malta also failed to elect any MEPs. The Cyprus Greens were fairly small, polling less than 1%. The green party in Malta, the Alternative Democrats, formed in 1989 but had found it difficult to undercut the dominance of the two major parties, Labour and the Nationalist Party. Having polled between 1% and 2% in national elections, their

2004 result of 9.3% was a huge success for the party, although it was not sufficient for an MEP to be elected. A major factor in this outcome was the popularity of party leader Arnold Cassola, who had been very prominent in the campaign for EU membership.[18]

Another success in Southern Europe was the first election of Green MEPs from Spain: in both cases, green parties had formed joint lists with larger parties. The Confederation of the Greens formed an alliance with the Spanish Socialist Party (PSOE) and had one MEP elected. The Catalan ICV stood in an electoral alliance with the United Left (IU) and also had one MEP elected.

Overall, the 2004 European elections were a success for the Greens. These were the largest European elections thus far, involving 25 countries (with Bulgaria and Romania added in 2007). The Greens generally weathered this period of government involvement well, and the first MEPs were elected in Spain and the UK. However, the elections also revealed the problems being faced by those attempting to establish successful green parties in East-Central Europe.

Austerity and populism, 2009–19

The global financial crisis that emerged in 2008 had a profound effect on the politics of the following decade, with policies of economic austerity becoming dominant in many European countries. It was a struggle for environmental issues to stay visible in this context. The 2010s also saw the rise of populist right-wing parties campaigning on immigration issues and opposition to the EU as well as promoting scepticism about climate change and rolling back environmental regulation. Austerity and the emergence of the extreme right provided the major challenges to green politics during this time.

At the time of the 2009 European elections, the full nature of the crisis and its resultant policies of austerity were yet to unfold fully, but the elections were nonetheless dominated by the threat of serious economic and social problems. A further complication was that green parties in several countries had joined national coalition governments, and – unlike in the 1990s – often with centre-right coalition partners.

This placed some green parties in positions of accountability with regard to the economic crisis and its ensuing austerity measures.

An early sign of problems for green parties associated with the economic crisis was the result in the Republic of Ireland. The Greens had entered a government coalition with the conservative Fianna Fáil party in 2007.[19] The Republic of Ireland was hit very hard by the financial crisis, and severe measures including radical austerity policies were taken in 2008. While no direct responsibility for the financial crisis could possibly be attributed to the Greens, the party got caught up in public outrage over the policies adopted. The 2009 European elections were thus fought under a cloud of austerity. The party only fought two of the four constituencies and polled just 1.9%, losing representation in the European Parliament. Dramatic losses were also experienced in local elections on the same day. The Greens carried on in government until 2011, when they lost all representation in the Irish Parliament.

Another case where a green party in government was negatively affected by the economic crisis is Latvia. The country was very badly affected by the global economic crisis and adopted radical austerity policies. The 2009 European elections were a first electoral test for the government after the crisis. Shortly before the European elections, in March 2009 the government collapsed. The Greens did not play a role in this collapse, but in the prevailing economic climate it was more difficult for the party to gain a hearing for ecological issues. The ZZS polled just 3.7% and again failed to earn enough votes to win representation.

A further case of government participation having a negative effect on electoral performance is the Czech Republic. Here, the Greens had entered a national coalition government in 2006 under a new leader, Martin Bursík. He won the leadership in 2005 despite resistance from the group of environmental activists who had successfully relaunched the party in the early 2000s. Bursík had been a member of other parties before and was seen as a charismatic leader with the media experience to promote the party more effectively. The Greens entered the Czech Parliament for the first time in 2006 with 6.2% of the vote and formed a coalition with two conservative parties, but internal opposition to government participation became a major problem. Alongside concern over the neoliberal economic policies pursued by the government, opposition to Bursík's leadership tore the party apart. After two Green MPs were expelled from the party, the coalition collapsed in March 2009. Two rival parties were formed to compete with the Greens in the European elections of June 2009, but none of them came close to winning representation: the Greens only polled 2.1%, and did little better in the national elections of 2010.[20] The experience of participation in government on this occasion proved to have a negative effect on the party's development.

Looking at other cases of green parties entering the 2009 elections following a period in national office, the Italian Greens had entered government again in 2006 as part of another broad centre–left electoral alliance called The Union. However, that government was very unstable and had collapsed by 2008. In the subsequent parliamentary election, the Greens were excluded from the main left-wing alliance and had to join a group dominated by two communist parties (the Rainbow Left), but they failed to re-enter parliament. The Greens thus entered the 2009 European elections from a position of weakness: this had little to do with the work they had done in government but was a result of the division of the Italian left and its failure to create a viable alternative to the right. In 2009 the Greens joined an alliance of New Left parties called Left Ecology Freedom. Gaining 3.1% of the vote, the list failed to win the 4% necessary to guarantee representation.

A contrary example to these cases of governments having an adverse effect on electoral performance is provided by Finland. The Finnish Greens had re-entered government in 2007 in a coalition led by right-wing parties. The European election of 2009 was the first electoral test of the new government. Fielding two very strong candidates (Heidi Hautala and Satu Hassi), who had played a leading role in Finnish green politics, the Greens did very well, with a result of 12.4% electing two MEPs. Environmental issues played some role in the party's campaign and, as before, green voters were obviously not put off by the Greens' participation in government, even with conservative parties.

Looking at other countries, the pattern of previous years was essentially repeated in this period. In general, the green parties of East-Central Europe did not do particularly well, while the green parties of more affluent Northern Europe maintained their strong position. In Southern Europe, the share of the vote was, again, fairly low, but the Greek Greens had some success. Following devastating forest fires in 2007 and a wave of riots directed against the political establishment in 2008, the Greens briefly became a force to be reckoned with, and the first Greek Green MEP was elected with 3.5% of the vote.[21]

The one outstanding result of 2009 was achieved in France, which elected 14 Green MPs with 16.3% of the vote. This French case has some unusual features. The success had been achieved by a list called Europe Ecology,[22] which was the brainchild of Daniel Cohn-Bendit. After achieving fame as the leader of the 1968 student movement in Paris, he was forced to leave France and came to play an important role in the German Green party. After steering the French Greens to their 1999 European election success, Cohn-Bendit became leader of the Green parliamentary group in the European Parliament. He was re-elected in 2004 on the list of the German Greens but expressed his interest in returning to the French political scene in early 2008. At that time, the French Greens faced a major internal crisis, mainly stemming from renewed discussions about its relationship with the Socialist Party. In opposition since 2002, the Greens had refused to enter a new electoral alliance with the Socialists in the 2007 legislative elections, and there was concern that the party was turning into a more 'fundamentalist' force. Cohn-Bendit had been a close ally of the German Greens' long-time 'virtual' leader, Joschka Fischer, and shared Fischer's reformist vision of green politics as the art of the possible; this put him at odds with the French Greens' new fundamentalist tendencies.

To help renew the French Greens, Cohn-Bendit's vision was to include people from outside of the green party, from civil society and other political movements. He managed to recruit prominent activists from civil rights and anti-globalisation movements, such as Eva Joly and José Bové, to a new movement called Ecology Europe. Politically, Cohn-Bendit sought to create a more centrist force, unburdened by the chronic divisions typical of far-left groups in France. However, Cohn-Bendit's initiative also included a threat to basic elements of green politics, such as grassroots democracy and the power of party activists to determine the party's development. In fact, Cohn-Bendit's vision featured major elements of an 'anti-party' attitude; he expected the Greens to eventually disband and be replaced by some kind of 'green collective'. However, given their weakness in previous years as well as Cohn-Bendit's charismatic personality and the outstanding role he had played in green politics over many decades, the Greens decided to go along with his initiative nevertheless. An agreement was reached by the Greens and Europe Ecology to run under the latter's name, but with half of all candidates being selected by the Greens and the other half being nominated by Europe Ecology, which included prominent recruits that Cohn-Bendit had collected from civic groups outside of green politics. The experiment worked: Europe Ecology was tremendously successful.

The case of Europe Ecology is a prominent example of European elections being used for what might be termed political experiments. Some critics saw this initiative as introducing a kind of green 'celebrity' politics, with democratic internal procedures being replaced by the choice of a charismatic leader. The effect of the 2009 'experiment' on the post-election phase was, however, less profound. The process of selecting candidates from civic society groups continued for the regional elections of 2010 but was then abandoned. Both groups joined to form a new party, Europe Ecology–The Greens (EELV), in 2010, and Cohn-Bendit withdrew from participation in 2011. The idea of having a nonparty structure in green politics seems to have been just an episode.

In the 2014 elections, the European crisis and austerity politics dominated the agenda. While the Fukushima nuclear accident in 2011 had contributed to a temporary electoral boom for green parties (particularly in Germany), by the time of the European elections environmental issues were marginalised. The Greens only won 38 seats in 2014, compared with 47 in 2009. Nevertheless, given the very unfavourable context, this election result can still be seen as a success.

The results again combined successes with some disappointments. The French victories of 2009 could not be repeated. In 2012, the French Greens had rejoined the Socialists in government, but they became more and more disillusioned with the increasingly right-wing nature of the government's policies and their own lack of influence. The Greens eventually left government again in 2014, shortly before the European election, in an attempt to distance themselves from the increasingly unpopular Socialists. On this occasion, the Greens could not even benefit from the charismatic leadership of Daniel Cohn-Bendit, who had retired from active politics. Given all of this, their result of 9% can be regarded as a respectable one.

Other countries with Greens in government at the time of the elections included Denmark, Finland, Latvia and Luxembourg. The Finnish Green League had previously done well in European elections, despite their long involvement in government, but this time the party suffered some losses. Continuously in government since 2007, the party had decided to stay, in spite of government decisions on nuclear power going against them. Austerity policies also played a role. The Left Alliance had departed government in protest against these policies, but the Greens had decided to stay. While the Left Alliance increased their share of the vote, the Green League experienced some slight losses.

The Danish Socialist People's Party (SF) had observer status with the EGP but decided before the election to apply for full membership. A few months before the elections, it had also decided to leave its government coalition over disagreements on what the party regarded as neoliberal policies pursued by the Social Democrats. With 11% of the vote, the SF lost almost 5 percentage points compared with its 2000 result.

In Luxembourg, the Greens had entered national government for the first time in 2013 as part of a coalition with Liberals and Social Democrats. All government parties lost votes, but green losses were fairly minor: they gained 15% of the vote (compared with 16.8% in 2009).

In Latvia, the Greens found themselves in government at the time of the elections after a brief period in opposition (2011–14).

The result of the Union of Greens and Farmers was again lower than in national elections but higher than in the previous European elections. One MEP was elected, but they were a representative of the Latvian Farmers' Union. Later in the year, the Union of Greens and Farmers polled 19.5% in the country's parliamentary elections. In 2015, Raimonds Vējonis was elected president of Latvia; this is the first time a green party member has held the post of head of state.

Another case where green government involvement played a role, this time at a regional level, was Belgium. Here, the Greens were, overall, slightly down on the 2009 result, but there was a major difference between the two green parties. While the Flemish Greens improved in their representation, polling 6.7% in Flanders (compared with 4.9% in 2009), Ecolo lost half of its 2009 votes, dropping from 8.6% to 4.3%. While the Flemish Greens had not been in government at the regional level, Ecolo appears to have been punished for its government involvement, losing voters mainly to a far-left party: the Workers' Party of Belgium.

Among green parties that did not have to defend a record in government, the picture was rather mixed. Greens in Germany and the Netherlands experienced slight losses. More serious losses were experienced in Greece, where the Greens only polled 0.9% and lost their MEP. Severe austerity policies had made it difficult for the party to make its mark. Italy was not a success story in 2014 either. Monica Frassoni, co-chair of the EGP, founded the movement Green Italia, which sought to unite people from a variety of political backgrounds, from left to right, as well as movement activists, green economic entrepreneurs and intellectuals. Green Italia and Italy's green party, the Federation of the Greens, entered the European elections on a joint list but attracted only 0.9% of the overall vote and secured no MEPs.

There were, however, a number of success stories. In the Republic of Ireland, the Greens finally appeared to have recovered from their experience in government. Competing in all four constituencies, the party polled at 4.9% and narrowly missed having one MEP elected. The Greens in Sweden and Austria recorded major successes, with a substantial increase in vote share, benefitting from the unpopularity of incumbent governments.

The Green Party of England and Wales also experienced some success. Largely ignored by the media, which preferred to concentrate on the euro-sceptic UK Independence Party (UKIP), the Greens only suffered minor losses in terms of vote share. A very strong performance in South West England nevertheless gave the Greens a third representative in the European Parliament: Molly Scott Cato. This successful outcome sparked renewed interest in the party, leading to a 'green surge' in 2014–15. Membership of the Green Party of England and Wales stood at around 16,000 before the 2014 European elections, but it had risen to 30,900 by the end of 2014 and more than doubled during 2015.[23] Campaigning on a strong anti-austerity platform, the Greens managed to attract many former Liberal Democrats voters disaffected by the party's governmental record in coalition with the Conservatives. In the general election of May 2015, the Green Party of England and Wales received more than one million votes and a share of 3.6%, the best result in its history.[24] This helped to re-elect its only MP, Caroline Lucas, with an increased majority, but any hopes of increasing its representation in parliament were disappointed.

The biggest success story of 2014 was that, finally, Green MEPs were elected in East-Central Europe. The Hungarian Politics Can Be Different party (LMP) managed to poll at 5%, which was just enough to elect its first MEP. The LMP probably benefitted from the weakness of the Hungarian Socialist Party. In Croatia, which was taking part in European elections for the first time, a new green party called Croatian Sustainable Development (ORaH) won a seat in the European Parliament with 9.4% of the vote. However, in other parts of Eastern Europe there was little for Greens to cheer about. The Czech Greens achieved a marginally better result than in 2009, polling at 3.8%, but otherwise results below 1% dominate the picture.

Overall, 2014 was a difficult election year for the Greens. The general trends did not fundamentally differ from previous elections. Green parties in Eastern and Southern Europe at the time were less successful, while Greens in Northwestern Europe mainly held their positions, with specific national circumstances determining upward or downward trends. The negative effect of government involvement was felt more strongly in 2014 than before, with all green parties campaigning as opposition parties and increasing their representation.

Conclusions

What can we learn from the history of green parties' participation in European elections? What influence, if any, did European elections have on the development of green parties?

The overall pattern of European election results for green parties reflects the economic and social conditions in each country. There is a strong correlation between the level of affluence and the support for green parties, which consistently do well in the economically stronger countries of Northern and Western Europe but find it more difficult to win support in the poorer countries of Eastern and Southern Europe. Nevertheless, there is considerable variation within each group of countries.

Other factors outside the control of green parties include the salience of environmental issues and the positioning of rival parties. Environmental issues were clearly the main driving force in the 1980s. Environmental scandals such as the forest fires in Greece have also helped green parties to win representation in the European Parliament. Many green parties have 'diversified' to cover many more issues and avoid being labelled 'single issue' parties. However, surveys show that voters generally associate green parties with 'the environment',[25] and it has been quite difficult for green parties, in some countries more than in others, to develop strong issue competence on nonenvironmental issues. In addition, efforts by established parties of both the left and right to lay claim to a 'green' identity have generally not been very successful.

Several green party successes in European elections may be explained, at least in part, with reference to the impact of green party leaders. The names Arnold Cassola (Malta), Paul Rosenmöller (the Netherlands) and Daniel Cohn-Bendit (France) have been mentioned. However, the dominance of charismatic leaders can also provide challenges for green parties. The principles of grassroots democracy seem to clash with the idea of green parties adopting popular leaders.

The case of Europe Ecology as an alternative model for green party organisation, promoted by Daniel Cohn-Bendit, is perhaps one of the more challenging ideas. The concept of Europe Ecology embracing nonparty movements and individuals had its successes in 2009, but its applicability to other countries and times seems questionable. Yet, this idea of moving away from a party model is shared by Emmanuel Macron and his *En Marche* movement, which succeeded in sweeping away the traditional parties of the left and right in France: Europe Ecology was perhaps an early forerunner of this development. It seems unlikely, however, that a similar model would resonate outside of France.

Charismatic leaders can also be a source of splits in the green movement. While this was avoided in France in 2009, competition between rival green parties had a devastating effect on the early fortunes of the Greens in France, with competing lists preventing green parties from winning representation in the European Parliament in both 1984 and 1994. Several other countries had more than one party claiming to be 'green', particularly in the early phases of green party development. In the EU, founder members Italy, the Netherlands and Luxembourg all saw more than one green party competing in elections. While these divisions were resolved by mergers in Italy and Luxembourg, in the Netherlands both GreenLeft and the Greens competed in European elections until 2014, although the Greens were the much weaker party and their electoral participation had only a negligible effect on GreenLeft.

Within new EU member states, competition between different green parties has occurred, for example, in Bulgaria and Spain. While competition between EGP member parties in 2014 was limited to Bulgaria and the Netherlands, green parties also have to contend with non-EGP member parties that claim to be 'green', in some cases as a result of splits within the green party. This occurred in 2014 in the Czech Republic, Hungary and the Republic of Ireland. Overall, though, divisions within the green party family have generally been resolved, and party splits are not a serious issue in most countries.

European elections had a positive effect on green party development when they were associated with the provision of additional resources and opportunities. The story of the German Greens benefitting financially from their participation in the 1979 European elections is perhaps fairly unique. More common were the benefits green parties could enjoy from taking advantage of the second-order character of European elections, in which voters felt more free to vote for a party they really preferred, or to cast a protest vote against an unpopular government.

The exact nature of such resource advantages depends, however, on the different opportunities provided by the electoral systems at both a national and European level. The advantages are particularly clear for countries that employ a majority voting system in national elections but a proportional representation system in European elections. The French and British Greens (after 1999) were the main beneficiaries. This situation is reversed for smaller countries, who are allocated a more limited number of seats in the European Parliament; even with proportional representation in place, the vote share required to win representation can be very high, which discourages voters from casting their votes for smaller parties, such as the Greens, who have relatively little chance of success. In certain circumstances, this situation can provide an incentive for smaller parties to join together to form a united green party with a chance of clearing the threshold, as was seen in the Dutch case.

France and the UK are the only countries in the EU that employ a majority electoral system at the national level and a proportional representation system at the European level. Small parties such as the Greens are severely disadvantaged in national elections in these countries, and European elections have been used successfully to win representation and boost the party's profile. However, there is a huge contrast between the two countries in terms of how electoral success in the European elections has been turned into success in national politics. The French Greens have had a continuous presence in the National Assembly since 1997 and participated in national government from 1997 to 2002, and again from 2012 to 2014. By comparison, the

British Greens had their first MP elected in 2010 but without any role in national government. Why did the major successes of both parties in the 1989 European elections lead to such different outcomes?

The key mechanism that allowed the French Greens to make a major impact was their entry into an electoral alliance. The French Greens' failure to translate victory in the 1989 European elections into success in the national parliamentary elections of 1993 led to a debate about their joining an electoral alliance with the Socialist Party. The huge success of the British Greens in 1989 did not have a similar effect. An alliance with other parties was not on the agenda. This only changed after the 2014 European and 2015 general elections, when the idea of a 'progressive alliance' became a major issue. However, the unwillingness of the Labour Party to enter such an alliance in the 2017 general election provided a huge obstacle.[26]

Several political factors explain this contrast. In the French electoral system of two rounds, electoral alliances are an integral part of electoral politics. In Britain, pre-election alliances are limited to specific historical cases (eg the SDP–Liberal Alliance of the 1980s) and are not a regular feature of party competition. The Socialist Party was in crisis and was eager to set up a broad coalition of left-wing forces to counteract the right in parliament. Moreover, candidate selection in France is centralised, allowing parties (including the Greens) to decide in which constituencies they will field candidates.[27] In Britain, the selection of green party candidates is exclusively a decision of constituency parties, making it far more difficult for national agreements to be made and implemented. However, the French experience has not been an unmitigated success. As the Socialists knew the Greens were dependent on them to ensure representation, they faced limited pressure to compromise on key issues. Many Greens were disaffected by the lack of influence the party had within the alliance, and there was strong opposition to its continuation during the 2000s and 2010s. Participation in the Socialist-led government after 2012 proved to be a frustrating experience, and the Greens decided to leave in 2014.

The role of green parties in national coalition governments has been another important element of the experience of Greens in

European elections. Green parties can benefit electorally from government participation. However, lack of competence, internal strife and the pursuit of unpopular policies such as austerity can have a strong negative effect on the electoral performance of green parties, in national as well as in European elections.

How large, then, is the influence of European elections on national politics? Analyses of the 'Europeanisation' of parties and party systems have generally expressed scepticism about a major effect.[28] Even in European elections, the national context still seems to be dominant. European Parliament debates and decisions usually attract very little media coverage, and for many green politicians, particularly those well established in their home countries, interest in European green affairs is often very limited. Green party successes in European elections can, but do not necessarily, have a positive impact on the fortunes of green parties. Even major successes, such as the record green vote in the UK in 1989, do not necessarily translate into success at a national level. It is still national institutions and politics that determine the influence of European election results.

Looking forward to the European elections of 2019, the Greens appear to be in a promising position in several of their traditional strongholds. On Green Sunday, 14 October 2018, a 'green wave' swept through Belgium, Luxembourg and Bavaria (Germany). Both the Flemish and Walloon Greens scored major successes in local elections.[29] In Luxembourg, the Greens polled 15.1% in parliamentary elections: 5 percentage points up from 2013, when they had joined a government coalition with liberals and socialists.[30] In regional elections in Bavaria, the Greens scored 17.5%, marking an increase of 8.9% since 2013. At a federal level, the poll rating of the Greens during October 2018 stood at between 16% and 19%, up from 8.9% in the federal elections of 2017.[31] Greens also appear to be doing well in the Netherlands and Finland, but recent elections have seen setbacks for green parties in Austria, France, Italy and Sweden. Increasing support for Greens in the Low Countries and in Germany provides a strong basis for continued success in European elections.

Appendix

Table 1. Green European election results, 1979–2014.

	1979	1984 (1987)	1989	1994 (1995–6)	1999	2004 (2007)	2009	2014	Avg
Austria	–	–	–	6.8	9.2	12.9	9.7	14.5	10.6
Belgium	3.4*	8.2*	13.9*	11.5*	16.0*	8.7*	13.5*	11.0*	10.8
Bulgaria	–	–	–	–	–	0.5	0.7	0.9*	0.7
Croatia	–	–	–	–	–	–	–	9.4‡	–
Cyprus	–	–	–	–	–	0.9	1.5	(7.7)	1.2
Czech Republic	–	–	–	–	–	3.2	2.1	3.8	3.0
Denmark	–	–	–	–	–	8.0‡	15.9‡	11.0	11.6
Estonia	–	–	–	–	–	–	2.7	0.3	1.5
Finland	–	–	–	7.6	13.4	10.4	12.4	9.3	10.6
France	4.4	6.7*	10.6	5.0*	9.7	7.2	(16.3)	9.0	8.6
Germany	3.2	8.2	8.4	10.1	6.4	11.9	12.1	10.7	8.9
Greece	–	–	2.6*	0.8*	1.5*	0.7	3.5	0.9	1.7
Hungary	–	–	–	–	–	–	(2.6)	5.0	–
Ireland	–	1.9	3.7	7.9	6.7	4.3	1.9	4.9	4.7
Italy	–	–	6.2*	3.2	1.8	2.5	(3.1)	0.9	3.0

Latvia	—	—	—	—	—	(4.3)	(3.7)	(8.3)	—
Lithuania	—	—	—	—	—	—	—	—	—
Luxembourg	1.0	6.1*	11.3*	10.9*	10.7	15.0	16.8	15.0	10.9
Malta	—	—	—	—	—	9.3	2.3	3.0	4.9
Netherlands	4.4*	6.9*	7.0*	6.1*	11.9	7.4	9.1*	7.2*	7.5
Poland	—	—	—	—	—	0.3	[2.4]	0.3	0.3
Portugal	—	[11.5]	[14.4]	[11.2]	[10.3]	[9.1]	[10.6]	[12.7]	—
Romania	—	—	—	—	—	0.4	—	0.3	0.4
Slovakia	—	—	—	—	—	[16.9]	2.1	0.5	1.3
Slovenia	—	—	—	—	—	(2.3)	2.0	—	2.0
Spain	—	0.9*	2.7*	0.8*	2.1*	[48.4]	[6.2]	[11.0]	1.6
Sweden	—	—	—	17.2	9.5	5.9	11.0	15.4	11.8
UK	0.1	0.5	14.5	3.1*	5.5*	6.1*	8.6*	7.7*	5.8

Note: The question of the inclusion or non-inclusion of parties can be difficult in countries where green party history has seen a lot of organisational discontinuity and rivalry between different parties claiming to be 'green'. In these countries, we have included all parties that could be considered possible candidates up to the foundation of the EGP in 2004. For 2004, 2009 and 2014 only the vote share of members of the EGP are given. For parties that had EGP observer status at the time of the elections, the election results are indicated by the sign *. For elections in which the results of several green parties are combined, this is indicated by an asterisk (*) and the names of the parties are included in the 'Parties and sources' section (pp. 40–4). A further question arises from the candidacy of green parties as part of electoral alliances also involving non-green parties in which the share of the vote of green parties cannot be identified. Results for electoral alliances in which green parties participated as major or equal partners are displayed in round brackets (). Results for electoral alliances in which green parties were junior partners are displayed in square brackets []. Electoral results of electoral alliances are not taken into account in the calculation of the average vote share. All values are given as percentages.

Table 2. Seats won in European elections by green parties, 1979–2014 (all values given as percentages).

	1979	1984	1989	1994 (1995-6)	1999	2004 (2005-7)	2009 (2013)	2014	Avg
Austria	–	–	–	1	2	2	2	3	2.0
Belgium	0	2	3	2	5	2	3	2	2.4
Bulgaria	–	–	–	–	–	0	0	0	0.0
Croatia	–	–	–	–	–	–	–	1	–
Cyprus	–	–	–	–	–	0	0	0	0.0
Czech Republic	–	–	–	–	–	0	0	0	0.0
Denmark	–	–	–	–	–	1	2	1	1.5
Estonia	–	–	–	–	–	–	0	0	0.0
Finland	–	–	–	1	2	1	2	1	1.4
France	0	0	9	0	9	6	14	6	5.5
Germany	0	7	8	12	7	13	14	11	9.0
Greece	–	–	0	0	0	0	1	0	0.2
Hungary	–	–	–	–	–	–	0	1	0.5

Ireland	—	0	0	2	2	0	0	0	0.6
Italy	—	—	5	3	2	2	0	0	2.0
Latvia	—	—	—	—	—	0	0	0	0.0
Lithuania	—	—	—	—	—	—	—	—	—
Luxembourg	0	0	0	1	1	1	1	1	0.6
Malta	—	—	—	—	—	0	0	0	0.0
Netherlands	0	2	2	1	4	2	3	2	2.0
Poland	—	—	—	—	—	0	0	0	0.0
Portugal	—	0	1	0	0	0	0	0	0.1
Romania	—	—	—	—	—	0	—	0	0.0
Slovakia	—	—	—	—	—	0	0	0	0.0
Slovenia	—	—	—	—	—	0	0	0	0.0
Spain	—	0	0	0	0	2	1	1	0.6
Sweden	—	—	—	4	2	1	2	4	2.6
UK	0	0	0	0	2	2	2	3	1.1
TOTAL	0	11	28	27	38	35	47	37	—

Parties and sources

Austria. 1996–2014: *Die Grünen–Die Grüne Alternative* (The Greens–The Green Alternative). URL: https://bit.ly/2F6iqgx

Belgium. 1979–2014: Ecolo and Agalev (renamed *Groen!* (Green!) in 2003 and *Groen* (Green, without exclamation mark) in 2012). URL: https://bit.ly/2yLdgAD. More information, URL: https://bit.ly/2SaAU5E

Bulgaria. 2007: Зелена партия (Green Party); 2009: Зелените (Greens); 2014: Зелена партия (Green Party) and Зелените (Greens). URL: https://bit.ly/2PaGm6U

Croatia. 2014: *Održivi razvoj Hrvatske* (Sustainable Development of Croatia, OraH). URL: https://bit.ly/2JCYhNv

Cyprus. 2004–9: Κίνημα Οικολόγων–Περιβαλλοντιστών (Movement of Ecologists–Environmentalists); 2014: the Cyprus Green party, renamed Κίνημα Οικολόγων–Συνεργασία Πολιτών (Movement of Ecologists–Citizens' Cooperation), formed an electoral alliance with the Movement for Social Democracy (EDEK). URL: https://bit.ly/2DjYd5b

Czech Republic. 2004–14: *Strana zelených* (Green Party, SZ). URL: https://bit.ly/1kCLuZV

Denmark. 2009–14: *Socialistisk Folkeparti* (Socialist People's Party, SF). URLs: https://bit.ly/2AKspE1, https://bit.ly/1tpXHST

Estonia. 2009–14: *Erakond Eestimaa Rohelised* (Political Party of Estonian Greens, ROH). URL: https://bit.ly/2sl222g

Finland. 1996–2014: *Vihreä liitto* (Green League). URL: https://bit.ly/2qv6nz4

France. 1979: *Europe Écologie* (Europe Ecology); 1984: *Les Verts* (The Greens) and *Entente Radicale Écologiste* (Radical Ecologist Accord, ERE); 1989: *Les Verts* (The Greens); 1994: *Les Verts* (The Greens) and *Génération Écologie* (Generation Ecology, GE); 1999–2004: *Les Verts* (The Greens); 2009: *Europe Écologie* (Europe Ecology); 2014: *Europe Écologie–Les Verts* (Europe Ecology–The Greens). URL: https://bit.ly/2OmuBF8

Germany. 1979–89: West Germany, *Die Grünen* (The Greens); 1994–2009: Germany, *Bündnis '90/Die Grünen* (Alliance '90/The Greens). URL: https://bit.ly/2ziZ01u

Greece. 1989: Οικολόγοι Εναλλακτικοί (Alternative Ecologist), Ελληνικό Δημοκρατικό Οικολογικό Κίνημα (Greek Democratic Ecological Movement) and Οικολογικό Κίνημα–Πολιτική Αναγέννηση (Ecological Movement–Political Rebirth); 1994: Ένωση Οικολόγων (Union of Ecologists), Πολιτική Οικολογία (Political Ecology) and Οικολογική Αναγέννηση (Ecological Renaissance); 1999: Οικολογικό Ελληνικό (Ecological Greek), Έλληνες Οικολόγοι (Greek Ecologists) and Οικολόγοι Εναλλακτικοί (Alternative Ecologists); 2004–14: Οικολόγοι Πράσινοι (Ecologists–Greens). URL: https://bit.ly/2Cg4cVC

Hungary. 2009: *Lehet Más a Politika* (Politics Can Be Different, LMP) and *Humanista Párt* (Humanist Party, HP) (joint list); 2014: LMP. URL: https://bit.ly/2Chr6vw

Ireland. 1984: *Comhaontas Glas* (The Green Alliance); 1989–2014: *Comhaontas Glas* (The Green Party). URL: https://bit.ly/2P6MFZg

Italy. 1989: *Federazione delle Liste Verdi* (Federation of Green Lists) and *Verdi Arcobaleno* (Rainbow Greens); 1994–2004: *Federazione dei Verdi* (Federation of the Greens); 2009: *Sinistra e Libertà* (Left and Liberty); 2014: *Verdi Europei*–Green Italy (Italian Greens–Green Italy). URL: https://bit.ly/2AIteNG

Latvia. 2004–14: *Zaļo un Zemnieku savienība* (Union of Greens and Farmers, ZZS), consisting of two parties, *Latvijas Zaļā partija* (Latvian Green Party, LZP) and *Latvijas Zemnieku savienība* (Latvian Farmers Union, LZS). URL: https://bit.ly/2CfkIFc

Luxembourg. 1979: *Alternativ Lëscht Wiert Iech* (Alternative List Resist, AL); 1984: *Gréng Alternativ Partei* (Green Alternative Party, GAP); 1989: *Gréng Lëscht Ekologesch Initiativ* (Green List Ecological Initiative, GLEI) and *Gréng Alternativ Partei* (Green Alternative Party, GAP) (separate lists); 1994: *Gréng Lëscht Ekologesch Initiativ–Gréng Alternativ Partei* (Green List Ecological Initiative–Green Alternative Party) (joint list); 1999–2014: *Déi Greng* (The Greens). URL: https://bit.ly/2Pz4xeO. More information, URL: https://bit.ly/2RFUS2I

Malta. 2004–14: *Alternattiva Demokratika* (Democratic Alternative). URL: https://bit.ly/2D2WGzf

The Netherlands. 1979: *Politieke Partij Radikalen* (Radical Party, PPR), *Pacifistisch Socialistische Partij* (Pacifist Socialist Party, PSP)

and *Communistische Partij Nederland* (Communist Party of the Netherlands, CPN); 1984: *Groen Progressief Akkoord* (Green Progressive Accord, GPA), electoral alliance of PPR, PSP and CPN, and *De Groenen* (The Greens); 1989: *Regenboog* (Rainbow), electoral alliance of PPR, PSP and CPN, and *Evangelische Volkspartij* (Evangelical People's Party, EVP); 1994: *GroenLinks* (GreenLeft) and *De Groenen* (The Greens); 1999–2004: *GroenLinks* (GreenLeft); 2009–14: *GroenLinks* (GreenLeft) and *De Groenen* (The Greens). URL: https://bit.ly/2yM69Is

Poland. 2004: *Zieloni 2004* (Greens 2004); 2009: *Koalicyjny Komitet Wyborczy Porozumienie dla Przyszłości–Centro Lewica* (*PD + SDPL + Zieloni 2004*) (Coalition Agreement for the Future–Centre Left (Social Democrats, Democratic Party and Greens)); 2014: *Partia Zieloni* (Green Party). URLs: https://bit.ly/2M3bHDO, https://bit.ly/2RGYh5v, https://bit.ly/2sv4DqJ

Portugal. 1984–2014: *Coligação Democrática Unitária* (Democratic Unity Coalition, CDU), consisting of two parties, *Partido Comunista Português* (Portuguese Communist Party, PCP) and *Partido Ecologista 'Os Verdes'* (Ecologist Party 'The Greens', PEV). URL: https://bit.ly/2AGpEDb

Romania. 2007: *Partidul Verde* (Green Party, PV); 2014: PV. URLs: https://bit.ly/2PcxIEU, https://bit.ly/2SJbfh3

Slovakia. 2004: *Strana zelených na Slovensku* (Green Party of Slovakia, SZS), one SZS candidate standing on the list of *Smer* (*tretia cesta*) (Direction (Third Way)); 2009: *Strana zelených* (Green Party, SZ); 2014: SZ. URLs: https://bit.ly/2F4Lip9, https://bit.ly/2RCidmG, https://bit.ly/2JGQTk4

Slovenia. 2004: *Stranka mladih Slovenije* (Party of the Youth of Slovenia, SMS) and *Zeleni Slovenije* (Slovenian Greens, SZ) (joint list); 2009: *Stranka mladih–Zeleni Evrope* (Youth Party–European Greens). URL: https://bit.ly/2AEYahl (accessed July 2009)

Spain. 1987: *Los Verdes* (The Greens) and *Confederación de Los Verdes* (Confederation of the Greens); 1989: *Lista Verde* (Green List), *Alternativa Verda–Movimento Ecologista de Catalunya* (Green Alternative–Ecologist Movement of Catalonia), *Los Verdes Ecologistas* (The Ecologist Greens) and *Vértice Español para la Reivindicación* *del Desarrollo Ecológico* (Spanish Vertex for Claiming Ecological Development, VERDE); 1994: *Els Verds* (The Greens) and *Los Verdes–Grupo Verde* (The Greens–Green Group); 1999: *Los Verdes–Izquierdas de los Pueblos* (The Greens–Leftist of the People) and *Los Verdes–Grupo Verde* (The Greens–Green Group); 2004: *Confederación de Los Verdes* (Confederation the Greens) formed an alliance with PSOE, ICV formed an alliance with the IU, *Los Verdes–Grupo Verde* (The Greens–Green Group); 2009: *Europa de los Pueblos–Verdes* (Europe of the People–Greens, alliance of CLV with left-wing nationalist parties), ICV formed an alliance with the IU, *Los Verdes-Grupo Verde* (The Greens–Green Group); 2014: ICV stood as part of the electoral alliance *La Izquierda Plural* (The Plural Left), which included the IU and various other regional parties, and EQUO stood as part of the electoral alliance *Primavera Europea* (European Spring, PE). URL: https://bit.ly/2Szru01

Sweden. 1995–2014: *Miljöpartiet de gröna* (Environmental Party the Greens, MP). URL: https://bit.ly/2FdITIK

UK. 1979–84: *Ecology Party*; 1989: *Green Party*; 1994–2009: Green Party of England and Wales (GPEW) and Scottish Green Party (SGP); 2004–14: Green Party of England and Wales (GPEW), Green Party in Northern Ireland and Scottish Green Party (SGP). URLs: https://bit.ly/2PJbLg8, https://bit.ly/2ALCNes, https://bbc.in/2ALVjU3, https://bbc.in/2ez89qs, https://bbc.in/2PCU9CI

Endnotes

1   For comparative overviews, cf. Ferdinand Müller-Rommel (ed.), *New Politics in Western Europe: The Rise and Success of Green Parties and Alternative Lists* (Boulder CO: Westview Press, 1989); Sara Parkin, *Green Parties: An International Guide* (London: Heretic, 1989); Dick Richardson and Chris Rootes (eds.), *The Green Challenge: The Development of Green Parties in Europe* (London: Routledge, 1995); Michael O'Neill, *Green Parties and Political Change in Contemporary Europe: New Politics, Old Predicament* (Aldershot: Ashgate,

1997); Jon Burchell, *The Evolution of Green Politics: Interpreting Development and Change Within European Green Parties* (London: Earthscan, 2002); Miranda Schreurs and Elim Papadakis, *Historical Dictionary of the Green Movement*, 2nd edn. (Lanham, MD: Scarecrow Press, 2007); E. Gene Frankland, Paul Lucardie and Benoît Rihoux (eds.), *Green Parties in Transition: The End of Grass-roots Democracy?* (Aldershot: Ashgate, 2008); Per Gahrton, *Green Parties, Green Future: From Local Groups to the International Stage* (London: Pluto Press, 2015); Emilie van Haute (ed.), *Green Parties in Europe* (London: Routledge, 2016).

2   Wolfgang Rüdig, 'The Greens in Europe: ecological parties and the European elections of 1984', *Parliamentary Affairs*, Vol. 38, No. 1, 1985, pp. 56–72; Mark Franklin and Wolfgang Rüdig, 'The green voter in the 1989 European elections', *Environmental Politics*, Vol. 1, No. 4, 1992, pp. 129–59; Neil Carter, 'The Greens in the 1994 European parliamentary elections', *Environmental Politics*, Vol. 3, No. 3, 1994, pp. 495–502; Neil Carter, 'The Greens in the 1999 European parliamentary elections', *Environmental Politics*, Vol. 8, No. 4, 1999, pp. 160–7; Neil Carter, 'Mixed fortunes: the Greens in the 2004 European parliament election', *Environmental Politics*, Vol. 14, No. 1, 2005, pp. 103–11; Neil Carter, 'The Greens in the 2009 European parliament election', *Environmental Politics*, Vol. 19, No. 2, 2010, pp. 295–302; Wolfgang Rüdig, 'The Greens in the 2014 European elections', *Environmental Politics*, Vol. 24, No. 1, 2015, pp. 56–62. Also very useful are the election briefings of the European Parties Elections and Referendums Network (EPERN); https://bit.ly/1pyeYXr.

3   Klaus G. Troitzsch, 'Die Herausforderung der "etablierten" Parteien durch die "Grünen"', in: Heiko Kaack and Reinhold Roth (eds.), *Handbuch des deutschen Parteiensystems*, Vol. 1 (Opladen, Germany: Leske Verlag + Budrich GmbH, 1980), pp. 260–94.

4   These election results refer to the percentage of votes in the regions of Belgium contested by these parties, not the overall percentage of all votes cast in Belgium as a whole.

5   In the academic literature, Herbert Kitschelt in particular conceived green parties as a type of 'left–libertarian' party, cf. Herbert Kitschelt,

'Left–libertarian parties: explaining innovation in competitive systems', *World Politics*, Vol. 15, 1988, pp. 194–234; Herbert Kitschelt, *The Logics of Party Formation: Ecological Politics in Belgium and West Germany* (Ithaca, NY: Cornell University Press, 1989). A similar approach is taken by authors who see green parties mainly as 'new politics' parties that emerged as a result of a so-called post-materialist value change, eg Thomas Poguntke, 'The "new politics dimension" in European green parties', in: Ferdinand Müller-Rommel (ed.), *New Politics in Western Europe: The Rise and Success of Green Parties and Alternative Lists* (Boulder, CO: Westview Press, 1989), pp. 175–94; Thomas Poguntke (1993), *Alternative Politics: The German Green Party* (Edinburgh: Edinburgh University Press). This approach has been mainly influenced by the work of Ronald Inglehart, *The Silent Revolution: Changing Values and Political Styles Among Western Publics* (Princeton: Princeton University Press, 1977). Conceiving of 'green parties' as 'left–libertarian' or 'new politics' parties, in my view, negates the 'ecological' element as the key identity-giving feature of green parties; see Philip Lowe and Wolfgang Rüdig, 'Political ecology and the social sciences: the state of the art', *British Journal of Political Science,* Vol. 16, 1986, pp. 513–50.

6   On the development of international co-operation of green parties from 1979 to the 1990s, see in particular Thomas Dietz, *Die grenzüberschreitende Interaktion grüner Parteien in Europa* (Opladen, Germany: Westdeutscher Verlag, 1997); see also Thomas Dietz, 'Similar but different? The European Greens compared to other transnational party federations in Europe', *Party Politics*, Vol. 6, No. 2, 2000, pp. 199–210; Elisabeth Bomberg, *Green Parties and Politics in the European Union* (London: Routledge, 1998); Eric H. Hines, 'The European Parliament and the Europeanization of green parties', *Cultural Dynamics*, Vol. 15, No. 3, 2003 pp. 307–25; Nathalie Brack and Camille Kelbel, 'The Greens in the European Parliament: evolution and cohesion', in: Emilie van Haute (ed.), *Green Parties in Europe* (London: Routledge, 2016), pp. 217–37.

7   The Danish electoral system is fairly generous to small parties (2% threshold), but there are considerable obstacles to being registered as a party entitled to compete in elections. For the 1984 European elections, the Greens had to collect signatures from around 20,000

voters supporting their candidacy, which they failed to achieve; Jør-gen Elklit, Anne Birte Pade and Nicoline Nyholm Miller (eds.), *The Parliamentary Electoral System in Denmark* (Copenhagen: Ministry of the Interior and Health and The Danish Parliament, 2011).

8   For a more detailed analysis of the 1989 European elections and its aftermath in Britain, see Wolfgang Rüdig, Mark N. Franklin and Lynn G. Bennie, 'Up and down with the Greens: ecology and party politics in Britain, 1989–1992', *Electoral Studies*, Vol. 15, No. 1, 1996, pp. 1–20.

9   Michel Pauly, '25 Jahre Déi Gréng', *Forum für Politik, Gesellschaft und Kultur*, Nr. 273, February 2008, pp. 30–41.

10   Wolfgang Rüdig, 'Green parties and the European Union', in: John Gaffney (ed.), *Political Parties and the European Union* (London: Routledge, 1996), pp. 254–72.

11   Karlheinz Reif and Hermann Schmitt, 'Nine second-order national elections – a conceptual framework for the analysis of European election results', *European Journal of Political Research*, Vol. 8, No. 1, 1980, pp. 3–44.

12   On the experience of Greens in government in these countries, see Ferdinand Müller-Rommel and Thomas Poguntke (eds.), *Green Parties in National Governments* (London: Frank Cass, 2002); Benoît Rihoux and Wolfgang Rüdig, 'Greens in power: a research agenda', *European Journal of Political Research*, Vol. 45, 2006, pp. S1–S33; Per Gahrton, *Green Parties, Green Futures*, op. cit., pp. 82–107.

13   Neil Carter, 'The Greens in the 1999 parliamentary elections', op. cit., p. 164.

14   Bryan Morgan and Richard Cracknell, *Elections to the European Parliament – June 1999*, House of Commons Library Research Paper 99/64 (London: House of Commons Library, 1999).

15   Wolfgang Rüdig, 'Is government good for Greens? Comparing the electoral effects of government participation in Western and East-Central Europe', *European Journal of Political Research*, Vol. 45, 2006, pp. S127–S154.

16   On the development of the Latvian Greens, see David J. Galbreath and Daunis Auers, 'Green, black and brown: uncovering Latvia's environmental politics', *Journal of Baltic Studies*, Vol. 40, No. 3, 2009,

pp. 333–48; Daunis Auers, 'The curious case of the Latvian Greens', *Environmental Politics*, Vol. 21, No. 3, 2012, pp. 522–7.

17 Anna Gora, *Europeanization of Green Parties in the New Members States: The Cases of Poland and the Czech Republic*, MA Thesis, Institute of European, Russian and Eurasian Studies, Carleton University, Ottawa, Ontario (Canada), August 2010.

18 Roderick Pace, 'The Maltese electorate turns a new leaf? The first European Parliament election in Malta', *South European Society and Politics*, Vol. 10, No. 1, 2005, pp. 121–36.

19 Dan Boyle, *Without Power or Glory: The Green Party in Government in Ireland (2007–2011)* (Dublin: New Island, 2012); Mary Minihan, *A Deal with the Devil: The Green Party in Government* (Dublin: Maverick House, 2011).

20 Petr Jehlička, Tomáš Kostelecký and Daniel Kunštát, 'Czech green politics after two decades: the May 2010 general election', *Environmental Politics*, Vol. 20, No. 3, 2011, pp. 418–25.

21 Kostas Gemenis, 'Winning votes and weathering storms: the 2009 European and parliamentary elections in Greece', *Representation*, Vol. 46, No. 3, 2010, pp. 353–62.

22 For a comprehensive account of Europe Ecology, see Roger Lenglet and Jean-Luc Touly, *Europe Écologie: Miracle ou Mirage?* (Paris: Éditions First, 2010); see also Bruno Villalba, 'La transmutation d'Europe Écologie–Les Verts', in: Pierre Bréchon (ed.), *Les partis politiques français* (Paris: La Documentation française, 2011), pp. 129–54.

23 The Scottish Green Party increased its membership substantially during 2014, but this was mainly a result of the referendum on Scottish independence in September 2014. Elections to the European Parliament have been less important for the Scottish Greens. Having the whole of Scotland as a European constituency, with just six MEPs elected (since 2009, seven in 2004 and eight in 1999), the share of the vote required for representation was well above the results the party achieved in Scottish parliamentary elections. However, the Scottish Greens came quite close in 2014, polling their best ever result with 8.1% of the vote, just 2.4 percentage points short of the share of the vote achieved by the list of the sixth MEP elected in Scotland.

24   James Dennison, *The Greens in British Politics: Protest, Anti-Austerity and the Divided Left* (Basingstoke: Palgrave Macmillan, 2017).

25   See Franklin and Rüdig, 'The green voter in the 1989 European elections', op. cit.; Wolfgang Rüdig, 'The perennial success of the German Greens', *Environmental Politics,* Vol. 21, No. 1, 2012, pp. 108–30.

26   Barry Langford, *All Together Now: The Progressive Alliance and the 2017 General Election* (London: Biteback, 2017).

27   See Rainbow Murray, *Parties, Gender Quotas and Candidate Selection in France* (Basingstoke: Palgrave Macmillan, 2010).

28   Peter Mair, 'The limited impact of Europe on national party systems', *West European Politics,* Vol. 23, No. 4, 2000, pp. 27–51.

29   'Une vague verte', *L'Echo,* 14 October 2018; https://bit.ly/2OrT9wD (accessed 16 October 2018).

30   'Luxembourg, Belgique, Bavière: les Verts ratissent de plus en plus large en Europe', *Le Quotidien,* 15 October 2018; https://bit.ly/2JHjZA2 (accessed 16 October 2018).

31   Wahlrecht.de, Wahlen, Wahlrecht und Wahlsysteme (Elections, Suffrage and Electoral Systems); https://bit.ly/2w7hLGN (accessed 16 October 2018).

Chapter 2

Proportional representation and Britain's democratic deficit

Klina Jordan and Owen Winter

Introduction

Britain is one of the few countries that still uses the first-past-the-post (FPTP) electoral system to elect its MPs. This chapter reflects on the use of proportional representation (PR) around the world, particularly for European elections; the implications this has for Britain's political system; and the case for moving to a system of PR. Since its conception in the Treaty of Rome in 1957, the European Parliament has evolved from an appointed assembly of six countries to a parliament of 28 nations, elected in transnational elections involving over 500 million people.[1] It offers a unique and overlooked perspective on the effect of electoral systems on voter behaviour and party systems, and shows how proportional electoral systems give rise to diverse multiparty systems, with many consequences for national politics. This has been crucial in the rise of green parties as a European movement, with Greens outdoing their UK Parliament performance in national elections across Europe.

The use of PR in the UK has exposed the failings of FPTP: recurring UK Parliaments have failed to represent how people have voted. This stands in stark contrast to our European neighbours, who have achieved better representation of women and minorities as well as greater satisfaction with democracy. In fact, PR countries outperform majoritarian ones in many areas, including climate policy, peacefulness and income equality.

Figure 1. Strasbourg European Parliament hemicycle, with MEPs elected to represent 28 nations and over 500 million people (5 February 2014). *Photo:* David Iliff (license: CC-BY-SA 3.0).

The use of PR for European and devolved elections has fundamentally altered British politics, making a reform of the House of Commons increasingly likely. With the rise of the Make Votes Matter movement – the single-issue campaign for PR led by activists and owned by everyone who wants democracy – the time is right to push for real democracy in the UK.

The history of European Parliament elections

The Treaty of Rome, signed in 1957, set out a vision for a European Parliament. This parliament would be like no other in existence: a cross-border assembly with representatives elected from across Europe. The inspiration for the Parliament came from the European Coal and Steel Community's Common Assembly; with the creation of the European Economic Community and European Atomic Energy Community in 1957, the Common Assembly was expanded to encompass all three European Communities. Initially, members of the European Parliament (as it was renamed in 1962) were appointed, but the wheels had been set in motion for the world's first transnational elections, eventually involving 28 nations representing 508 million people.

The treaty proposed that the Parliament be elected 'by direct universal suffrage using a uniform procedure in all member states'.[2] This line, it turned out, would be difficult to implement. The Council of Europe, made up of ministers from member states, stalled on the election of the Parliament for almost two decades. Politicians feared that uniform transnational elections would undermine their national political systems, leading to the creation of a European public politics in which they would play only a marginal role. As Hoskyns and Lambert argue, their reluctance to embrace elections with a uniform system undermined the legitimacy of the Parliament at a formative stage in its development.[3]

After the European Parliament threatened to take the Council to the European Court of Justice, they relented. At the Paris summit of 1974, ministers agreed to a European election in or after 1978. The European Parliament drew up proposals for the first elections to be held in 1979. Crucially, however, the Council only agreed to elections on the condition that the requirement for a uniform procedure would not be implemented. As a result, it fell to national legislatures to draw up electoral systems for their MEPs.

Despite the lack of a uniform system, it was generally felt across Europe that PR would be the most appropriate method for electing MEPs. Of the nine countries that participated in the 1979 elections, seven (Belgium, Denmark, Ireland, Italy, the Netherlands, Luxembourg and West Germany) already used some form of PR for their national legislature, so it was well established as the electoral system of Europe.[4] The primary purpose of the Parliament was representative, and PR was the best way of ensuring the broad range of public opinion would be heard. Devoid of any government-forming function, this system's usual perceived disadvantages no longer existed, so – despite lacking a uniform procedure for elections – a broad consensus emerged for PR.

It is in this context that Britain's Home Secretary, Merlyn Rees, introduced the European Parliamentary Elections Bill in 1977. The bill proposed that elections to the European Parliament take place under a system of PR, similar to those systems being simultaneously adopted by the UK's continental counterparts. Although the government did not think PR was appropriate for House of Commons elections, they argued that with just 81 constituencies, the distorting effect of FPTP would be even more pronounced, with small swings in the vote resulting in huge upheavals for MEPs. As a representative body without a government-forming function, the Home Secretary argued, PR could be adopted without fear of 'weak coalitions' or frequent early elections. Rees also pointed out that PR would bring the UK into line with the other EU nations holding elections, arguing in the debate:

> The hon. Member for Mid-Oxon talked about the regional list system as being unusual. The hon. Member for Guildford called it bizarre. The regional list system is to be used in many countries in Europe; it is proposed to be used for elections for the European Assembly. Bizarre it may well be, in which case we are in good company. Unusual it is not.[5]

MPs, however, were not impressed. Labour MP Dennis Skinner asked, 'why is it that [EU nations] have tried to impose their system of election upon us? Why do not they accept our first-past-the-post system?' When another MP responded that a common electoral system was subject to negotiation, Ulster Unionist MP Enoch Powell interrupted with 'No, leadership.' Clearly, a newfangled electoral system from Europe was too hard to stomach for many MPs.

An amendment was put forward to remove the commitment to PR, and a heated debate followed. Pro-FPTP MPs argued that a PR system would increase distrust in the new elections and mean electing MEPs with no constituency link. Unsurprisingly, self-interest played a part in their opposition. Labour MP Fred Willey, who proposed the amendment, admitted to supporting PR as a child but altered his view when 'Labour swept County Durham and, apart from the debacle of 1931, has done so ever since.' Labour and the Conservatives were not prepared to give up their duopoly of the electoral system, even for European elections.

In the end, the government granted MPs a free vote and, despite opposition from three prime ministers (Harold Wilson, Ted Heath and Jim Callaghan), the amendment passed by 97 votes. Elections were held in June 1979 and, predictably, Labour and the Conservatives won every seat. With 48% of the vote, the Conservatives won 60 out of an available 81 MEPs.

However, that was not the end of the story for Britain's European electoral system. Through the 1990s the Liberal Democrats, on the back of disappointing results in the 1989 European elections, set their sights on European elections as the most likely route to installing PR in the UK. In 1993 the Liberal Democrats challenged the European Parliament in the European Court of Justice for failing to make proposals for a uniform electoral procedure, as it was mandated to do by the Treaty of Rome. Although this legal action failed, it did spur the European Parliament into discussing the issue; this led to approval of the De Gucht Report, which called for common criteria to be agreed on by the Parliament. The final report specified that the UK should elect at least one-third of its MEPs by PR: a gradualist approach to unifying the electoral system. Karel De Gucht, who authored the report, was quoted at the time as saying, 'I have tried to make it as difficult as possible for Britain to say no.'

No action was taken by the UK government in time for the 1994 European Parliament elections, but it became Labour's policy, in opposition, to move to PR for electing MEPs. In the lead-up to the 1997 general election, Labour and the Liberal Democrats set up the joint Consultative Committee on Constitutional Reform and agreed to common policies on constitutional reform, including PR for European Parliament elections. When Tony Blair won a landslide election victory in 1997, many assumed that the policy would be kicked into the long grass, but Home Secretary Jack Straw introduced the European Parliamentary Elections Bill in October that same year. As in the debate 20 years earlier, some MPs were hardly subtle about their partisan interests. For example, Gerry Berming-ham of the Labour for FPTP group said in the debate:

> Many MPs are concerned about the loss of constituency identity by going for a regional list of candidates. In my own region in the North-west, it is bound to lead to the Tories regaining a foothold.

However, despite concerns about the nature of the system selected by Labour's leadership, and opposition from the Conservatives and some Labour MPs, the bill was passed into law in time for the 1999 elections. This act brought Britain into line with the rest of Europe, with all MEPs being elected by some form of PR; the result is a European Parliament that broadly reflects the range of opinions held by the people it represents.

The effect of proportional representation in European elections

For those interested in the effects of electoral systems, the European Parliament offers some unique insights, allowing us to test the theory that electoral systems can lead to radically different party systems. European Parliament elections also affect our national politics, giv-ing a platform to different issues and political parties. This effect is particularly relevant for green parties across Europe, who have ben-efitted from the exposure of European elections and used them to overcome structural barriers to success. We can compare the effect of different electoral systems on green parties with particular reference to the UK pre-1999, France, the UK post-1999 and Germany. PR, at all levels of government, is key to the success of green parties across Europe and has fundamentally altered British politics.

It is well known that countries with proportional electoral sys-tems tend to have more political parties. The European Parliament allows us to test whether this relationship is causal. Maurice Duverger famously theorised that FPTP tends to favour a two-party system, whereas proportional electoral systems are favourable to many more parties.[6] This theory came to be known as Duverger's Law, and it operates by two processes. First, there is the 'mechanical effect' of different electoral systems. FPTP has the effect of suppressing smaller parties because you must win a plurality of votes in a constituency to win any MPs. A party could win 10% or 20% of the votes in every constituency but be left with no MPs because they did not come first in any. This process is compounded by a second process: the 'psychological effect'. This is the practice of voters and elites strategically supporting preferred candidates from larger parties who are more likely to win. Over time, smaller parties drop out as they struggle to win support, and the system is whittled down to two major parties. Conversely, in proportional systems, the mechanical and psychological limits to the number of parties are much higher, so more parties emerge, more accurately representing the range of views held by the people.

However, some political scientists have questioned Duverger's approach. They argue that countries with multiparty systems are more likely to adopt PR, so it is not the electoral system that leads to multiparty systems. Some even go as far as to argue that it is multiparty systems that lead to the introduction of PR.[7,8,9,10] As the product of a transnational, exogenous election, the European Parliament offers a chance to test this theory. That is the approach taken by Christopher Prosser of the University of Manchester.[11] He finds that the number of parties winning votes at European elections grows over time, but the number of parties grows *more* when the electoral system used for European elections is more proportional than that used for national elections. This supports Duverger's claim that more proportional systems lead to a greater number of political parties.

To illustrate this, it is useful to look at the difference between the UK's national and EU elections between 1979 and 1997, and between 1999 and 2017. A relatively similar number of people voted for the main two parties at general elections and EU elections between 1979 and 1997, with an average of 74.6% for the former and 73.9% for the latter.[12] However, from 1999 onwards a big gap emerged, with an average of 71% for general elections and 49.4% for EU elections.

This figure may be slightly skewed by the 2017 election, which had a particularly high vote share for Labour and the Conservatives; but even accounting for that, the average for general elections is 68.1%: a gap of 18.7%.

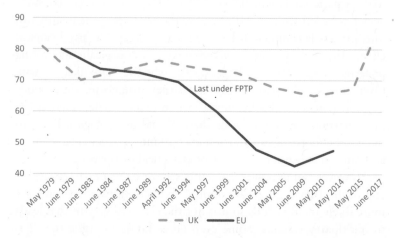

Figure 2. Percentage of votes cast for Labour or the Conservatives in general elections and EU elections, 1979–2017.

According to Prosser, this expansion of political parties in EU elections has been fed back into national political systems. This point is picked up by Patrick Dunleavy, who argues that voters and parties have changed their behaviour to reflect the changing electoral systems used in the UK.[13] Since 1999, PR has been used for EU elections and devolved assemblies in London, Scotland and Wales (since 1973 in Northern Ireland), while the supplementary vote (SV) system is used for mayoral and police and crime commissioner elections, and FPTP is used for the House of Commons and English and Welsh local elections. There is extensive evidence of vote splitting within and between these electoral systems, with voters supporting parties that possess a broader range of ideological positions. As party leaders try to adapt to this new multiparty-voting Britain, FPTP continues to fail at representing the people's preferences in Parliament.

What this means for Greens

As a smaller party that has struggled to fit into the restrictive British party system, this realignment is key for the Green Party. With the adoption of PR for EU elections in 1999, the Greens won their first national representation for the UK: Caroline Lucas and Jean Lambert were both elected as MEPs that year. Across Europe, PR elections to the European Parliament have provided an important opportunity for Greens, and often entry into national politics. European elections allow green parties to overcome structural obstacles and better reflect the fact that the green movement is genuinely pan-European.

In 2011 Andrew Knapp and Vincent Wright identified three main structural obstacles for Greens, aside from the electoral system. First, there is the electoral problem that green policies tend to have more localised or long-term benefits than other parties' policies. Many people who support Greens on principle do not vote for them in national elections because they are more concerned with the short-term, national issues that more fully preoccupy traditional parties. Second, Greens tend to be averse to the hierarchical leadership structures that are used by conventional parties and are entrenched in many national political systems. Third, Greens face a strategic choice between remaining isolated or joining alliances, which may lead to unacceptable compromises. The European Parliament has been crucial in overcoming these structural obstacles by allowing people to vote based on their principles, without altering their national government, and by having structures that are much better suited to Greens' organisation.

The European Parliament has also been important to Greens as a way of reflecting their status as a pan-European movement. While European elections are usually made up of mostly separate campaigns in each country, green parties often collaborate across borders and raise issues that are relevant globally. A prime example of this is the 1989 European Parliament election. As John Curtice noted at the time, everywhere the Greens put up candidates, they increased their share of the vote.[14] Across Europe, the green vote more than trebled from 2.5% to 7.7%. Surprisingly, the Greens' biggest jumps in support occurred in countries where they were not already represented in the national legislature, such as France and the UK. In France, *Les Verts* won 10.6% of the vote and nine MEPs: the party's first representatives in a national election. In the UK, the Green Party won 14.5% of the vote (2.3 million votes). This remains the Greens' best result in UK history. However, due to the FPTP system in use at that time, this did not win the party a single MEP. Across Europe, the Greens' 7.7% resulted in 5.2% of MEPs, with most of the disparity caused by the UK's disproportional system.

The European Green Party has continued to grow and establish itself – in coalition with regionalist and left-wing nationalist parties – as a significant bloc in the European Parliament. The use of PR for a transnational election to the European Parliament has been transformative for many green parties, particularly those that compete in majoritarian electoral systems in national elections (eg in the UK and France). We can compare the effects of European elections on green parties in countries that have majoritarian electoral systems for both national and EU elections (UK pre-1999), those with majoritarian national elections but proportional EU elections (France, UK post-1999) and those with PR for both national and EU elections (the rest of the EU).

Before 1999 Greens in the UK, under a number of different banners, did not make a big impact in most national elections. The party hovered between 0.1% and 0.5% from 1979 to 1987. As part of a European-wide phenomenon, the party surged at the 1989 European elections, winning 2 million votes: 14.5% of the total. However, with no representation under FPTP, the party could not sustain this growth in the way that other European green parties did. In 1992 the party fell back to 0.5% in the general election and 3.1% in the 1994 European elections. While the party clearly performed better in European elections, perhaps for the reasons discussed above, the FPTP system for MEPs meant that the party could not establish a foothold.

This changed in 1999, a year that saw the first national election using PR held in the UK. The party won 5.8% of the vote and Caroline Lucas and Jean Lambert were elected MEPs. This offered a vital platform from which the party increased its vote share at the next two European elections. In 2014, despite a slight fall in vote share, the party won its third MEP, Molly Scott Cato, in South West England. However, the party struggled to convert this into success at Westminster under the FPTP system. While the party increased its vote share with greater exposure after 1999, it was consistently lower than in European elections, peaking at 3.8% in 2015. Nevertheless, Caroline Lucas managed to win a place in the House of Commons in 2010, aided by her experience and platform as an MEP. European elections allowed the Green Party of England and Wales to greatly increase its exposure and status, but because of FPTP this did not translate into a group of MPs.

France, the other EU nation that uses a majoritarian system for its National Assembly, has had a similar experience, with French Greens significantly overperforming in EU elections but struggling to break into the National Assembly. France uses a two-round electoral system for its National Assembly, with all candidates other than the top two being eliminated and facing each other in a second round. While this means all *députés* are endorsed by a majority of their constituents, it results in Assemblies that are often even more disproportionate than FPTP ones, with smaller parties struggling to make it to the second round or defeat mainstream candidates.

In proportional EU elections, the green and ecology parties have regularly recorded over 10% of the vote collectively, winning many MEPs. In 2009, *Les Verts* won over 16% of the vote and matched the *Partis Socialiste* with its number of MEPs. In legislative elections, Greens usually win between 4% and 7% of the vote and struggle to win significant numbers of *députés*. When they have made breakthroughs, it is usually the result of electoral pacts such as in 1997 and 2012, as part of the *Gauche Plurielle*.

Interestingly, both Britain and France have proportionally elected regional assemblies in which Greens perform much better than at a national level. In the UK, green parties have won seats on all the devolved parliaments and assemblies other than Wales, having a significant presence in Scotland, London and Northern Ireland. It is clear that in both Britain and France there is a significant level of support for green politics, at every level of government, but majoritarian electoral systems constrain voters and suppress green support.

This effect is mirrored in the few other countries that use FPTP around the world. In New Zealand, which used FPTP until 1996, the world's first green party – originally called the Values Party – won over 5% of the vote in 1975 but did not elect a single MP. In Canada, as in the UK, Greens have only ever won one MP, despite winning almost 7% of the vote in 2008. The US Green Party has no nationally elected representatives and only a scattering of local representatives, with Greens famously being criticised by those on the left for supposedly splitting the vote and allowing George Bush to become president in 2000.

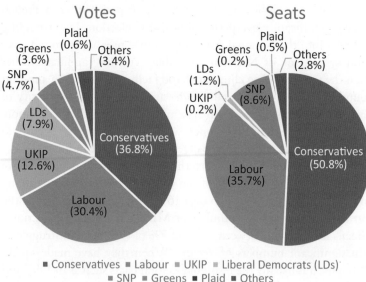

Figure 3. Vote share and seat share by party, 2015 general election.

The examples of Britain and France stand in contrast to most EU nations, which use forms of PR for both national and European elections. In Germany, for example, while the Greens perform slightly better in European elections, the gap is far smaller, with *Die Grünen* being a significant party in the *Bundestag* at every election since 1983 (1994 excepted). In the *Bundestag, Die Grünen* has had significant achievements, including the phasing out of nuclear power, the liberalisation of immigration laws and the legalisation of same-sex marriage. By looking at German electoral results regionally, we can see that the Greens have only ever won one local constituency, suggesting that even with high levels of support they would not have won nearly as many MPs without Germany's proportional system. The same is true of many countries with significant green parties, including Belgium, Denmark, Finland, the Netherlands, New Zealand (since 1996) and Sweden.

European countries that use PR make the UK look outdated. In the vast majority of such countries, parties win MPs in proportion to the votes they receive. They are far more responsive to new political movements – such as green parties – and genuinely represent the public.

The many failures of the first-past-the-post system

FPTP has led to successive parliaments that do not reflect how people have voted. The best example in recent times is the 2015 general election. This was the most disproportionate election in British history, with a parliament that looked virtually nothing like what people voted for being elected. The Conservatives won 37% of the vote and received a majority of MPs, while the UK Independence Party (UKIP), the Green Party and the Liberal Democrats won almost a quarter of the vote between them but ended up sharing just 1.6% of seats.

The reason for this discrepancy is that FPTP is based on constituencies that each elect a single MP. This means that general election results are decided by the geographical distribution of votes, rather than by the amount of support a party receives overall. A party wins an MP provided they have at least one more vote than every other candidate in that constituency, regardless of whether they won 20% or 80% of the vote.

This means larger parties, or parties with concentrated geographical support, win far more MPs than their proportion of the vote. In 2015 the Conservatives received only 37% of the vote but won the most votes in 51% of constituencies. This meant they could form a government despite 63% of people voting for other parties. In 2005 the same effect meant Labour could win 55% of MPs with just 35% of the vote. This leads to governments that most people did not vote for carrying out policies that most people do not support.

On the flip side, parties with evenly distributed support often struggle to win any MPs, despite being given a significant chunk of the vote. Historically, this has been most harmful for the Liberal Democrats. In 1983, the SDP–Liberal Alliance (forerunner of the Liberal Democrats) received 25.4% of the vote but only won 23 MPs: less than 4%. With the rise of multipartism, this effect has become more pronounced. In 1951 Labour and the Conservatives won 96.8% of the vote between them, but by 2010 this had fallen to 65.1%. Although Labour and the Conservatives have performed slightly better since 2010, the arrival of devolved assemblies and European elections means the two main parties are unlikely to recover their monopoly on political debate. New political parties have grown in support but are unable to secure election success under the current system.

By any reasonable measure, therefore, we can see that votes do not count equally. At the last general election in 2017 it took 28,000 votes to elect a Scottish National Party (SNP) MP compared with 526,000 for the Green Party, while 594,000 votes for UKIP won no MPs at all. In fact, *most* votes do not count towards the final election result. Because a candidate needs only one more vote than their nearest opponent to become the sole MP in a constituency, votes for losing candidates and votes for winning candidates above the amount needed to win have no impact. These are called 'wasted votes'. At the 2017 general election, 68% of votes were wasted in this way.

Because of this, many people decide that it is not worth voting, while others try to avoid wasting their vote by voting tactically. Tactical voting is when someone votes for a candidate other than their favourite because they are more likely to beat another candidate that they like even less. This is an unhealthy feature of British democracy, which finds millions of people feeling unable to express their views at the ballot box. In 2017 tactical voting was endemic, with between 20% and 30% of voters saying that they planned to vote tactically.

The issue of unequal votes is compounded by the inequality between 'safe' and 'marginal' constituencies. Rationally, parties realise that many votes are wasted, and try to maximise the efficiency of their campaigning. They do this by targeting 'winnable' seats, where their party has enough support to overtake the incumbent, and defending 'loseable' seats, where their party is at risk of being overtaken. Constituencies where two or more parties are in with a chance of winning are called 'marginal' seats. General elections are decided in these seats, with a small number of swing voters in each marginal constituency ultimately deciding the result of the whole election. Accordingly, parties disproportionately campaign in these areas and design policies to please the voters in these seats.

FPTP can also result in MPs being elected with very little support from their constituents. The record for the lowest share of the vote received by a candidate was set in 2015, in Belfast South, where a Social Democratic and Labour Party MP was elected with less than 25% of the vote. When 75% of people voted for another candidate, it is difficult to argue that the MP can genuinely claim to represent their constituents. Again, this effect has been exacerbated by the rise of multiparty politics in the UK. When there are two candidates standing, the winner requires at least 50% of the vote plus one. When three stand, this goes down to 33.3% plus one, etc. In 2017 there was an average of 5.1 candidates in each constituency, meaning candidates could potentially be elected with just 20% of the vote. In 2005 a record 15 candidates stood in Tony Blair's Sedgefield constituency, meaning an MP could theoretically have been elected with as little as 6.7% of the vote.

At the other end of the spectrum are safe seats, where one party is particularly popular. These seats are highly unlikely to change hands, meaning MPs have a job for life. Even when MPs are particularly unpopular, party loyalty makes it almost impossible to remove them. West Dorset, for example, has been a Conservative seat since 1885.

Voters in West Dorset have very little ability to influence the final election result because the local result is a foregone conclusion.

The other effect of marginal and safe seats is that general elections can hand victory to a party that did not win the most votes. Parties can stack up thousands of votes in safe seats but lose the election if they are not popular enough in marginal ones. These so-called wrong winner elections are a frequent occurrence under FPTP. In the UK, there have been two wrong winner elections since 1945 (in 1951 and 1974); Canada has also had two (in 1957 and 1979), and New Zealand scrapped its FPTP voting system after two wrong winner elections in a row (in 1978 and 1981).

On all counts, FPTP fails as a system for electing MPs. It fails to represent individual constituencies effectively, to ensure MPs are accountable to voters and to produce governments that have the support of a majority of voters. It even fails to give the party with the most votes the most seats. This is not just an issue for political anoraks or obsessives; it influences every decision that politicians make.

The solution: proportional representation

Thankfully, Britain is in the minority using FPTP. Among the 35 members of the OECD, for example, at least 85% use some form of PR. Of those that don't, just three use FPTP: the UK, Canada and the US. The vast majority of democracies (80%) use some form of PR, making the UK look seriously outdated.

The international trend is also towards more proportional systems. Belgium (1899), the Netherlands (1917), Germany (1918), Denmark (1920), Ireland (1921), Malta (1921), South Africa (1994) and New Zealand (1996) have all moved from FPTP to PR. The Institute for Democracy and Electoral Assistance (IDEA) found that 31 countries had changed their electoral system over a 20-year period. Of these, 27 increased the level of proportionality, while just one (Madagascar) reduced it. There is no reason why the UK couldn't also change its system.

There are a number of different methods of PR, which we outline below. It must be noted, however, that debating which PR system is best can distract us from the fact that, if accurate representation is important in a democracy, then all proportional voting systems are clearly more democratic than disproportionate ones. As we will see later in this chapter, proportional democracies also tend to enjoy better socioeconomic outcomes than their disproportional counterparts. For many decades, much of the energy of the electoral reform movement has gone into systems debate, to the detriment of generating adequate interest and action to bring about change. Having said that, it is important for those who want to see UK politics become more democratic to understand what the alternatives to our antiquated FPTP system actually are. Table 3 summarises the main groups of proportional electoral systems that have been adopted in order to demonstrate how PR has been put into practice in the UK and around the world.

Some people frame the debate between PR and FPTP as a choice between fairness or representation and effective government. This could not be further from the truth, as numerous studies by political scientists have found that PR countries outperform those which use FPTP in both representation *and* effective policymaking.

For a start, it is not just political parties that are more proportionally represented under PR. Proportional electoral systems produce parliaments that more accurately reflect the public and their preferences in a number of ways. First, PR has been found to enable a better gender balance in politics. Every single country that has more than 40% female MPs in its primary legislature uses some form of PR. This can be explained by the fact that PR encourages political parties to put forward a range of candidates that will appeal to more voters, while parties that fail to do so are punished. Under FPTP, where a single candidate is nominated in each constituency, the priority is not to maximise diversity but simply to win over enough voters to defeat the opposition. FPTP also locks in historic disparity in representation: the Electoral Reform Society recently found that safe seats are overwhelmingly held by male MPs, reducing opportunities for new female MPs to be elected.

Table 1. Summary of common proportional voting systems in use around the world.

Electoral System	Examples	Definition
Additional member system (AMS)	Germany, London, New Zealand, Scotland, Wales	Half of MPs are elected in single-member constituencies, as with FPTP. The other half are elected to represent larger regions and are elected from lists to ensure that the overall result is proportional.
Closed-list	Italy, Israel, Portugal	MPs are elected to multimember constituencies. Voters choose which party to support and seats are allocated so that parties receive a proportional share, with individual MPs decided by a list provided by the party.
Open-list	Denmark, Finland, Iceland, Norway, Sweden	MPs are elected to multimember constituencies. Voters choose which party to support and which candidate is their favourite. Seats are allocated so that parties receive a proportional share and the most popular candidates from each party are elected.
Single transferable vote (STV)	Ireland, Northern Ireland, Malta	MPs are elected to represent multimember constituencies. Voters rank the candidates in their constituency and once a candidate has reached a certain share of the vote they are elected. If no candidates have enough support, the candidate in last place is eliminated and their second preferences are reallocated until all positions are filled.

A similar effect applies to black, Asian and minority ethnic (BAME) representation. There are very few UK constituencies in which the majority are from BAME groups, so white candidates may (subconsciously or otherwise) be seen as a safer bet in majority-white constituencies. PR encourages political parties to select candidates who can reach out to the broadest range of voters. While PR would not, of course, instantly resolve the issue of female and minority representation, it would mean a system that encourages diversity rather than penalises it.

PR also encourages a broader range of people to participate in politics, with PR countries reporting higher turnout figures than countries that use FPTP. Logically, this effect has obvious causes. At every election under FPTP, the vast majority of votes has no impact on the final result. For many people, their constituency has always been held by the same party, so voting is seen as pointless. FPTP also stifles choice by suppressing smaller parties and new entrants. Political scientists have found that countries which use PR have 5–8% higher turnouts than those which use disproportional systems such as FPTP.[15,16,17]

Similarly, Arend Lijphart found in his study *Patterns of Democracy* that citizens in countries with PR are more satisfied with the performance of their country's democratic institutions, even when the party they voted for is not in power. That may be because PR produces a more collaborative political system, which often results in cross-party initiatives and consensus-based policymaking. PR leads to more parties being represented and coalition governments. In addition, the governments formed will more likely have the support of a majority of voters, and the policies put forward will require the support of parties representing a majority of voters in order to be passed.

How proportional representation leads to better policymaking

Some people argue that PR leads to weak coalitions that are unable to get things done. In reality, the opposite is the case. Because coalition governments under PR base policymaking on consensus, they are actually more decisive and effective than single-party governments under FPTP.

Political scientists have theorised a number of explanations for this. Markus Crepaz argues that a greater proportion of voters are represented in government, so government policies are likely to carry more public support and are therefore more likely to be implemented.[18] This is supported by Arend Lijphart's argument that while policymaking might take longer under PR, the creation of a broader base of support for policies means they are longer lasting and more consistent.[19] Under FPTP, governments frequently change from one single-party government to another, leading to policy instability. Under PR, governments are far more likely to retain policies from the previous government, and ideological swings are less pronounced. Patrick Dunleavy expands on this by looking at the UK's record of policy disasters such as the poll tax.[20] He argues that part of the reason why the UK is disproportionately affected by policy disasters is that policymaking happens too rapidly, with single-party governments able to dominate the legislature, and that FPTP incentivises adversarial policymaking.

In the UK, we are used to political parties reversing the policies of the previous government, but if policies are based on a broad range of support they are far harder to reverse. This allows politicians under PR systems to take a longer-term view, rather than being concerned with the next general election and how to win support in marginal constituencies.

Better policymaking under proportional representation leads to better socioeconomic outcomes

The effect of PR on both representation and policymaking is not purely academic; it leads to concrete political outcomes that affect our everyday lives. How we elect our politicians is absolutely fundamental to the decisions they make, so our electoral system should not be a debate for political anoraks and partisan obsessives alone. PR can facilitate a better country for everyone, with evidence from around the world showing that PR countries take faster action on climate change, are more peaceful, have lower income inequality and are more likely to have welfare states. FPTP reserves political power for the small number of swing voters in marginal constituencies, meaning political decisions are made in the interest of an over-represented minority. PR means genuine political power for all voters and policies that are created in the interests of the country as a whole.

The increased capacity for long-term policymaking under PR has particular relevance for climate policy. While the effects of climate change are becoming increasingly apparent, it is still not a top priority for most voters, so parties are not incentivised to prioritise it under FPTP. Under PR, however, long-term policymaking is possible, and voters who prioritise climate change are able to express this at the ballot box. The rise of green parties under PR systems has been crucial for climate policy in many countries, with green parties making environmentalist policies central to coalition negotiations and other political parties prioritising green policies to win over green voters. Lijphart and Salomon Orellana find evidence supporting this, showing that on average countries with PR score 6 points higher on the Environmental Performance Index.[21] Using data from the International Energy Agency, Orellana found that between 1990 and 2007, when carbon emissions were rising everywhere, the statistically predicted increase was significantly lower in countries with proportional systems: 9.5% compared with 45.5% in countries using winner-takes-all systems. Orellana found use of renewable energy to be 117% higher in countries with fully proportional systems. There is also evidence that PR countries were faster to ratify the Kyoto Protocol.[22] PR countries are more predisposed to deal with the challenge that climate change poses.

Action on climate change is also deeply related to the nature of special interests and public goods under different electoral systems, a point explored by Vicki Birchfield and Markus Crepaz.[23] According to Birchfield and Crepaz, PR legislatures are what is known as a 'collective veto point', meaning they require collective agency and collective responsibility, leading to reduced partisanship. Because of multipartism and coalition governments under PR, policies that are 'diffuse' (ie have many contributors and benefactors) are better represented. This is the inverse of FPTP, which is a 'competitive veto point' in which parties are encouraged to compete for power. Under FPTP, policies supported by powerful special interests have more sway. Such special interests (eg well-funded lobbyists) are likely to be opposed to policies tackling climate change and are more able to influence single-party governments than coalitions that represent a broad range of society.

This line of thinking extends to many policy issues, notably policies to reduce inequality. PR is better at representing a broad range of people who are affected by, for example, public welfare schemes. It is also better at representing minorities – particularly those who are geographically spread out – who are more likely to call for action on inequality. This leads to PR countries having higher levels of social expenditure, on average, and lower income inequality. Lijphart finds that 'consensus democracies' (of which PR is a key component) have an average social expenditure that is 4.75% higher.[24] This lends itself to lower income inequality. Numerous studies have found strong, statistically significant relationships between income inequality and disproportionality. Comparing the Gini coefficient (a measure of economic inequality) of the 35 Organisation for Economic Co-operation and Development (OECD) nations, we can see this relationship in action. The 14 nations with the lowest income inequality all use PR, while those that use FPTP come 20th (Canada), 29th (UK) and 33rd (US). According to Lijphart, the average consensus democracy has a Gini coefficient 9 points lower than the average majoritarian democracy. He finds a similar relationship with measures of gender inequality.[25]

Perhaps most surprisingly, political scientists have found that electoral systems also have a significant effect on whether countries go to war. Steve Chan and David Leblang go as far as to say:

> Among the various distinctions considered (such as parliamentary versus presidential forms of government, rule by a single dominant party versus a coalition government, and phases of the electoral cycle), a country's electoral system turns out to be the most important institutional factor that dampens war involvement. Established democracies with a Proportional Representation system tend to have significantly less such involvement according to three alternative measures.[26]

This, again, is because of the representation of a broad range of interests and a consensual approach to policymaking. Under PR, it is far harder to take reckless military action based on minority support. While Chan and Leblang recognise that this is an area which requires more research, it is certainly a striking finding.

By nature, proportional electoral systems lead to policymaking that is in the interests of a broader section of society. When political power is put in the hands of a greater number of voters, politicians are incentivised to make decisions that are beneficial to a greater number of people. Policymaking is more effective, because politicians can work in the long term, rather than simply focussing on the current electoral cycle, and policies are passed with a greater base of support, so they are harder to dismantle. While PR is not a panacea, it facilitates the creation of a better, more equal society that is better equipped to protect the planet. We would go so far as to say that moving to PR – to real democracy – is the single most important thing we could do to make the world a better place.

Why do we not have proportional representation already?

Given the well-known problems with FPTP and the effective use of PR around the world, a fair question to ask is 'why haven't we already adopted PR?' The truth is that, as democracy emerged in the UK – a process that began hundreds of years ago – our electoral system developed with no proper scrutiny or discussion. FPTP evolved directly from the ancient seats in the House of Commons, which could be bought by the aristocracy. As voting rights were expanded and constituencies equalised in size, FPTP emerged as the system for electing MPs.

So, what about the Alternative Vote (AV) referendum? In 2011 the public rejected a proposal to adopt the AV system, with 68% voting 'no' to change. While this was considered a major setback for electoral reformers, it absolutely does not represent a rejection of PR by voters. The AV system is not a proportional system. AV allows voters to rank candidates so that the latter require the support of a majority of electors to be elected; however, it retains the single-member constituencies that lead to the same disproportional electoral results seen under FPTP. In fact, if AV had been used for the 2015 general election, it is likely that the result would have been even less proportional. Even Nick Clegg, who negotiated the referendum for the Liberal Democrats, described AV as 'a miserable little compromise'. When Caroline Lucas proposed a cross-party amendment to include proportional systems as options in the referendum, it was voted down by MPs.

For the opponents of PR, the referendum on AV had two obvious benefits. First, it made the chance of reform far less likely, as there was no public demand for AV. Second, had AV been adopted, it would have retained the essential aspects of FPTP. The results of the referendum were as you would expect for a Hobson's choice between two bad voting systems: most people stayed at home. Turnout was less than 42%, meaning that less than 29% of the electorate voted to defend FPTP. Hardly a ringing endorsement.

Through much of British history, disinterest has categorised public opinion towards electoral reform. Attempts to change the electoral system have lacked the interest required from the public to become a reality, and the issue has been confined to the most committed political activists. However, this has changed dramatically in the last few years.

As Dunleavy argues, the adoption of PR for elections to the European Parliament and devolved assemblies has fundamentally changed British politics.[27] Voters occupy a more diverse range of positions and are represented by a broader range of political parties. This diverse multipartism is incompatible with the FPTP system at Westminster and has exposed the system's failings. More people than ever before are aware of the disproportionality of elections, the pressure to vote tactically and the failure of MPs to adequately represent their constituents. This is backed up by polling, which has shown PR consistently enjoying support from the majority of voters, with opposition being as low as 6–12% in some polls. It is in this context that a renewed push for PR has emerged, one that is genuinely grassroots, based on overwhelming demand from the public and determined to change Britain's politics.

Make Votes Matter

The 2015 general election – the most disproportionate in British history – sparked a surge of support for PR. Millions of voters did not see their views reflected in Parliament, and it was clear that FPTP had grossly distorted the election result. Almost half a million people signed petitions for PR in the aftermath of the election, and politicians from across the political spectrum came together to push for reform.

By all accounts, the response to the 2015 general election was different to previous spikes in interest for PR. The rise of parties such as the Green Party, UKIP and the SNP transformed the political landscape and, as Patrick Dunleavy predicted, made the failings of FPTP even more obvious. The election of a majority Conservative government – with just 37% of the vote – shocked voters and commentators, who had predicted a hung parliament. Public interest in reform following the election was maintained for far longer than after previous elections.

Figure 4. The Great Gathering for Voting Reform, London, July 2015. *Photo*: Laurie Taylor.

It was in this atmosphere that a grassroots campaign began to emerge. Thousands of people expressed an interest in campaigning or taking action. Through his Change.org petition, which amassed almost a quarter of a million signatures, 16-year-old Owen Winter invited supporters to join a Facebook group, initially called the 'Voting Reform Team', which quickly grew to over 7,000 members. From this group, a core team of activists agreed to establish an ongoing campaign. Our group then organised the Great Gathering for Voting Reform in July 2015, which saw over a thousand people meeting to demonstrate outside Parliament. Local branches of supporters appeared, with Joe Sousek leading the formation of the first, South East London for Electoral Reform, which had its inaugural meeting in October 2015.

As is inevitable with new groups, the Voting Reform Team went through a process of forming, storming, norming and performing. During one of the 'storms', when a key organiser left the group, it became clear that Klina Jordan would need to take a more leading role if the group were to continue, and within months it was taking up most of her time. In the autumn of 2015 we had our first face-to-face team day, and a few of us were elected as co-facilitators to lead the campaign. As we developed the campaign into a more long-term project, it became clear to us that we needed a stronger name. So, in November, we agreed to crowdsource a new one. Over 8,000 people voted to select 'Make Votes Matter' (MVM): a suggestion that came from Owen's lovely mum, Alison.

MVM is an example of grassroots organising in a digital age, with online petitions and Facebook groups giving way to a democratically organised core activist team, supported by local groups across the country. It is a genuine expression of a surge in support, based on volunteers and crowdsourcing. This is the feature that sets it apart from pushes for PR that have come before, and it reflects a fundamental shift in support for PR since 2015.

With thousands of people taking action to win real democracy, the path is being laid to reach PR in the next few years rather than decades. To secure PR, a grassroots movement must have the strength across the country to campaign and persuade people to back PR; the Labour Party must abandon its indifference on the electoral system, as it did when it changed the electoral system for European elections in 1998; and an alliance of politicians and organisations must form that spans the breadth of British politics and society, eventually making up a majority of MPs and introducing PR. Progress towards these goals is well underway, but it will require sustained action by supporters and volunteers to ensure success, and avoid losing the progress that has already been made.

The path to proportional representation

With a relatively small central team, it is volunteers and activists who take the MVM message to the public. Across the country, local MVM groups and individuals are taking action for PR. At the time of writing, there are at least 20 active MVM groups, all locally run and democratically organised. The groups choose how to take action, lobbying MPs, holding street stalls and organising events. In Totnes, for example, activists met their local MP in costume as suffragettes and were featured in the local press. MVM North London holds a regular 'roadshow' stall, signing up supporters and persuading the public to take action. In June 2018 MVM called a national day of action – Demand Democracy Day – featuring over 60 street stalls across the country, hosted by local people from Truro to Aberdeen. Local action like this reaches many more people than national campaigns ever could, and it engages people who would otherwise never have considered the way we elect MPs. With new local groups emerging and the MVM activist network expanding, these local actions will extend to every part of the country, building support among the public and coordinating the continued lobbying of politicians.

However, grassroots action alone is not enough to bring about change, which is why local action is supported and coordinated by the MVM Alliance of parties, politicians, organisations and celebrities. A perfect example of this collaboration is 'Hungry for Democracy', which was held in February 2018 and saw 407 individuals joining a 24-hour 'hunger strike' to commemorate the centenary of the Representation of the People Act. Among the hunger strikers were MPs, such as Stephen Kinnock; MEPs, such as Molly Scott Cato; and political leaders including Jonathan Bartley, co-leader of the Green Party of England and Wales. Activists and politicians took collective action to push the issue up the agenda.

At the time of writing, the MVM Alliance includes all British opposition parties aside from Labour, and it is continually growing. It is also supported by individuals including Shadow Chancellor John McDonnell, actor Michael Sheen, comedian Frankie Boyle and campaigner Helen Pankhurst. The Alliance brings together politicians, parties and campaigning organisations such as Compass, Unlock Democracy and the Electoral Reform Society at regular meetings to coordinate strategy and actions, and to lay the groundwork to introduce PR into the House of Commons.

Figure 5. Activists in Totnes meet their MP Sarah Wollaston, in costume as suffragettes, for Demand Democracy Day (30 June 2018). *Photo:* Laurie Taylor.

While different parties within the Alliance have different system preferences, all parties (the Greens, Liberal Democrats, Plaid Cymru, SNP, UKIP and the Women's Equality Party) have signed up to a 'Good Systems Agreement'. The MVM Alliance pooled collective knowledge and carried out extensive research to agree on the principles that are required of 'good' voting systems. We drew on the work of official expert panels and consultations from around the world as well as a wide range of academic literature and a wealth of knowledge from other expert sources. The aim of the agreement is to sidestep the debate about which PR system is best by agreeing principles common to all 'good' voting systems, and to avoid a possible future situation in which the opportunity to introduce PR arises but electoral reform MPs are split about which system to bring in.

As one of the two biggest parties and the only British opposition party that does not back PR, Labour is key to this process. As can be seen from Labour's support for PR in Scotland, Wales, London and European elections, there is a strong case for feeling optimistic about Labour backing PR. In recent years, support within the party has ballooned, making 'Labour for PR' the third key strand of the MVM campaign. Over 80 Labour MPs have come out in support of PR, with a much smaller number saying they are opposed. By far the largest group of Labour MPs constitutes those who are undecided or undeclared.

Figure 6. Save Our Democracy rally, London (24 June 2017). *Photo*: Klina Jordan.

In isolation, these efforts for PR could be doomed to fail, but together they represent the biggest mobilisation for PR in British history. It now falls on all of us – as voters, party members and activists – to ensure that the move to MVM succeeds. We know we can achieve *real* democracy in the next few years, but we need your help. To find out how, search online for 'Make Votes Matter' and we'll show you. Together, we can transform the UK into a *real* democracy and give people the power to build a country for the common good, with a stronger society, a more equal economy and a much healthier environment. Join us and help create a positive, genuinely democratic future.

Endnotes

1   Udo Bux, *The European Parliament: Historical Background*, March 2018; https://bit.ly/2AQgZ1s.

2   Oonagh Gay, *The European Parliamentary Elections Bill*, House of Commons Library Research Paper 98/102 (London: House of Commons Library, 1998).

3   Catherine Hoskyns and John Lambert, 'How democratic is the European Parliament?', in: Catherine Hoskyns and Michael Newman (eds.) *Democratizing the European Union: Issues for the Twenty-first Century (Perspectives on Democratization)* (Manchester: Manchester University Press, 2000).

4   Matt Golder, 'Democratic electoral systems around the world', *Electoral Studies*, Vol. 24, No. 1, 2005, p. 103.

5   HC Deb (13 December 1977), Vol. 941, Col. 1977 (accessed 11 July 2018); https://bit.ly/2yZZCtH.

6   Maurice Duverger, *Les Partis Politiques* (Paris: Librairie Armand Colin, 1951).

7   Kenneth Benoit, 'Electoral laws as political consequences: explaining the origins and change of electoral institutions', *Annual Review of Political Science*, Vol. 10, No. 1, 2007, p. 363.

8   Stein Rokkan, *Citizens, Elections, Parties: Approaches to the Comparative Study of the Processes of Development* (Oslo: Universitetsforlaget, 1970).

9   Octavio Neto and Gary Cox, 'Electoral institutions, cleavage structures, and the number of parties', *American Journal of Political Science*, Vol. 41, No. 1, 1997, p. 149.

10 Carles Boix, 'Setting the rules of the game: the choice of electoral systems in advanced democracies', *The American Political Science Review*, Vol. 93, No. 3, 1999, p. 609.

11 Chris Prosser, 'Second order electoral rules and national party systems: the Duvergerian effects of European Parliament elections', *European Union Politics*, Vol. 17, No. 3, 2016, p. 366.

12 Richard Cracknell and Bryn Morgan, *European Parliament Elections – 1979 to 1994*, House of Commons Library Research Paper 99/57 (London: House of Commons Library, 1999).

13 Patrick Dunleavy, 'Facing up to multi-party politics: how partisan dealignment and PR voting have fundamentally changed Britain's party systems', *Parliamentary Affairs*, Vol. 58, No. 3, 2005, p. 503.

14 John Curtice, 'The 1989 European election: protest or green tide?', *Electoral Studies*, Vol. 8, No. 3, 1989, p. 217.

15 Arend Lijphart, *Patterns of Democracy: Government Forms and Performance in 36 Countries* (London/New Haven: Yale University Press, 2012).

16 Dennis Pilon, *The Politics of Voting: Reforming Canada's Electoral System* (Toronto: Edmond Montgomery Publications, 2007).

17 International Institute for Democracy and Electoral Assistance, *Voter Turnout in Western Europe* (Stockholm: 2004).

18 Markus Crepaz, 'Constitutional structures and regime performance in 18 industrialized democracies: a test of Olson's hypothesis', *European Journal of Political Research*, Vol. 29, 1996, p. 87.

19 Arend Lijphart, *Patterns of Democracy: Government Forms and Performance in 36 Countries* (London/New Haven: Yale University Press, 2012).

20 Patrick Dunleavy, 'Policy disasters: explaining the UK's record', *Public Policy and Administration*, Vol. 10, No. 2, 1995, p. 52.

21 Saloman Orellana, *Electoral Systems and Governance: How Diversity Can Improve Policy Making*, (New York: Routledge Press, 2014).

22 Darcie Cohen, *Do Political Preconditions Affect Environmental Outcomes? Exploring the Linkages Between Proportional Representation, Green Parties and the Kyoto Protocol*, Thesis, Simon Fraser University, 2010; http://summit.sfu.ca/item/10084 (accessed 12 July 2018).

23 Vicki Birchfield and Markus Crepaz, 'The impact of constitutional structures and collective and competitive veto points on income inequality in industrialized democracies', *European Journal of Political Research*, Vol. 34, 1998, p. 175.

24 Lijphart (2012).

25 Ibid.

26 Steve Chan and David Lebland, 'Explaining wars fought by established democracies: do institutional constraints matter?', *Political Research Quarterly*, Vol. 56, No. 4, 2003, p. 385.

27 Patrick Dunleavy, 'Facing up to multi-party politics: how partisan dealignment and PR voting have fundamentally changed Britain's party systems', *Parliamentary Affairs*, Vol. 58, No. 3, 2005, p. 503.

Part II

The UK's Green MEPs: in their own words

Chapter 3

London, Brussels and beyond: my work as a Green MEP

Jean Lambert

Welcome at last

'Welcome at last'. This was the greeting from Juan Behrend, Co-Secretary General of the Green Group in the European Parliament, when I arrived at the Group's first meeting after the 1999 European election. It was the first in the UK to be held by a method of proportional representation. I knew Juan, and many others at that meeting to set up the Group for the 1999–2004 term, through my years as a UK Green Party of England and Wales representative to the European Green Coordination (forerunner of the European Green Party) and as my party's 'guest' MEP in the 1989 Green Alternative European Link (GRAEL) group, which was the first coordinated group of its kind led by the Greens. For two-and-a-half years, I had been a member of the Group's executive body (the Bureau), had attended and voted at meetings of the Group, and had represented it at times, such as supporting the then Czechoslovakian Greens (*Strana Zélèny*) in the first election after the collapse of the Soviet Union.

How had this come about? It was the result of the 1989 European election, when, under the previous disproportional electoral system (first-past-the-post), the UK Greens gained an average of 14.5% of the vote but no MEPs.[1] Under a proportional system, we would have been the largest national green delegation. The European Greens wanted to acknowledge the injustice of the result, and Sara Parkin (Secretary of the European Green Coordination) negotiated an honorary position in the Group for our party. This was offered to me and I took it without hesitation. It proved to be a very valuable apprenticeship. This meant that when the Labour government introduced the regional list system of proportional election in 1999, I had a good idea as to how the Group worked and why the Greens really mattered in the European Parliament. I knew I wanted to join then and that it could be possible in the ten-MEP-member region of London.

I was fortunate enough to be voted in as number one on the London Green Party list. We ran the London campaign on the basis of 'Your Vote Counts': if one in ten voters votes green, a Green MEP will be elected. We could show that we were part of a European political family that was already elected at the European level and getting results. People understand that environmental issues cross borders, so cross-border.working is essential. The proportional electoral system meant voting Green was not a wasted vote.

The election of two Greens (myself in London and Caroline Lucas in South East England) was also a momentous moment for the Green Party, although it was largely unnoticed by the British press, which seemed to be more taken up with the election of UKIP: a recurrent problem, as it has turned out. At that point, we had only two Green councillors elected in London (but more in the country generally), and the Greater London Authority had yet to come into being; its first elections were held the following year. However, a month earlier, in May 1999, we had seen the election of Scottish Green Robin Harper to the new Scottish Parliament.

Arriving in the European Parliament with real MEPs in 1999, the UK Green Party had a clear view on our priorities in terms of committee membership when it came to negotiations in the Group. We wanted my wonderful colleague, Caroline Lucas, on the Trade Committee, as she was a policy advisor on trade at Oxfam. The Party had (and still has) a highly critical approach to the World Trade Organization (WTO) agenda, and we wanted those objections raised.

I had prioritised the Constitutional Affairs Committee, as we knew major EU Treaty changes were being contemplated. As a council member of the UK campaign group Charter 88, I had a strong interest in constitutional issues such as introducing a written constitution for the UK (how useful that would have been in many of our national issues with the EU, not least in determining the basis on which we could change that relationship) as well as the entrenchment of international human rights standards and electoral systems.

However, any negotiation means being prepared to give ground on some things if you can achieve your main aim, so Caroline joined the Committee on Industry, External Trade, Research and Energy and I agreed to join the Committee on Employment and Social Affairs. I also managed to secure a 'substitute' position on the Citizens' Freedoms and Rights, Justice and Home Affairs Committee, arguing that, as I represented the EU's most diverse city, it would be useful to be on the committee dealing with anti-discrimination,[2] asylum and immigration. Plus I've had a long-standing commitment to anti-racism.

I also picked up a working seat on the Petitions Committee. All EU residents have the individual Treaty right to petition the European Parliament if they feel that their rights under EU legislation have not been upheld, or that legislation has not been properly applied by EU or national authorities. The Petitions Committee proved a very useful place to learn about areas of EU law that I was not engaged with through my committee work. It also meant I could support particular petitions in the committee and help individual citizens or groups to address the committee at times.

I worked with objectors to plans for developments at Crystal Palace to bring their case to the committee.[3] Partly as a result of this, the Commission engaged with the UK government to improve the quality of training and guidance for local authority planning officers in terms of implementing the Environmental Impact Assessment Directive. The petitioners may not have got everything they wanted from the EU, but they had an impact.

As an elected Green who was not on the environment or agriculture committees, finding a point of contact on such issues needed consideration and some adaptation to take into account the very welcome election of three Greens to the Greater London Authority's London Assembly in 2000: Darren Johnson, Jenny Jones (now Baroness Jones of Moulsecoomb) and Victor Anderson.

I decided to focus on the directives coming on stream that were linked to the Aarhus Convention (2005/370/EC) and commissioned the Environmental Law Foundation (ELF) to conduct an analysis of how UK planning law matched up with existing EU law as well as new proposals. One of the benefits of being a Green MEP is the information monies we have to promote and explain our work and to develop ideas. For me, planning law shapes our environment and is very much underestimated as a tool for giving the latter a greener design.

Figure 1. Jean campaigning to save Queen's Market, East London.

I also became involved in the Thames Gateway 'green' initiative under the leadership of Professor Mark Brearley (of the University of East London), which promoted the concept of a green grid running through the development in order to provide nature corridors as well as walking and cycling possibilities. This concept was taken up by my green colleagues on the London Assembly and has now become an official London government strategy.

In the early days after the election, I found people would contact their Green MEP as a sort of 'higher court of appeal' for local environmental issues, such as their neighbouring restaurants' emissions. My London staff generally answered those letters, pointing people to the appropriate authority or advice service. Maybe it's my teaching background, but it's always been important to me to help people understand which level of government is appropriate to help with their problem. The EU is not the overall control body that many assume it is.

When I first started out, I also found that I had a big question to answer: 'Who you do represent?' I believe it is a myth that you represent all of your constituents when you clearly can't. I decided that London – as in the territorial City and big business – had enough people representing its interests in the EU (which is partly at the root of our current problems), but London's poorer communities did not. Also, if you're a lone MEP trying to represent what the EU can offer, you need to get your voice out, and the best way, I felt, was to work with communities of interests across London, as it was not possible to represent everyone. I felt, too, that there were many people who never thought the Greens had anything to say to them; they saw us as only caring about sea and trees, not about equality – whether between people or within societies – or tackling poverty. Given the committees I was on, there was a clear opportunity to reach out.

A major recipient of the EU Social Fund is London, as, while it is one of the EU's richest regions, it has areas of significant deprivation, a skills shortage, relatively high youth unemployment and the highest rate of child poverty of any English region. So, a good way to get to know London was to visit EU-funded projects, often meeting people who had never met 'a real MEP' before, let alone a Green one. I learnt about how EU money works at the grassroots, through training older workers in computer skills (which are essential in today's labour market), providing nursery assistant training for female refugees, teaching people English or training young men as gym instructors. I saw how that money was being used to help civil society organisations meet local needs, and to assist local authorities in delivering more services through matching EU funding.

The then Mayor of London, Ken Livingstone, was active in both promoting London and securing EU funding through London House in Brussels. A number of EU regions and cities have set up such bodies. London House was used to showcase the work of London's policies and voluntary sector. London's MEPs were included as part of the capital's representation and that helped our visibility.

All that ended when Boris Johnson became Mayor of London. London no longer had a visible presence in the Parliament. I remember receiving one letter from the Mayor: he was asking me not to support the introduction of any financial transaction tax (FTT), as it would be bad for London's financial sector. Unfortunately for Mayor Johnson, Greens are long-standing advocates of an FTT.

I also received one invitation to the launch of a Joint European Support for Sustainable Investment in City Areas (JESSICA) funded project: setting up the London Green Fund (LGF). This included finance for the improvement of energy efficiency in London's social housing stock. The Commissioner for Regional Affairs, Danuta Hübner, was introduced by the Mayor, in his usual charming fashion, as he muttered that he really didn't think we should be in the EU. Nevertheless, London took the money and it has proved to be a very valuable initiative. Ironically, Danuta Hübner is now an MEP and chairs the Constitutional Affairs Committee, which is responsible for the European Parliament's Brexit response.

Green jobs

Obviously there have been ongoing, major environmental issues in London with a clear EU dimension: air quality and airport expansion, particularly Heathrow, for example. This has been shared work for the Greens at various levels of government both in and around London.

I was involved from its early days in the Clean Air in London campaign, led by the inspiring Simon Birkett. However, the London Assembly Greens were able to have a more immediate impact on policy in London from the get-go, helped early on by then Mayor of London Ken Livingstone. He needed their votes to get his budget through, which resulted in £500 million for cycling initiatives.[4] This impressive work has been continued by current Green Assembly Members Caroline Russell and Sian Berry. As members of the European Parliament's Environment, Public Health and Food Safety Committee, Caroline Lucas and Keith Taylor (successive Green MEPs for the South East) have pushed Clean Air initiatives in the EU. I have written to and raised air quality issues with the Commission, responded to numerous consultations at the EU, UK and London levels, spoken in public meetings and produced London-focused information materials.[5]

Figure 2. Green jobs: Jean visiting a recycling plant in London.

We've developed a similar pattern of work in opposing airport expansion, where the issue of air quality joins with the pressing issue of combatting climate change: air transport is one of the fastest growing sources of greenhouse gas emissions. The Committee on Employment and Social Affairs has also offered an opportunity to consolidate our work on climate change, environmental protection and jobs.

In the earlier days of the environmental movement, there was an attitude among many trade unions and certain businesses that environmental goals and the Greens were bad for jobs. Nothing could be further from the truth. We have always argued that an ecological transformation of society would open the door for new industries, and that many would be more locally based as opposed to offshore.

While wider industrial policy is covered by the European Parliament's Industry, Research and Energy Committee, the Committee on Employment and Social Affairs has a role in employment strategy, setting targets, determining skills input, and identifying particular groups that are vulnerable on the labour market and how to work with them.

In my work on green jobs, I have aimed to get the environment and climate included in strategic planning and to address a wider need to feature both in employment policy as a whole. I managed as early as 2006 to get an environmental dimension included and recognised as a key component in the educational part of the EU's sustainability strategy. In 2004 I also commissioned a study from Capacity Global, *Integrating Social Inclusion and Environment: Exploring the Potential for Joined-up Thinking*,[6] to examine how well the EU's proposals for National Action Plans for employment and social inclusion actually integrated economic, social and environmental strands. Unsurprisingly, the main conclusion was that, while the economic and social strands complemented each other, the environment came a very poor third. Part of the study included focus group discussions with young people from deprived areas in London and Hamburg, which looked at their experience of training and education. A number of those taking part said they wanted to know more about the environment and how their work training could help to improve this. However, they felt they had been taught little or nothing on the subject. An issue raised by the adults involved was that they would like to do more, but 'who trains the trainers?'. A good question and one I've worked to help answer.

I began to ask questions of commissioners and the EU agencies linked to the Employment Committee. These included the European Centre for the Development of Vocational Training (Cedefop), the European Foundation for Living and Working Conditions (Eurofound), the European Training Foundation (ETF) and the European Agency for Safety and Health at Work (EU-OSHA). 'What is your strategy to promote investment and/or training in green jobs?', I asked. It was interesting, and sometimes depressing, to hear the replies. For some, especially ministers representing Council or nonemployment commissioners, I was speaking a foreign language politically. However, the answers have improved over time as policies have developed and understanding has grown. Greens have certainly played an important role in that. I took the requests from the Capacity Global study and, in 2006 (during my second term), commissioned a DVD from Redcurrent Films to show how ideas from the grassroots could be taken into and heard by the Parliament and various agencies.[7]

EU4U! was made by college students and filmed mainly in the European Parliament. It looked at the committees' work and how their requests were now, partly, in the EU Sustainability Strategy and could be taken further. It seemed to me to be really important to show young people that they are not voiceless in the European Union. This was also why I was happy to help support the setting up of the European Parliament's cross-party Youth Intergroup at the start of my third term in 2009.[8] We also produced a publication in London to highlight what could be done in the capital to increase energy efficiency in the city's housing stock: *Hothouses* (2007).[9] This linked the job creation potential across all skill levels with the Energy Efficiency of Buildings Directive (2010/31/EU) and the need to deliver on targets for reducing climate change emissions.

In 2008 I produced another publication: *Green Work: Employment and Skills – The Climate Change Challenge.*[10] This tied in well with the publication of a major report from the United Nations Development Programme and the International Labour Organisation, *The Green Jobs Initiative: Towards Decent Work in a Sustainable Low-carbon World,* in September that year.[11] This powerful report showed the large opportunities in employment there would be in a world that took climate change seriously. It also stressed the importance of decent work, fair pay and good working conditions rather than exploitation and rock-bottom pay. This fitted with work I'd been doing on the Working Time Directive (2003/88/EC) as well as the Temporary Agency Work Directive (2008/104/EC). The United Nations (UN) report also stressed the need for 'just transition' in terms of providing support and investment in and for those whose jobs would disappear as greenhouse gas emissions reduced, such as workers in the fossil fuel industries. This report aligned with what Greens had been saying for years and gave a new dynamism to those in the 2009 Commission, which came forward with *Europe 2020: A European Strategy for Smart, Sustainable and Inclusive Growth*.[12]

I wanted the Greens to add to the momentum created by the UN report. I had the opportunity to do this with the UK-based Campaign Against Climate Change, which helped me to strengthen connections with some of the UK trade unions such as the Public and Commercial Services Union (PCS) and the National Union of Teachers (NUT). These were committed to making progress on tackling climate change and wanted to do more in the workplace. I gave talks to professional bodies (such as the Royal College of Occupational Therapists) keen to make changes in their own working environments. The active engagement of people at work is crucial to embedding environmental thinking throughout an organisation.

I used some of the information monies available to me as an MEP to produce a DVD on green jobs.[13] This used three London businesses – the Arcola Theatre, Calverts Press and Acorn House Restaurant – to show that an environmentally conscious business can take many organisational forms: a charity, a workers co-operative, a social enterprise. The DVD was launched at the Arcola Theatre and inspired a lot of interest, including from a local kebab takeaway. The EU Commissioner for Employment and Social Affairs, Lazlo Andor, even used the DVD for in-house training on 'what is a green job?'. Along with Trades Union Congress (TUC) General Secretary Frances O'Grady, he spoke at a major conference I organised on this subject the following year.

With the change of Commission in 2014, at the start of my fourth term, many of us felt there was a risk of the 'just transition' concept fading in importance as we slid back to the old 'growth and jobs' agenda. So, we decided, as the Greens–European Free Alliance, to push for what's known as an 'own initiative' report (INI for short), which is nonlegislative, to respond to the outgoing Commission's proposals on the 'Green employment initiative: tapping into the job-creation potential of the green economy' (2014/2238(INI)). We managed to convince the coordinators in the Committee on Employment and Social Affairs (representatives from each of the political groups in the Parliament) that it would be good for us to have an official response. My group was assigned the report and I took it on as rapporteur.

Figure 3. Our green economic future: event with Commissioner Andor and TUC General Secretary Frances O'Grady. *Photo*: David Connolly.

The group and I used this opportunity to talk to a range of experts and interested parties on the issue. We ran two roundtables, one in London and one in Brussels, and invited academics, trade unions, green businesses, business bodies for small and large companies, students, representatives from education and training establishments and relevant professional bodies to contribute ideas. Generally, the committee backed my key points, for example, on the need for an education and training framework that moves from a general awareness of the need for resource efficiency and emissions reductions to sectoral and specific work training, and for strategic investment in the wider setting of needing to aim for a green economy in general. We held a Green Group Conference to reinforce the report's influence.

I was invited by the EU's environmental commissioner to speak at the Commission's Green Week in 2017, which focused on green jobs and made a written contribution to a European Trade Union Confederation (ETUC) conference on the topic later that year. At the UK end, we used much of the work from the report to strengthen our response to the UK government's consultation on its proposed industrial strategy.[14] It was disappointing – to put it diplomatically – to see the government fail to have a clear focal point for a resource-efficient, climate-emissions-compliant strategy. However, this is indicative of the inability of so many politicians to get their heads around the way in which political goals need to change in light of the challenges facing us.

South Asia

Apart from my committee work in the European Parliament, I also chair one of its permanent delegations to countries with which the EU has trading relationships. I am responsible for the Delegation for Relations with the Countries of South Asia (DSAS). This covers six countries around India (which has its own delegation): Bangladesh, Bhutan, the Maldives, Nepal, Pakistan and Sri Lanka. While Bangladesh and the Maldives are well known as being vulnerable to climate change in terms of rising sea levels, Sri Lanka has ranked fourth in Germanwatch's latest Global Climate Risk Index top ten, and Pakistan has ranked as the seventh most vulnerable country for *long-term* climate risk, just below Bangladesh.[15] The governments and people of the six countries covered by DSAS will all tell you that they are already seeing the effects of climate change. They will also point out that, as a nation, they are not significant contributors to global greenhouse gas emissions.

The Himalayas provide the world's 'third pole' and are the source of fresh water for approximately 1.4 billion people. Increasingly, hydroelectric power is a source of energy and income for the countries and regions of the Himalayas. As a delegation chair who is also a Green, I have tried to give this part of the world a voice in the Parliament on climate issues. Until recently, the Maldives chaired the Association of Small Island States (AOSIS), which acts as an informal grouping within the UNFCC. I invited their chair to speak to us and asked environmental NGOs and other ambassadors to contribute. We have also invited the International Centre for Integrated Mountain Development (ICIMOD) to address us, and we have created other opportunities in the Parliament and with the Commission. Of course, climate change is not the only pressing issue in the region, but it will affect all other policy areas, and it puts additional pressures on the existing tensions within society.

I have also focused heavily on the garment and textile industry in South Asia and beyond. The horrors of the Tazreen fire and the collapse of the Rana Plaza building on the outskirts of Dhaka, Bangladesh, which killed over 1,000 people, raised many questions as to how global companies take responsibility for their supply chains.[16] This scrutiny also provides a challenge to developing countries to look at how their governments can take more control over the quality of their industries yet remain competitive in global markets, where companies often have more effective power than national governments.

The Delegation has returned to the issue over the years since the tragedies, in both Brussels and Bangladesh as well as on visits to Pakistan, now a beneficiary of the EU's GSP+ trading scheme (an extension of the Generalised Scheme of Preferences). Corporate social responsibility and supply-chain compliance are important areas of debate in the European Parliament, where many of us have been pushing the Commission and Council to go further to make companies more transparent and more responsible for their supply chains. The voluntary approach is not enough, as bad practices will always undermine good. It should be noted that UK Conservative MEPs have always voted for the voluntary approach.

I have hosted a number of events in the European Parliament on the ready-made garment (RMG) sector: some with NGOs such as

CARE International and the Clean Clothes Campaign, and others where I have set the agenda, such as arranging a screening of *The True Cost* (a film directed by Andrew Morgan). I also put on an exhibition in the square outside of the European Parliament, comprised of photos taken by Bangladeshi photographers of both the Rana Plaza collapse and some of the survivors, taken after treatment. The EU Commissioner for Trade, Cecilia Malmström, also agreed to speak at a conference I hosted, to set out her commitment to improving supply chains.

Figure 4. With Rebecca Harms MEP and Malala Yousafzai – Pakistani activist, Sakharov Prize winner and Nobel laureate.

The delegation connection has given me the opportunity to speak about the fashion industry and supply chains at demonstrations, at universities including Harvard, and with manufacturers, brands, trade unions and governments. It has provided me with an opportunity to question the way the industry works, the issues of consumption and disposal, and the environmental cost of the fashion industry – reckoned to be the second most-polluting industry in the world. I also drafted the Committee on Employment and Social Affairs's response to the Commission Flagship Initiative on the garment sector, where we were able to comment on labour and factory inspections and draw attention to the poor conditions and pay in many EU garment factories. This is a global issue and many of the measures now being taken in Bangladesh should provide an example for the way forward.

Chairing the DSAS has also given me the opportunity to travel to these countries along with colleagues from other political groups. I am always impressed by the support we get from the EU Ambassadors and European External Action Service (EEAS) when we travel, and the willingness of ministers, MPs and civil society activists to meet with us.

These meetings can be very sensitive. Official EU delegations are charged with raising issues of human rights, including the death penalty, to which, I am pleased to say, the EU has a principled objection. It can be difficult to raise that with MPs who have just lifted their national moratorium after over a hundred children have died in a terrorist attack, as at Peshawar, or a few days after the execution of those convicted of the murder of family members of the nation's prime minister, as in Bangladesh. Yet we raise it.

It is also difficult to raise questions around the impunity of military personnel or police officers in times of conflict, as in Sri Lanka, or of repressive laws against human rights defenders. We are sometimes accused of promoting a 'Western agenda', but I always stress that these are international conventions and values that we are upholding, designed to improve the lives and security of the citizens of any country. As a Green, I can also point out that we hold the EU and our governments to those same standards: this is not so easy for some from other parties.

While travelling with the delegation, we also visit projects supported by the EU. Many of these are concerned with women's empowerment, from small microcredit schemes to advocacy for marginalised groups, such as the Dalits or the indigenous communities of the Chittagong Hill Tracts in Bangladesh.

International aid matters and, done well with local communities and governments, it transforms lives. The EU is seen as an honest partner that supports people and good governance without 'dictating' to governments in the way that some other global powers do. But there are those who remind you that 'we have other friends', as it was once put to me, who don't make demands regarding human rights and better democracy. That is why it is important to meet ministers and politicians on their own ground. In my experience, it really helps you to understand the context and culture within which they are working and to find a way forward that can work for the benefit of the people. The EU's broader work supporting democracy internationally is also important, which is why I've participated in EU election observation missions in Africa and Asia.

Asylum, displacement and diversity

When talking about the EU's Common European Asylum System, or the development of its immigration policy, I often feel like a living history exhibit. Both of these areas were introduced in the Treaty of Amsterdam (adopted in 1997).

One of the earliest trips I took was to represent the Committee on Employment and Social Affairs at a meeting of the Migrants Forum in Casablanca in October 1999. Wondering what to say about the EU's position on third-country nationals (non-EU citizens) in the EU, I was helped by the timely adoption of the Tampere Council Conclusions (named after the Finnish city where they were adopted).[17] It sent out a political message on the creation of 'an area of freedom, security and justice in the European Union' under the Treaty of Amsterdam. It also set up the mechanism for drawing up a draft Charter of Fundamental Rights. The Conclusions are worth reading in their own right for those who think the EU is a valuable institution. They declare that the rights of third-country nationals should be 'approximated to [those] of Member State nationals', the caveat being that said nationals should be legally staying within a member state.

The statement of intent from Tampere is something I have taken seriously in all of my work on migration within the Parliament – and

I have done a lot of it, both in terms of legislation and in other ways. I have also worked on the rights of undocumented migrants, for whom many governments have the single, public solution of 'deportation', neglecting to examine why so many people find themselves in this situation. This is one reason why I have supported the European Network on Statelessness (ENS) since it was set up in 2012. I find it shocking that so many governments still have no effective system for tackling this issue of people existing like ghosts in our societies, as they have no documentation to establish an identity. Quite rightly, people are aghast at Myanmar's treatment of the Rohingya, who have been settled in the country for generations but denied citizenship and basic rights.

Figure 5. EU election observation mission, Sierra Leone. *Photo*: Press office, EU Election Observation Mission Sierra Leone.

Yet there are many people living within our own countries without an identity or a country they can legally claim is theirs. I helped the ENS bring their concerns before the Parliament via a study I proposed the Committee on Civil Liberties, Justice and

Home Affairs should commission, along with a hearing to follow up and reinforce the work of the 2015 Luxembourg Presidency on the issue. At least it is now seen as a priority for children's rights, as I have also helped the Parliament's cross-party group on children's rights (of which I'm a founding member and vice-president) to invest in working to ensure that no child is stateless. In addition, I have supported organisations such as the Platform for International Cooperation on Undocumented Migrants (PICUM) and Doctors of the World in their work to ensure that no-one in need of health-care is left untreated. To me, it makes no sense to deny primary healthcare to children or refuse to treat people with life-threatening conditions or infectious diseases because they cannot provide the right documents.

In the Parliament, and outside it, I am viewed as one of the few MEPs who provides a strong voice for asylum seekers and refugees. Even before I was elected as an MEP, I had a keen interest in the topic and had been following a professional development course on 'language acquisition for young people of migrant backgrounds and asylum seekers' at my local Further Education college. Asylum seekers are some of the world's most vulnerable people. They are not all fleeing conflict in boats but come from a wide range of countries and social circumstances. The world is a mess and people are forced to move, sometimes alone and sometimes en masse. I find it difficult to understand why 'asylum seeker' is often seen as such a dirty term by many in politics and society as a whole.

I appreciate that we need to help prevent conflict and promote good governance and human rights elsewhere in the world so that people do not have to flee oppression. In which case, it would be great if governments were more willing to donate to help those countries supporting the most refugees: Tunisia or Lebanon in our own neighbourhood, or Bangladesh and Pakistan elsewhere, for example. As you can probably sense, this issue makes me angry, so – along with others in the Parliament and outside – I channel that emotion to affect policy and legislation. Over the years, I have been responsible for a number of parliamentary reports, some legislative, for the Common European Asylum System.

I was the rapporteur on the regulation that set up the European Asylum Support Office (EASO). This assists member states and the EU in implementing our asylum system properly, which is an uphill struggle. I was pleased we managed to keep and strengthen the role of the Consultative Body for EASO, which gives them a range of expertise – from academics, NGOs, local authorities (thanks to input from the Committee of the Regions rapporteur) and others – to draw on.

My work on the Qualification Directive proved frustrating, as the Parliament's progressive views are held back by national governments in Council. This directive sets out the grounds on which people can qualify for, or lose, international protection. We achieved a parliamentary majority for a progressive report on the first version of the directive, but the Parliament was only consulted at that stage. When we received the reissued (recast) directive to consider in 2011 and I was again the rapporteur, there were parts the Parliament was not allowed to amend; so, although it was then a co-decision process, we had less chance of winning. We did, however, manage to introduce 'gender identity' into the text as grounds for consideration. This was a first in asylum legislation and was achieved through working with the International Lesbian, Gay, Bisexual, Trans and Intersex Association (ILGA), who lobbied specific national governments to get a majority in Council – a strategy often neglected by NGOs, who tend to concentrate on the European Parliament alone.

Hopefully, as Greens, we will have a major impact on the new version of the Dublin Regulation, which determines the member state responsible for handling an asylum claim. This is a dossier I have worked on throughout my time in the Parliament and have generally voted against. We feel the current version denies asylum seekers any element of agency in deciding which country they wish to claim asylum in, ignoring any links they might have (apart from some family ties) and 'trapping' them in the first EU country or safe country they come to.

Over the years, it has become clear that some countries end up dealing with many more cases than others, as different trouble spots erupt and travel routes shift. In my visits to reception centres in the Canaries, North Africa (Ceuta and Melilla), Malta and Italy, I have seen systems struggling to cope on the ground, while other member states find reasons not to support them and send asylum seekers back to their country of entry if they have moved on. So, I was one of the Greens that commissioned a report from Richard Williams, former EU representative for the European Council on Refugees and Exiles (ECRE), to look at how we could redesign the Dublin system to make it more *solidaire* and share the responsibility around. This proposal has now strongly influenced the official position of the Parliament.

So, one legislative institution of the EU is doing its job to deliver a Common European Asylum System, while too many member states cling to their national arguments. Member states do need to be pushed to deliver on the legislation they have passed. The issue of safeguarding children in the asylum system has become ever-more important, not least due to the total failure of the French and British governments to find a way of ensuring under-18s are helped to join family members in the UK, as they are entitled to do under the law. A key initiative was recently taken up by Citizens UK (a brilliant organisation, in my view), which set up Safe Passage to help those children, filling the gap left by state authorities. French Green MEP Karima Delli and I nominated this organisation for an EU Citizens prize, which enabled it to gain access to the Commission and governments to help make progress.[18]

I was also instrumental in providing legal text to improve the protection of children in asylum law and legislation on the return of illegally staying third-country nationals. I have mixed feelings about this, as I always thought the returns text on detention was inadequate; however, it proved to be an improvement on the proposed text for the Receptions Conditions Directive! It is at points like these that I value the Green Group's approach of constructive engagement with the legislative process. We may only make small gains at times, but these gains can have a positive effect on people's lives.

Of course, in addition to changing legal text, there is the wider issue of changing the overall culture in which decisions about asylum and immigration are made. There has been a growing movement in some countries, reflected in the governments coming to power, that wishes to close borders to those seen as not fitting their 'national' identity. This is spoken of as the need to protect national cultures, with those seeking asylum (or immigrants – the choice of word is often indicative of a political position) being viewed as a threat to that culture, particularly if they are Muslim. This thread of thinking is not specifically Eastern European, although statements from the so-called Visegrád Group (Hungary, Poland, Slovakia, Czech Republic) may give that impression. I can remember sitting in the Parliament hearing then Spanish Prime Minister José María Aznar speaking of a 'clash of civilisations' after the horrific Madrid bombings. We have also seen the way in which UKIP have instrumentalised 'Turkey' as code for 'Muslim', to stoke fear of 'the other'.

This perspective denies the role of Islam in Europe's history and assumes that culture is static: if it were, I – a woman – would not be sitting in the European Parliament. This is a fact I like pointing out to those such as the Swedish Democrats, whose female member sits in the Committee on Civil Liberties, Justice and Home Affairs (now as a member of the ECR Group, founded by the British Conservatives). Working on the issue of cultural shifts is one reason why I am a co-president of the intergroup on anti-racism and diversity, which works with civil society to promote diversity and equality within the EU. We have hosted events on tackling Islamophobia and Afrophobia, and on promoting greater diversity within the EU's own institutions.

Migration

Throughout my time in the Parliament, I have worked on legislation tackling discrimination on various grounds, whether in the workplace or in society more generally, and in promoting the work of the EU's national equality bodies set up under that legislation. These bodies were largely modelled on the UK's sectoral commissions, such as what was the Commission for Racial Equality, and make a significant contribution to protecting people's rights within the EU. In the UK, we have seen the merging of agencies and significant funding cuts. Despite the UK's decision to leave the EU, I hope that the UK Equality and Human Rights Commission (EHRC) will remain within the European Network of Equality Bodies (Equinet), as we have a lot to offer other countries. I have aimed to bring that experience into the EU via my work on integrating migrant workers, tackling terrorism and combatting hate speech.

Figure 6. Sangatte Red Cross refugee centre, near Calais in northern France.

Immigration is also a field in which I have worked on much of the EU's legislation, despite the UK opting out of virtually every piece of legislation that might affect the rights of third-country nationals to cross our borders (even in terms of providing support to victims of trafficking, on which the UK has adopted parallel legislation!). I worked with my London Assembly colleague Jenny Jones to help shift the government's position so that victims of trafficking would be supported and not just deported.[19] I have used the Tampere Conclusions as my guide, along with the question 'what would we want as migrants?'. The answer is to bring the rights of immigrants and nationals as close together as possible.

My contact with migrant organisations in London, such as the Migrants' Rights Network, has also been valuable in forming my views on migrants' rights. One key factor for me is the right to good administration (first championed in the Parliament's Petitions Committee). The total inefficiency and hostility of the UK's own Home Office is breathtaking at times, as the casework in my office shows. We have fed into numerous consultations on this. We have worked with groups such as Brides Without Borders to support the right of married couples to stay in the UK when the Home Office wants to deport one spouse, for example. I am proud to be a patron of the ice&fire theatre company, which has tackled this and a wide range of human rights issues through works such as *My Skype Family*.

There have been some minor successes in EU legislation, for example, on increasing the portability of pension rights, on providing better access to training and on achieving more rights for family members to accompany migrants from outside the EU. But there have been some failures as well. Most migrant workers are still not allowed to change jobs, which ties them to one employer, on whom they are dependent, and thus potentially leaves them open to exploitation. We may make some progress on this for domestic workers through the Parliament championing the International Labour Organization (ILO) Convention on Domestic Workers, which I worked on in the Committee on Employment and Social Affairs.[20]

We (the Greens) have still not managed to get a full understanding of circular migration: the ability to come, go and return more flexibly. The EU still works on a model of short-term migration, rather than offering a smooth path to potential settlement, which is not good for migrants, employers or society as a whole. Governments are very reluctant to see that migration is a fact of life and that development is not a substitution for migration. Rather, migration is a part of development; it changes the choices and the balance of power for countries and individuals. Many governments still place so many barriers in the way of recruitment, even for highly qualified people, that the EU risks missing out in many ways.

One area of change is in the growing recognition of the effect of climate change on population movements. This is a subject that has been close to my heart throughout my time in the European Parliament. I was one of the first politicians to work on the issue.

In 2002, I published a report titled *Refugees and the Environment: The Forgotten Element of Sustainability*.[21] This was partly a response to those who couldn't understand why a green party politician was working on immigration and asylum: I wanted to show that there was a direct connection. Over the years, my views have shifted as I have come to understand the issues better. Although the environmental and climate pressures causing population displacement are increasing, I would no longer argue for a separate category of 'environmental refugee' or 'climate refugee'. However, the Green Group and some other organisations do sometimes still use this language.

I became disturbed by the way the prospect of many people being displaced, by rising sea levels in particular, was being portrayed as a threat by a number of development and environmental organisations to push for action on combatting climate change, playing into the view of refugees so often pushed by right-wing politicians. I felt this posed a risk to the better treatment of asylum seekers without necessarily shifting policy on climate. Fortunately, I was able to link up with the Climate Outreach and Information Network (COIN), since renamed Climate Outreach, and we co-hosted a number of meetings at the European Parliament office in London to discuss these questions with a range of organisations. This led to the setting up of the Climate and Migration Coalition, which has worked on the topic ever since.

I have continued to work on the issue, most recently speaking to the Women Ambassadors group in Brussels at the invitation of the ambassador for Pakistan. It is now included in the UN's climate framework, and the European Parliament included it in our response to the UN's migration forum conference, held in Morocco in December 2018. However, inclusion does not imply solution, so there is still work to be done. I also believe that free movement within the EU will become a method of managed adaptation for climate displacement within the EU. The UK is opting out of this possibility.

The first piece of legislation I worked on in the Parliament was a revision of Regulation 1408/71 on the application of social security schemes to employed persons and their families moving within the Community (a title so snappy you were asleep before you reached the end!). This is one of the oldest pieces of EU legislation and concerns the rights to social security for EU nationals working, residing or trav-elling in another member state. It is a key piece of law for millions of people. The European Health Insurance Card (EHIC) that entitles you to urgent healthcare in another member state (on the same basis as a national of that country) when you're on holiday, for example, is linked to this legislation. The ability to pool, say, your German and UK state pension rights is also part of this, as is your access to fam-ily benefits if you are working in another EU/EEA country. It took five years' work to revise this major piece of legislation in a procedure where the Parliament theoretically had co-decision yet unanimity in Council was also required. I then went on to work for another five years on the implementing regulation that accompanies what is now Regulation 883/04, which sets out the rules to be followed. Improving the rights of citizens to be informed was a key change we got through.

During those ten years there was a marked difference in how that regulation was viewed. It was initially seen as boring and technical (which was why the Greens were allowed to work on it!) but was eventually presented by UKIP and the *Daily Express* as a 'new law' that would allow millions of Eastern Europeans (adapted to include Bulgarians and Romanians during the next phase of enlargement) to get their hands on British social security payments. A very partial truth, stretched almost far enough to break the elastic. No-one from the UK government corrected this over-the-top view or pointed out that this was a reciprocal arrangement, as is free movement.

The regulation became a focus of David Cameron's activity when he was seeking a 'better deal' from the EU and chose child benefits as an area for change. Instead of standing firm and saying 'this is a small sum and goes to people who are overwhelmingly contributing to the UK economy to support their families', he played into the view that it is 'unfair' for people to get benefits for children who are not in the UK. That 'deal' is now contaminating the latest revision of the regu-lation that I am currently working on – not as rapporteur, though, as big political groups now think it is politically important rather than technical, so the Greens are no longer allowed to be in charge.

The failure to manage and explain the rules of free movement has proved to be a monumental failure of successive UK governments.

The UK was not consistent in the advice it gave to people arriving in the UK after 2004 about registering with the authorities. Local housing bodies were being asked for advice, for which they were given no additional resources. Indeed, it has been known for years that many EU nationals have no right to Housing Benefit (it's not social security under the regulation), and the resources of many voluntary bodies have been strained because of this.

Figure 7. Trade union demonstration in Strasbourg on the Working Time Directive.

I managed to get a funding line opened up in the EU's Social Fund, which helped support a project between the London Borough of Westminster and Polish organisations such as Barka to try to deal with this, but there is still no real answer or prospect of bridging this gap between national systems. I have been working with FEANTSA, the EU network of organisations dealing with homelessness, on a recent project on the issue. This supported challenges in the UK courts when the Conservative government decided that homelessness was grounds for deporting EU nationals, regardless of whether they were employed or should have been receiving social security or other payments. A real shame that the government decided to opt for deportation rather than solve the real problems.

I am a champion of free movement within the EU. Only about 3% of EU nationals use that right, but it broadens understanding, opens up many opportunities, and has economic and social benefits. However, it needs government and local authority support to work properly. The rules are there but the British government has chosen not to implement them. The government could choose to really implement the law that ensures employers pay at least the minimum wage, but it doesn't. The Conservative government has indicated that it wants to step back from the law on protecting temporary agency workers, which I helped to negotiate in Brussels. The Working Time Directive is another law unpopular with this British government (and its predecessors) that I – along with many in the Trade Union movement – have fought to improve and defend. I published a report titled *I Must Work Harder?* to make the case for this health and safety legislation in the face of opposition from the then Labour government.[22] I also leafletted outside London Bridge station to encourage people to respond to the Commission's consultation before they proposed a revision, which has never made it to the statute books.

In another area, I was the rapporteur for a report by the Committee on Employment and Social Affairs covering access to care for groups vulnerable because of the financial crisis. The report proposed measures to protect care services in the face of government cuts, including a proposal that asked for EU legislation to guarantee 'carer's leave' from work. As a result, this was proposed in the Directive on Work–Life Balance, which is under negotiation at the time of writing. This could see the right to carer's leave protected in law.[23]

As we face the prospect of leaving the EU, all this work and the positive effects the EU has had on people's lives in the UK needs to be protected and, hopefully, improved. We must not compete on the international stage on the basis of lowering workers' rights and protections. It is essential that we safeguard the rights of those who have exercised their right to free movement, and who are now seeing those rights removed. We set a precedent with the Windrush-era migrants and should uphold that principle, but we need a fully functioning Home Office that looks to say 'yes, these are your rights' rather than finding ways to dismiss them.

What happens next?

Brexit is a constitutional crisis, in many respects stemming from an England used to seeing itself as superior and powerful being unable to come to terms with a changing world in which it is no longer dominant. The desire to go for stronger Commonwealth links is indicative of that. I can envisage the UK split apart by a shift to a united Ireland or an independent Scotland, leaving a divided England with a disconnected and discontented Wales.

Brexit was fuelled by austerity, inequality, underinvestment, misinformation and political complacency, partly derived from the first-past-the-post voting system. Brexit's multiple negative effects are already being felt and will continue to be felt across the country for years, probably decades, after leaving the EU. This will include the loss of important EU funding and connectedness to the continent.[24] This is why Greens have continued to strongly oppose Brexit. It doesn't help that our electoral system is a denial of diversity. It's a major challenge in the UK, exacerbated by potential boundary changes and the Tory and Labour addiction to first-past-the-post.

We can see in the European Parliament how it is possible for parties to work together on certain issues and find a way forward, while still retaining their identities. Compromise is not a dirty word, as it seems to be in UK politics. This British perception of how politics is done is part of what has contributed to the mess of the Brexit negotiations: too many old-style politicians see negotiations as a battle with one winner rather than a way to deliver a positive future working relationship. One thing is clear: there's so much that UK politicians could learn from their neighbours in Europe. I would prefer that we do this as part of the EU. We are stronger together.

Endnotes

1   European Parliament, *The European Elections in 1989*; https://bit.ly/2DsOMQC (accessed 17 September 2018).
2   A competence introduced in the Treaty of Amsterdam.
3   Green MEPs, *Storm Hits Brussels over Crystal Palace – MEPs Congratulate Local Activists for Forcing EU Court Action on UK Planning Law*, News Release (20 February 2003); https://bit.ly/2DrXPS7 (accessed 17 September 2018).
4   Pippa Crerar, 'Super-highways in Ken's £500m cycle revolution', *Evening Standard* (11 February 2008); https://bit.ly/2SUr2JF (accessed 17 September 2018).
5   Jean Lambert, *Air Pollution – London's Unseen Killer*, Report (2015); https://bit.ly/2DsB5RM (accessed 18 September 2018).
6   Maria Adebowal and Christoph Schwarte, *Integrating Social Inclusion and Environment: Exploring the Potential for Joined-up Thinking*, Working Paper (2004); https://bit.ly/2Dq5ujV (accessed 17 September 2018).
7   Redcurrent Films, *EU4U!* (2006); https://bit.ly/2F7p4D9 (accessed 17 September 2018).
8   Jean Lambert, *Jean Lambert Calls for the Formation of a New Cross-party Intergroup on Youth Issues in the European Parliament*, Press Release (2009); https://bit.ly/2QwgrU0 (accessed 17 September 2018).
9   Jean Lambert, *Hothouses: Climate Change and London's Housing*, Report (2006); https://bit.ly/2zy0G7D (accessed 17 September 2018).

10 Jean Lambert, *Green Work: Employment and Skills – The Climate Change Challenge*, Press Release (2008); https://bit.ly/2QmPWjK (accessed 17 September 2018).

11 Worldwatch Institute (for UNEP), *Green Jobs: Towards Decent Work in a Sustainable, Low-carbon World*, Report (2008); https://bit.ly/2D66p84 (accessed 17 September 2018).

12 See http://ec.europa.eu, *Europe 2020: A European Strategy for Smart, Sustainable and Inclusive Growth*, Report (2010); https://bit.ly/KMnOnV (accessed 17 September 2018).

13 Jean Lambert, *What Is a Green Job?*, YouTube Video (2011); https://bit.ly/2OsRMxv (accessed 17 September 2018).

14 Jean Lambert, *Response to Government's Industrial Strategy Green Paper*, Press Release (2017); https://bit.ly/2JMFnUz (accessed 17 September 2018).

15 David Eckstein, Vera Künzel and Laura Schäfer, *Global Climate Risk Index 2018*, Report (Germanwatch 2017); https://bit.ly/2F9yxKa (accessed 17 September 2018).

16 BBC News, 'Bangladesh factory collapse toll passes 1,000', Article (10 May 2013); https://bbc.in/2Ox8YCf (accessed 17 September 2018).

17 European Parliament, *Tampere European Council 15 and 16 October 1999: Presidency Conclusions*, Report (1999); https://bit.ly/2wD2f1s (accessed 17 September 2018).

18 Esmat Jeraj, 'Citizens UK awarded European Parliament prize for work on refugee crisis', Article (Citizens UK: 6 June 2016); https://bit.ly/2JLQzkh (accessed 17 September 2018).

19 Jean Lambert and Jenny Jones, *Silent Slavery: Stop the Trafficking of Women and Children for Sexual Exploitation in London*, Conference Pamphlet (2003); https://bit.ly/2JXpAT7 (accessed 17 September 2018).

20 International Labour Organization, *Decent Work for Domestic Workers: Convention 189, Recommendation 201*, Report (ILO: 2011); https://bit.ly/Ngl3Mw (accessed 17 September 2018).

21 Jean Lambert, *Refugees and the Environment: The Forgotten Element of Sustainability*, Report (2002); https://bit.ly/2D7qyum (accessed 17 September 2018).

22 Jean Lambert, *I Must Work Harder? Britain and the Working Time Directive*, Report (2006); https://bit.ly/2D5H2TI (accessed 17 September 2018).

23 Jean Lambert, *Access to Care in a Time of Crisis*, Report (2013); https://bit.ly/2yXpuq9 (accessed 18 October 2018).

24 Jean Lambert, *Losing It Over Brexit: What Does the End of EU Funding Mean for London's Communities and Projects?*, Report (2017); https://bit.ly/2BBqWOQ (accessed 17 September 2018).

Chapter 4

From Brussels to Westminster: how corporate power captured politics

Caroline Lucas

Introduction

> Globalisation…is about power and control. It is the reshaping
> of the world into one without borders ruled by a dictator-
> ship of the world's most powerful central banks, commercial
> banks and multinational companies. It is an attempt to undo
> a century of social progress and to alter the distribution of
> income from inequitable to inhuman.
>
> – **Paul Hellyer** (former Deputy Prime Minister of Canada)

The first British Green MEPs were elected to the European Parliament at a time of global political unrest. A corporate-led international trade system was being intellectually unpicked by a growing,
colourful movement of protests from the opponents of economic
globalisation. Battles were taking place on the streets outside of trade
negotiations. This peaked in late autumn 1999 in Seattle, where
activists clad in everything from clowns' costumes to black bandanas
brought the city to a standstill in the face of brutal policing and fierce

condemnation from a political elite that desperately wanted us all to believe there 'was no alternative' to corporate globalisation. It was an inspiring time to be involved in campaigning, not only because the 'One No, Many Yeses' of the anti-globalisation movement allowed us to work with new friends across the world, but also because the demands on the streets were so closely aligned with a growing appetite for green politics. It felt like something was changing, and it was happening fast.

I first walked into the European Parliament on a mission to bring the voices of the movement on the streets into the halls of power; I spent much of my time in subsequent years trying to play a part in building on the protests in Seattle and beyond. I felt then, as I continue to now, that we needed to make space for an opposition to a global race to the bottom that focussed as much on what we'd do differently as it did on what *they* were doing wrong. But before I started all that, I had to win an election: and that was by no means guaranteed.

Winchester Town Hall

The night of 10 June 1999 is one I will never forget. After months of gruelling campaigning across a constituency that stretched from Dover in the South East around London to Milton Keynes in the North, I sat in Winchester Town Hall waiting to see if the Green Party had finally broken out of local politics and into the mainstream. The results came in over the course of the evening on a number of big screens that detailed the vote tally in each part of the region; we knew pretty quickly that it was going to be *very* close. When the screens suddenly went down before the last few constituency results were reported, we sat in excruciating limbo, and I increasingly believed that we weren't going to make it across the finish line. As the minutes passed by and we sat in nail-biting silence, I remember Mike McCarthy, then a journalist at the *Independent*, turning to me and saying 'It's not over till the fat lady sings.' He was right to remain optimistic, and I somehow managed to keep myself together enough to be able to compute that I had indeed scraped in, by about 250 votes in an electorate of over one million.[1]

It was a sweet victory, not just because we'd worked so hard for it, or waited such a long time, but because we still felt sore from the injustice of the 1989 European election, which saw the Green Party gain 15% of the popular vote[2] but fail to pick up a single seat because of the deeply unfair voting system. We'd always told people that we'd break through with fair elections, and, following the introduction of a more proportional electoral system, the victories in London and the South East in 1999 proved we were right. I wasn't the only politician from a smaller party to take the stage at Winchester Town Hall that night; but I didn't know then that Nigel Farage's entrance to the European Parliament would bring with it such attention and be an early sign of the upswing in dangerous, populist nationalism that would sweep the country and the continent in the years to come.

For the Green Party as a whole, 10 June 1999 was a seismic moment. It wasn't just ten years after our most famous electoral defeat; it was also two years into a New Labour government, which often sang from the same hymn sheet as the Tories on the issues we cared about. On subjects as wide apart as the treatment of asylum seekers, defence spending, environmental protection and trade policy, it was clear that there was a huge opportunity for green ideas.

For me, being elected to the European Parliament meant big changes. With my children still very young, we decided to move the whole family to Brussels and be based there most of the time, to give them some stability. So, alongside my husband, Richard, and my two sons, I boarded the Eurostar in London that summer to begin a new life as an MEP.

The work of the European Parliament

Before the European election campaign, I had been working as the head of the trade policy team for Oxfam and had visited the EU institutions in Brussels on a number of occasions. Indeed, it was sitting in meetings with MEPs and lobbying them on trade that first made me think that perhaps I'd like to be sitting on their side of the table.

Figure 1. Caroline Lucas in the European Parliament, 2004.

What struck me first upon my arrival as a new MEP was the efficiency of the induction process. I was given some working space immediately and greeted with huge signs telling me what to do. I felt like I was being welcomed into a political family alongside the hundreds of other newly elected MEPs. The buildings themselves create an incredible sense of space and grandeur, with high ceilings and balconies suspended across huge expanses. So long are the corridors and hallways that a number of Green MEPs started using skateboards to get around the Parliament quicker – until the parliamentary authorities put a stop to it. It was big and complicated, but it was built for the modern world and I quickly found my feet.

The main chamber of the Parliament itself really is magnificent. MEPs sit in a semicircular formation, which creates a far less confrontational arena than one that sees representatives facing each other directly. At the front sits the president of the Parliament, and all around the edges are the many boxes where translators sit and allow people with different languages to be on the same page as each other.

Though the architecture was stunning, it was what was happening inside those grand buildings that most excited me, starting with the Green Group. Jean Lambert and I joined a group of Green MEPs that was vibrant, diverse and a powerful force to be reckoned with. Not only were there dozens of us in the European Parliament, but my fellow Greens had colleagues elected in national parliaments too – and even some in government. For us Greens from the UK, who had reached our highest ever office upon election to Brussels, it was awe-inspiring to see people who shared our politics putting their ideas into practice right across the continent. Those were heady days, and I certainly spent a fair amount of time thinking about how Greens in the UK might soon have a seat at the top table of British politics.

Of course I had my disagreements with the Green Group, not least because I continually found myself on the left of a group that, at times (in my opinion), drifted a little too close to the neoliberal consensus that was beginning to take root in European politics. I was a proud member of a small group of agitators (alongside Irish independent Patricia McKenna and Per Gahrton, one of the founders of the Swedish Greens) who consistently tried to drag the Green Group towards a more radical politics. Despite robust arguments within the group and a genuinely wide range of views in the party, we always managed to keep the political and personal separate, and to remain focussed on the bigger political goals outside of the internal meetings.

The politics in the group wasn't just split across left/right lines, of course. Perhaps more central to our disagreements was the split between those who I saw as fairly hard-line federalists and those, like myself, who were suspicious of European institutions' tendency to centralise power without upgrading democratic checks. The Green Party of England and Wales has always believed in subsidiarity – a technical-sounding word for the simple concept of ensuring that a central authority should perform only those tasks which cannot be performed at a more local level. Those federalising instincts of the EU, and particularly the Commission, weren't just concerning for democratic reasons; they risked undermining the very foundation of the EU as a force for peace and prosperity that required the support of the people for whom it was working. While the task of increasing the transparency and accountability of the EU institutions continues, the Green Group did ultimately play a big part in implementing crucial democratic checks such as allowing European citizens to bring continent-wide petitions to the Parliament for debate.

Like the internal politics of the Green Group, the wider culture of the Parliament was also generally collegiate; this was in part because no one party held all of the power, and in part because MEPs tended to think of themselves as a collective, with our 'enemy' in common often being the European Council, or at times the Commission. I frequently found myself working closely with MEPs from the Socialists, the far left and sometimes the Liberals to further the causes we believed in. It was a sign of a grown-up approach to politics that Eurocommunists, Greens and Social Democrats, speaking many different languages, could so often work together towards the best outcomes for those who elected them.

Such cross-party working was particularly crucial in parliamentary committees. In the European Parliament, some of these committees hold real power; many of them co-legislate on European law, giving MEPs the power to sit across the table from EU Council members and make their case on behalf of the whole Parliament. I sat on two committees: transport and trade, and later on the environmental committee. Each committee would appoint rapporteurs for specific draft proposals, thereby giving one named MEP the responsibility of piloting a piece of legislation through the whole legal process, and the opportunity to really delve into the details of a topic. For us Greens, that meant the chance to push for truly progressive policies across the board. Some of my most satisfying moments as an MEP occurred when I was a rapporteur – from my work banning illegally logged timber from being sold in the EU to pushing for aviation to be included in the EU's Emissions Trading Scheme.[3] It was genuinely a joy to be able to focus in detail on one policy issue for a long period of time as well as get to know all the key players working in that area.

Europe's failures

Though the working culture of the European Parliament was positive, it was clear to me from the very beginning that the EU was facing serious challenges. The first of those challenges, which was particular to Britain, was that no-one at home had any idea what the EU did. Every morning, I'd walk through the newsagents in the European Parliament, where I'd spot key EU stories being given front-page coverage by newspapers across the continent yet being ignored by the British media, unless it was some sort of scandal. Such was my frustration at the lack of coverage of our work – and my concern that the legitimacy of the EU was being undermined – that I literally begged political shows, particularly on the BBC, to give MEPs a slot. The broadcasters' refusal to cover the work of the EU seriously and the print media's stance of either ignoring the EU or printing often inaccurate stories about the laws we made were incredibly frustrating – and can, with the benefit of hindsight, be identified as a major contributor to the attitudes that led to Brexit.

But it wasn't just the coverage of the European Parliament that was problematic; so was much of what was happening in Brussels. The politics in the EU obviously reflected the dominant politics in European member states at the time (centrist social policy mixed with neoliberal economics), but with a cloak of secrecy particularly surrounding the actions of the unelected Commission. The EU had also, I argued at the time, lost its sense of purpose and risked simply becoming a vehicle for free trade. Writing in 2007, I said:

> Many of today's European citizens are no longer sure what the EU is for. The ambitious free trade project at the heart of the original treaties has, for many, become an end in itself. The debate about the future of the Union has been dominated by 'economism' – the idea that the overriding goals of European integration are economic, and that the progress of the EU should be judged in terms of economic growth and the removal of market barriers alone. As a result, the EU has failed to address fundamental questions of political culture and strategic purpose – and, therefore, has also failed to inspire the mass of citizens with a sense of enthusiasm and common cause, calling into question its own legitimacy.[4]

During key treaty negotiations, such as in Nice, it became even more apparent that the British public had very little idea what the EU actually did. But it wasn't just a lack of purpose that plagued the EU: it was actively partaking in a project that, I believe, may have been its undoing. That project was the economic and corporate-led globalisation which Tony Blair described as 'irreversible and irresistible'.[5] Inside the EU, that meant further embedding the single market, but it also meant 'activism in opening markets abroad'.[6] The downsides of such globalisation are well documented, from the tearing-up of working communities because of corporate outsourcing, to sweatshops in the Global South, to environmentally calamitous trade policies that saw Britain importing 61,400 tonnes of poultry meat from the Netherlands in the same year that it exported 33,100 tonnes of poultry meat *to* the Netherlands. We also imported 240,000 tonnes of pork and 125,000 tonnes of lamb, while at the same time exporting 195,000 tonnes of pork and 102,000 tonnes of lamb.[7] Not only does such perverse trade policy exacerbate climate change – by exporting food that we could have eaten to countries from which we're buying the very same product – it also risks pulling down food and animal welfare standards, and it contributes to disasters such as foot-and-mouth and bovine spongiform encephalopathy (BSE).

Figure 2. Caroline Lucas with Vandana Shiva in Cancun, 2003.

As a member of the Committee on International Trade, I saw first-hand that the EU was purposefully positioning itself as a beacon for global free trade, and I feared that in doing so it risked undermining its position as a force for cross-border solidarity as well as protecting the environment and human rights. The EU was an incredible peace project, a triumph of humanity over barbarism, and the most successful cross-border project ever invented; but it was also desperately in need of reform as well as a new, bold vision. My argument then was simple: we needed the EU to be a force for relocalisation:

Localisation is the very antithesis of globalisation, manifest in the EU's emphasis on ever more open markets, and which emphasises a beggar-your-neighbour reduction of controls on trade and contorts all economies to make international competitiveness their major goal. Localisation involves a better-your-neighbour supportive internationalism where the flow of ideas, technologies, information, culture, money and goods has, as its goal, the protection and rebuilding of national and local economies not just within Europe but worldwide. Its emphasis is not on competition for the cheapest, but on cooperation for the best.[8]

Despite some serious Green wins in the European Parliament and some major steps forward for environmental protection, the direction of travel in the EU at the time was very clearly towards corporate-led globalisation. We also faced the continued primacy of the unelected Commission over the elected Parliament, the ongoing expensive farce of moving the whole Parliament to Strasbourg every month, and the plight of the British press having very little idea how the whole operation worked. It wasn't hard for the europhobic media to find examples of EU excess and bureaucracy – and they didn't hold back.

The European Parliament passed many positive laws that were all but ignored by the mainstream media. Laws like the Working Time Directive, which stopped employers from forcing workers to undertake a dangerous number of hours, and the Habitats Directive, which has done so much to protect endangered species and our countryside, were forgotten by a media only looking for stories about 'bendy bananas'. They were given even less prominence by a European elite whose main focus remained opening up markets. One of the EU's greatest achievements – the removal of borders between nations in favour of free movement of persons – was all too often reluctantly accepted by governments as part of the single-market package, rather than being celebrated in and of itself. For my own part, I do regret not spending a little more time praising the EU for what it had done right, such as free movement and bringing lasting peace to Europe, while still not letting up on a robust critique of where goals needed to be changed and institutions improved.

It struck me then, as it does now, that there is a paradox at the heart of the EU. It has championed serious improvements in workers' rights and environmental protection, while at the same time being a vehicle for the neoliberal consensus that has gripped the continent for a generation. The tragedy we saw in my time at the European Parliament was that it was the neoliberal vision of EU governments that almost always won when the two competing sides faced each other. Ultimately, it was national politics and the almost cross-continental political support for neoliberalism that shaped the politics of the European Union; the institutions of the EU would only bend further towards social and environmental justice if progressive politicians at a national level shifted in that direction too.

I was also becoming increasingly concerned that the impact of having a Green presence in Europe simply wasn't getting through to people in Britain, and that the real power in politics lay in Westminster. The Green Party had begun to get a small amount of media coverage, but we continued to be all but ignored most of the time and were still seen as being on the far fringes of politics. Fighting for a seat in the UK Parliament seemed like the natural next step – not only to give the Green Party the recognition it deserved, but because I felt that the causes I cared most about would be best served if I could sit directly opposite the prime minister and make the case for a real alternative.

Westminster

The political context for my election to Westminster was shaped by the defeat of social movements in the preceding decade. Despite years of hard work, on the streets and in the halls of power, those of us arguing for alternatives to globalisation were nearly defeated. The UK's globalised finance system, liberalised trade and economic policies, and political appetite for slashing regulation were the result of a 'no alternative' attitude that we'd heard from those in power for years; these led directly to the economic meltdown and public spending crises that framed my election to Westminster in 2010. Unlike every other major party, the Greens had run a campaign demanding investment, not cuts. I took my seat in Parliament on a manifesto that promised to rebuild the public realm and transform the economic system to ensure that such a collapse wouldn't happen again.

Taking the seat wasn't easy. Though Brighton Pavilion was the Greens' strongest constituency, thanks in particular to the incredible work of the previous candidate (and later MEP) Keith Taylor, we still had a mountain to climb in order to win there because of the grossly unfair first-past-the-post electoral system. Unlike in the European elections, where we needed around one in ten voters to choose us across a huge region, we had to persuade at least one in three people to back my bid for Parliament and make history by electing the first Green MP. We couldn't just focus on a handful of core policies, either, which is what we tended to do for EU elections. Instead, I needed to demonstrate to the people of Brighton Pavilion that I cared as much about their child's school place, the state of the railways and the potholes on their street as I did about genetically modified crops and nuclear power. I've always had a politics that goes beyond environmental protection, but persuading people that the Green Party could be trusted with bread-and-butter issues was always going to be a challenge. Thankfully – and after a bruising campaign – I was elected to the House of Commons with a majority of 1,254 votes.[9]

Although the different nature of this election campaign was a shock to the system, it was nothing compared with the upside-down world I was about to enter in Westminster. Not only was I entering Parliament without any Green Party colleagues, I was going into a world that seemed to be based more on Oxford colleges than on any sort of modern democracy. Despite my work as an MP beginning immediately, it took an age to be allocated an office, with the more sought-after ones being given out first to reward previous 'good behaviour'. I was forced to work around a table in one of Parliament's cafes. As I wrote in my book *Honourable Friends? Parliament and the Fight for Change* (in 2015):

> So at the end of my first day I have been given a pile of House of Commons stationery, but have nowhere to store it; a pigeonhole for my letters but no computer to read my emails;

and a pink ribbon in the Members' cloakroom on which to hang my sword before entering the chamber. The Member for Brighton Pavilion is open for business.[10]

Though I was the only Green MP, I wasn't entirely isolated. Plaid Cymru and the Scottish Nationalists (SNP), who I had worked with closely in our shared group in the European Parliament, were on hand to point me in the right direction. With the Labour Party still very much in the political centre, and wilful cheerleaders for austerity, it really did feel very politically lonely at first as the one English MP representing a party of the left.

That loneliness was exacerbated when I entered the parliamentary chamber. Not only was the room incredibly loud, but many MPs purposefully shouted over me as I spoke. I also had to try to remember the absurd conventions around calling fellow MPs 'Honourable Member', or members of the Privy Council 'Right Honourable Member'. (You're only entitled to call someone an Honourable Friend if they are from the same party as you, which means it isn't a phrase I've had call to use so far, sadly.) We weren't allowed to mention the House of Lords in the chamber, either, and instead had to refer to it as 'The Other Place' by convention. Though English was always spoken in this Parliament, I couldn't help but think that I had arrived in a place where they spoke a language more foreign than anything I had heard in Brussels.

When you finally did get to speak in the chamber, there was often no set rule as to how long you would have: that was up to the Speaker. Unlike in the European Parliament, where speeches are just a few minutes, this meant that some senior MPs would be allowed to drone on for hours, while backbenchers like me would only be given a brief chance to say a few words.

Then there was the voting. In the European Parliament, we voted electronically, meaning we could get through huge amounts of legislation in a matter of minutes. In the British Parliament, we vote by walking though the 'aye' or 'no' lobbies – a process that can take over 15 minutes for each vote and often keeps us traipsing through lobbies until the early hours of the morning. In a report I wrote in 2010,

The Case for Parliamentary Reform, I found that an MP with an 85% voting record would have spent over 250 hours just queuing up to vote in a single parliament.[11] And it isn't just the process of voting in Westminster that's infuriating: the way the party whips cajole their MPs into the lobbies is downright intimidating and utterly undemocratic.

Despite the clear deficiencies of the Westminster system in comparison to the European Parliament – from the electoral system right through to the adversarial setup of the chamber – some clear positives have come from having a Green presence near the heart of British political power. First, there's no doubt that we've managed to hugely increase the coverage of our work in the media and to really make a splash with our efforts in, for instance, the area of personal, social, health and economic education (PSHE), where I managed to push the government into committing to statutory sex and relationship education for all children and raise awareness regarding the objectification of women by *The Sun* newspaper's 'Page 3'. Though we still aren't given a fair showing, I suddenly found myself on *Question Time* more frequently, and being asked to comment on environmental stories both in the printed media and on high profile TV and radio shows.

Being in Parliament has also given me the opportunity to build alliances with MPs from other parties on specific issues. Indeed, the issues on which I've had the most success – from serious PSHE reform to securing more family-friendly sitting hours, starting a debate about evidence-based drugs policy, challenging the idea that NHS privatisation is inevitable and fighting for an Environment Act – have been successful largely because I was able to work on them across party lines alongside MPs with whom I don't always see eye to eye.

Brexit and beyond

Being an MP with insight into how EU institutions work during the European referendum campaign has been a fascinating and frustrating experience. It's been particularly eye-opening to see the rank

hypocrisy of elites in the Brexit campaign pour scorn on the undemocratic nature of the EU, while many of them sit in a parliament
with an archaic voting system for one chamber and no elections for
the other. Similarly, I've heard Brexiteers shout about how British
people have no say on what the EU does, while ignoring the fact that
MPs outside of government in the UK are often powerless, and that
the divisive nature of our politics and the whips system essentially
preclude any large-scale cross-party working. A cursory look at the
government's plans for its new trade policy post-Brexit reveals that
ministers don't intend to give MPs even as much say as MEPs had,
and that the deals will essentially be done in backrooms without
proper oversight. So much for taking back control.

If the distortions of the Brexiteers weren't enough to drive people
towards Brexit, then the disingenuous Remain campaign certainly
did the trick. In particular, the Remain campaign utterly failed to
talk about the positives of freedom of movement across Europe – one
of people's main concerns.

Despite my pleas at Stronger In board meetings and in public,
the official Remain campaign looked like an establishment stitch-up.
Instead of spearheading a 'remain and reform' agenda, with proposals to democratise the institutions of the EU and address the genuine
grievances of people in this country, the liberal elite screamed about
the 'risks' of leaving the EU to many who increasingly felt they had
nothing left to lose. It's no accident that the 30 regions the Social
Mobility Commission has identified as the worst coldspots for social
mobility all voted Leave.

And that's where the final piece of the Brexit puzzle comes in. Ultimately, people were right to think that an unaccountable elite was
increasingly failing the vast majority. Wages had stagnated, bankers'
bonuses had sky-rocketed and town centres up and down the country were increasingly coming to resemble ghost towns as corporate
giants sucked business elsewhere and small firms shut after the recession. People were told that voting for Brexit would free them from the
shackles of bureaucracy as well as restore their pride and ultimately
their humanity. It was a simple lie – and, given the context, it was
almost bound to work.

I started this essay by talking about corporate globalisation: the burning political issue when I was elected to Brussels in 1999. I want to end my contribution by coming back to that, because it's my belief that by failing to implement a workable solution to problems caused by economic globalisation we left the door open to a populist right-wing politics based primarily on using migration as a proxy for the challenges we face. Imagine if more progressives had questioned corporate globalisation earlier on. Imagine if they'd allowed themselves to think outside of the economic box and to question the logic of a system that at once strips workers of their pay; sends goods thousands of miles across the world, when they could be made locally; and allows international trade deals designed to enable companies to sue elected governments for passing regulations to protect workers and our environment. The question that progressives should be asking themselves is how did they end up surrendering the debate on globalisation to a resurgent and dangerous strand of populism that fails to offer any real solutions?

I am proud of the contribution that Green MEPs from the UK made to the European Union in our 20 years there. In an increasingly divided political world, we fought for what was right, and we did so while swimming against the tide more often than not. Nobody knows what will happen next – and there's still a very real chance of Britain not leaving the EU, if the campaign for a People's Vote is successful, or of re-entering it later on. If we are to remain, though, then it's up to Greens in particular to learn the lessons of these recent decades and to redouble our efforts to present a workable alternative to the corporate capture of European politics.

In the year 2000 I wrote:

As more consumers, farmers and workers are feeling the downside of destructive globalisation, now is the time to consider how we replace this with a localisation that protects and rebuilds local economies around the world...It is the race for ever greater international trade and competitiveness that should go up in smoke, not animals and the future of our farmers and countryside.[12]

I'm committed to this cause as much now as I was then. I hope that others will join me in using this moment to seriously question the fundamentals of the economy, and carve out space for something altogether new.

Endnotes

1   For a list of the 1999 election candidates, see https://bit.ly/2QGHRXj (accessed 25 October 2018).

2   European Parliament (Liaison Office in the United Kingdom), 'The European elections in 1989', Table of Results: United Kingdom; https://bit.ly/2DsOMQC (accessed 25 October 2018).

3   Helena Spongenberg, 'Airlines should have own emissions trading scheme, MEPs say', *EUobserver*, 4 July 2006; https://bit.ly/2OITXNB (accessed 25 October 2018).

4   Caroline Lucas MEP and Colin Hines, *After 50 Years: A New Direction for Europe – An Alternative Berlin Statement*, Report (2007); https://bit.ly/2rIAeor.

5   World Trade Organization, *UNITED KINGDOM Statement by The Rt. Hon. Tony Blair, MP, Prime Minister*, Geneva WTO Ministerial 1998: Statement; https://bit.ly/2T73EsC (accessed 25 October 2018).

6   EU Directorate General for Trade, *Openness, Trade and the European Union*, Speech by Peter Mandelson (Chambre de Commerce et de l'Industrie, Paris: 30 June 2007); https://bit.ly/2zRohQK (accessed 25 October 2018).

7   Caroline Lucas MEP, *Stopping the Great Food Swap: Relocalising Europe's Food Supply*, Report (2001); https://bit.ly/2zRt30H (accessed 25 October 2018).

8   Caroline Lucas MEP and Colin Hines, *Time to Replace Globalisation: A Green Localist Manifesto*, Report (The Greens/European Free Alliance in the European Parliament: 2004); https://bit.ly/2z9sArb.

9   *BBC News*, 'Election 2017: Brighton Pavilion results'; https://bbc.in/2FvgP46 (accessed 25 October 2018).

10   Caroline Lucas MEP, *Honourable Friends? Parliament and the Fight for Change* (London: Portobello Books, 2015).

11 Caroline Lucas MEP, *The Case for Parliamentary Reform*, Report (UK Parliament Website: 2010); https://bit.ly/2z6MdQr (accessed 25 October 2018).

12 Caroline Lucas MEP, *Stopping the Great Food Swap: Relocalising Europe's Food Supply*, Report (2001); https://bit.ly/2zRt30H (accessed 25 October 2018).

Chapter 5

Changes

Keith Taylor

Memory of a Free Festival

As the end of my time as an MEP approaches, I want to take the opportunity to reflect on the experiences that led me to the most exciting and challenging job I have ever had – a job that has afforded me the potential to influence change for over 500 million EU citizens.

I was born in 1953 in sunny Southend on Sea, the son of a baker's roundsman and a chemist's shop assistant. I lived a fairly cosseted life, with cakes featuring heavily in my diet and no wound ever remaining undressed for long. I spent a few miserable years at a secondary modern school but was more interested in the arts. It was during these years that I established a life-long love of music, from blues to psychedelia and all points in between. That was largely due to the wonderful pirate radio stations and my hanging around shady clubs that I was too young to be in. Well, it was the sixties, and Southend was good for music, with regular visits from bands such as Status Quo, John Mayall, Fleetwood Mac, Dr. Feelgood and The Nice.

The high point of those years was getting the chance to see the 'debut' of a not-yet-well-known David Bowie at the Cricketers Inn. He was brilliant. Never one to let the grass grow under my feet, after the show, I went up to that (by now, very sweaty) musical shape-shifter. I explained that I was helping to organise a free concert in aid of Shelter and asked whether he would like to come and perform. David was very gracious, but it was his wife, Angie, who after a few questions said, 'Yes, David will do it'. I was stunned. Angie Bowie gave me her phone number and asked me to call the next week to fill them in on the details. The idea for the concert came from my charismatic RE teacher, Dave Lawrence, who later went on to run a successful mail-order vinyl business. When I arrived at school on the Monday after the gig and told Dave and the rest of the class who I had managed to book for the festival, the response was a mixture of disbelief and (I think) admiration.

Figure 1. Baby Keith Taylor had no plans to become an MEP.

And, sure enough, on my birthday – 1 August 1970 – David arrived at the Eastwood Free Festival field in his campervan, driving himself and wearing a beautiful white kaftan offset by his flowing, curly blond locks. He captivated the crowd and played practically all of what would later become the iconic *The Rise and Fall of Ziggy*

Stardust and the Spiders from Mars album. It was a knockout event, with performances from not only David Bowie but also Roger Ruskin Spear (ex-Bonzo Dog Doo-Dah Band), the Edgar Broughton Band, Michael Chapman and Surly Bird. To cap it all, when I asked David, whose *Space Oddity* single would hit number five in the charts the following month, how much money we should give him, he replied: 'It's for Shelter, just £15 to pay for the petrol.' What a guy! (To set this in context, John Peel asked for £180 to emcee the festival.) I went to bed that night a happy 17-year-old. The event taught me a valuable lesson about fearlessness and the importance of hard work. Having more 'front' than Southend helped too.

Figure 2. David Bowie made his Southend debut in July 1970 (attribution unknown).

Absolute Beginners

My early adulthood was spent helping rear my two gorgeous children, and generally having a good time, with a succession of boring
jobs and a period of self-employment. In that time, I moved to the
place I still call home: Brighton. My active political journey didn't
start until I was 45 years old. It was the, frankly, stupid plan to
build a huge Sainsbury's on a city-centre site next to Brighton station
that unleashed the political animal in me. To me, sacrificing a huge
city-centre area to yet another chain supermarket showed a pau-
city of civic imagination.[1] I was depressed by the idea the people of
Brighton needed yet another outlet for toilet rolls and baked beans,
and a giant surface level car park to ruin whatever else might remain.

When I heard that Brighton & Hove Council were recommend-
ing approval for the project, I thought to myself, 'blow that, even
I can do better than those monkeys in the Town Hall'. Unknow-
ingly, I was moving away from calling for someone to do something
about that towards realising that I should try to do something about
it myself. So I joined Brighton Urban Design and Development
(BUDD), a funky community group based around a wood business
on the station site. Many of the good people I met there remain
friends to this day. With a lot of hard work, and a bit of cheek (and
the support of an active community group), we managed to get the
application thrown out. After that success, the local Green Party
suggested I run for council in the 1999 local elections. Not without
some reservations, I decided I should try to embrace the opportunity
to build a better future for my town. Luckily, 1,488 voters from St
Peter's ward thought that was a good idea too. Thus, I made my
entry into the vicious world of local politics, alongside fellow Greens
Pete West and Rik Child.[2]

From the very start of my elected journey, I have been determined to represent people by making their future better as a priority,
while also striving towards a fairer future for the planet and all living
things on it. And, while I understand both how the media works and
the Green Party's struggle to break the mainstream stranglehold of
Labour and the Conservatives, I've never wanted to be the kind of

politician that approaches every situation with an open mouth. The local authority world was incredibly tribal and adversarial. We three Greens joined a Labour-run council (45 Labour, 27 Conservative, 3 Liberal Democrat). It was very New Labour: selling off schools to private finance initiative projects and stoking damaging disputes with public services and unions. In Brighton, a traditional left-leaning town, the Labour group were out of step with the community. Greens became a thorn in their side and continued to win Labour seats for the next decade.

A Better Future

I think one of the essential functions of the Greens is to act as a monitor: to check and challenge where necessary, and to tell the community what is being done in their name in the practice of power. Too often there is a failure of imagination in local authority decision-making, and a disconnect between the actions taken and their real effect on people. One such example is the Palmeira Project in Hove, a residential home the council set up for severely autistic young people, delivered in partnership with the charity National Children's Homes (NCH). Until 1998, these children had been housed in a variety of facilities that were meeting the needs of neither the children nor their families. The idea of opening a centre of excellence, therefore, was a good one, and the families agreed to the council's offer to rehouse the children. The trouble was, there was no coordination in setting the service standards, needs and costs of the NCH/council contract. After the children moved into Palmeira, NCH realised their needs could not be met by the budget set out in the council contract.[3]

The council realised they had made a mistake, but Labour's solution was to end rather than extend funding. This decision would have taken effect in August 2000. The plan was unconscionable: the council was about to let down the families that most needed our support. When I got wind of what was happening, I contacted the parents and pledged to take up their fight. The council had promised families a rosy future, but just a couple of years later these same families were being told Palmeira would be closing. Rather than admitting their mistake and pledging to find the funds to keep the service running, the Labour administration decided the balance sheet took primacy. The families would have to lump it. It was a decision that, in my view, was immoral and an abdication of responsibility. Working alongside parents and their legal teams, Greens attempted to hold Labour to account in the council chamber. In the end, we were left with no option but to support the parents' legal battle. After a three-day hearing in the High Court in October 2000, the judge ruled the council should find the necessary funds to keep the project open, at least until the children were 19 years old.[4] Ultimately, it had taken five autistic children and a High Court judge to teach the council the difference between right and wrong.

One of Labour's dafter ideas, handed down from Westminster, was to push for a directly elected mayor (DEM) to act as a 'strategic figurehead for the city'.[5] The plan was to centralise decision-making powers at the expense of representative local democracy. The party selected two of the best-known Labour figures to champion the idea. We judged the concept wasn't popular with the public. To win any argument, you need to understand the details. I scoured the fine print of the terms of the referendum that Brighton was required to hold on the issue. Hidden away was a condition outlining that the council must have a 'fallback' position in the event of a 'no' vote. After some wriggling with council lawyers, I secured a fallback option that would see the council return to a committee-based decision-making system. (We had been working under a much less democratic Cabinet system.)

The Greens in Brighton & Hove played an important role in the anti-DEM campaign group Allies for Democracy, which was made up of politicians and activists from across the political spectrum. We ran a good campaign and, on 18 October 2001, the people of Brighton & Hove voted 62% to 38% against a DEM. The idea was booted out and the council, consequently, reverted to committee-based decision-making.[6] This more representative system helped to shape the future of city politics for years to come, for the better. After an expensive and failed bid for European Capital of Culture, spearheaded by a New Labour council more focused on image and trying to spin a rosy picture of the future than on actually building one, there was a lot of local anger. At the time, I was quoted in the local paper, *The Argus*, being characteristically honest about my views on the process: 'From start to finish the whole campaign has been like an experimental ride on a balloon – lots of hot air and going nowhere.'[7] In 2001, Brighton & Hove was granted city status.[8] Many people in the know saw this as a consolation prize for losing out on the culture bid. By the time of the local elections, May 2003, local anger had been dwarfed by the national response to Tony Blair's illegal invasion of Iraq, launched just two months prior. With the largest ever UK political demonstration, which saw more than a million people take to the streets of London in protest against the Iraq War, it was no surprise that Labour took a hammering in the polls.[9] In Brighton & Hove, Labour collapsed, its lead of 18 seats over the Tories dwindling to just four in total. We Greens doubled our councillors to six. (Greens would go on to continue this trajectory in the city, doubling representation to 12 councillors in 2007 and almost doubling it again in 2011, when voters elected 23 Green councillors.)

Figure 3. Keith Taylor and Caroline Lucas in Brighton.

Fantastic Voyage

We Greens spent our time working hard, developing our green priorities, building proactive policies, positively influencing the council agenda, and doing loads of casework for our constituents. As group convenor, I proudly acknowledged the essential roles our councillors played in shaping Brighton & Hove politics and the enormous fun we had doing it. Our efforts, policies and approach were rewarded at the ballot box by the city's voters – the ultimate performance indicator – despite our being hamstrung by an archaic first-past-the-post electoral system.

Nationally, 2004 was a sad year for the Green Party of England and Wales. It was the year we saw the tragic death of Mike Woodin, one of the party's first elected councillors and our joint principal speaker alongside Caroline Lucas. It was Mike who inspired me with his visionary take on the interconnectedness of all things, where causes and effects were acknowledged and met with sustainable solutions. The whole UK green movement was intensely saddened by his death. We will be forever grateful to Mike.[10] After Mike died, I was appointed his replacement as a principal speaker for the Green Party of England and Wales, a position that was confirmed by a members' vote in November 2004. Neither your usual party leader (though that position did not exist in the Greens officially for another four years) nor your usual Green, the *Guardian* described me as 'defying the stereotype of Green politicians as earnest or bookish academics'.[11] I was just a normal, straight-talking chap, who now had the privilege and the responsibility of representing the Greens at a national level. With the support of a magnificent team, I was also the Brighton Pavilion general election candidate in 2001 and 2005. In my first attempt, I received 9% of the vote. I had built on a 2.6% vote share for the Greens in 1997, saving the party's deposit for the first time.[12] In my second attempt, I scored 22% of the vote.[13] At the time, it was the highest ever vote share for the Greens in a general election.

Alongside being a hard-working councillor, I also spent five years working with Caroline Lucas, one of the Green Party's two MEPs at the time. My job was to promote the work of Greens in Europe. Arranging constituency visits, contributing to policy and strategy, and working alongside Caroline was enormous fun and very instructive. I learned a lot and left with the impression that Caroline had more hours in her day than anyone else, and a burning ambition to deliver social and environmental justice. Following a decade of service as an MEP, Caroline made history by being elected Britain's first-ever Green MP in 2010.[14] Caroline was elected to the Brighton Pavilion seat with a whopping 31% of the vote. Since that momentous day, she has become a national opinion-former, a force for good and a beacon of hope for many inside and outside the green movement. Caroline punches well above her weight. She's a special person.

After Caroline's election, she had to vacate her seat in the European Parliament: one can't be an MP and an MEP at the same time. European elections are run on a regional party-list proportional representation system.[15] Parties put forward candidates in rank order, with the number of candidates matching the number of seats available in each region. In the 2009 elections the Green Party's South East list ranked Caroline first; I was second on the ten-candidate list.[16] Under the party-list system, the next candidate on the list is the first choice to replace an MEP who resigns their seat. So, I joined the European Parliament on 2 June 2010. I remember entering the building for the first time as an MEP – it was big and bustling with people, all of whom seemed to know what they were doing – and I instantly felt like a very small part of something huge. When I entered politics, I represented the 8,000 voters in Brighton's St Peter's ward. Now I was suddenly representing more than six million voters across the South East of England. (Almost one in ten of those voters chose me to represent them again as one of the South East's ten MEPs elected to the European Parliament in 2014.)

It Ain't Easy

I have learned, after 20 years as an elected politician, that success relies on building a good team, and I have been lucky in my choices of staff. Simply put, I could not do my job as well as I do without the excellent support my colleagues provide, for which I will always be incredibly grateful.

Explaining what an MEP actually does calls to mind a childhood memory of looking into a Woolworths shop window, which was crammed with different items, and seeing a sign that read 'impossible to show all we sell'. A significant amount of an MEP's work is dictated by the committees they join. European Parliament committees play a vital role in creating, scrutinising and amending EU laws. In my first term, from 2010 to 2014, I served on the development, transport and tourism, international trade, and petitions committees. In my second term, 2014–19, I stayed on the Committee on Transport and Tourism and joined the Committee on the Environment, Public Health and Food Safety. I also joined a number of intergroups that, although not official European Parliament bodies, are hugely important for bringing MEPs from different political groups together to work collaboratively on key issues. I have been a long-time member of both the LGBTI rights and animal welfare intergroups, becoming vice chair of the latter in 2014. Additionally, I have been a member of delegations for developing relations with Afghanistan and Palestine.

Since becoming an MEP, I have also taken on a variety of positions outside of the European Parliament, including being animals spokesperson for the Green Party of England and Wales, European chair of the Climate Parliament, vice president of the Local Government Association, vice chair of the European Alzheimer's Alliance, and a member of both the MEP Heart Group and the Irish Peace Process Support Group. There is certainly enough work to keep me on my toes.

Nature Boy

We need to live on this planet as if we mean to stay. As a member of the Committee on Environment, Public Health and Food Safety, I have continued to learn about and understand the challenges we all face while, I hope, helping to identify and influence the solutions to them. Other chapters in this book cover the key victories we have achieved as UK Green MEPs; therefore, to avoid regurgitating a list of legislative achievements, I want to reflect on the overriding issues that continue to motivate the work I do as an MEP, both inside and outside the European Parliament.

Our climate is changing due to greenhouse gas emissions. At the same time, our oceans are choking on plastic, and global deaths associated with air pollution are being measured in the millions. Rich countries are plagued by food waste but are suffering an obesity epidemic, while some developing countries face famine and land loss caused by rising sea levels. Similarly, the abundance of wildlife on our planet has decreased by 58% in just 40 years.[17] Biodiversity continues to be threatened by resource exploitation and habitat loss. All of these problems are self-made, and there is still time to reverse the damage. The task is huge; but it should be the top priority for every politician, government and corporation in the world. As a European parliamentarian, I have contributed to policies that are helping to address these issues and their effect on the way more than 500 million Europeans live and work. For me, a good starting point and an invaluable guide is the EU's Precautionary Principle (when an activity poses a threat to human health or the environment, it must not be allowed to continue until that threat is removed), allied with its polluter pays principle (which is pretty self-explanatory).

The Paris Agreement was groundbreaking, and the EU played a vital role in pulling it together. For over 190 countries to agree that there was both a problem and a solution was a significant step forward.[18] I was in Paris in 2015. I had travelled as the European chair of the Climate Parliament and spent my time working with governments from around the world. I was a proud and vocal champion for renewable energy. I spoke alongside former Deputy Prime Minister John Prescott with representatives from China and India: countries that, at the time, were investing heavily in sustainable energy. It is hard to overstate the significance of the Paris Agreement, despite its flaws. The agreement failed to set any of the firm targets or monitoring or reporting requirements essential for tackling greenhouse gas reduction in a meaningful way. Nevertheless, there was an agreement that countries would set 'national determined contributions', which, together, had to demonstrate how global temperature increases could be limited to 1.5°C.[19]

In the aftermath of the Paris Agreement, the EU set CO_2 reduction targets of 20% by 2020, and 40% by 2030.[20] Greens have argued strongly for greater ambition in these targets, and this is a fight we will not give up any time soon. The European Parliament is well placed to set the regulations that will help reduce greenhouse gas emissions across the EU, especially in the energy creation, transport and manufacturing industries. When it comes to taking action, however, we cannot ignore the strong industry lobbying, supported by some political groups with vested interests, opposing climate change action and pushing a deregulation agenda.

Neighbourhood Threat

Throughout my political career, I have tried to make the future better, not worse. But I have been told that this mantra is redundant because, hey, who *does* want to make the future worse? Sadly, all I can say is that, after rubbing shoulders with industry lobbyists and self-interested politicians, it has become clear that plenty of people want to trash your future. I think all politicians have a duty to their constituents to challenge what their governments are doing in their name and to resist pressure from multinational corporations who want to make money through activities that damage our environment. Fracking is a good example of an environmentally destructive industry supported by politicians with vested interests. I have written tomes on the case against fracking (but I won't rehearse them all here). Suffice to say, unconventional oil and gas extraction is responsible for emitting the most climate-destroying greenhouse gases: methane and CO_2.[21] It is a water-intensive industry that poses a risk to the water supplies of the local communities on which it is foisted. It also causes air and noise pollution and generates large volumes of heavy traffic on, usually, small, rural road networks.

I first became aware of fracking at Balcombe, West Sussex, in 2011. Like the majority of people, I was not sure about the process, but I quickly learned it was bad news. And the more people, like me, learned about its operation, impacts and risks, the less they wanted to see fracking in their communities. The whole idea of fracking concerned me greatly. In September 2013, I travelled to Pennsylvania in the US, where the number of fracking wells had mushroomed, to see the effects for myself. I met families suffering from sick livestock and polluted and unsafe water supplies. I saw roads damaged by the daily passage of huge trucks that also polluted the air. Armed guards protected the fracking sites I visited, which choked the air and pierced the rural peace with deafening sounds. I returned clear-minded: there was absolutely no way this should happen to our South Downs. Make no mistake, oil and gas companies see the US as a model for the UK. They want to take the profits and leave the communities they devastate to pay the price.

Figure 4. Keith Taylor joins Green Party councillors at the Balcombe anti-fracking protection camp in 2013.

The plans for Balcombe became national news after Reclaim the Power set up a protection camp at the proposed fracking site in August 2013. I was proud to be among the 2,000 local and national protesters who came to support the camp. Fracking hit the headlines; people power was starting to strike fear into the hearts of developers. Following the protest and the earthquakes linked to an exploration site in Blackpool run by Cuadrilla (who was the operator at Balcombe too), the frackers' designs on Balcombe were rebuffed.[22] And, despite government enthusiasm, unconventional oil and gas extraction was set back years. However, even though France, parts of Spain and Germany, Bulgaria, the Netherlands, Ireland and Scotland have all instituted bans or moratoriums on fracking in the interim, the threat of fracking has returned to England and Wales, and Balcombe.

The UK government has been a shameless cheerleader for the industry. In 2018 it released a report revealing the extent of fracking's contribution to pollution just days after it had given a green light to the first fracking operation in England in almost a decade.[23] To add insult to injury, this report had been drawn up in 2015 but deliberately suppressed by ministers. In those intervening three years, the government was promoting fracking, changing the planning laws to fast track it and cutting out local authorities from the decision-making processes concerning it, all the while accusing campaigners of being 'ideologically-driven scaremongers'.

I support and cherish the brave environmental protectors who have put their lives on hold to safeguard our future. From joining protesters on the front line to commissioning reports, linking up campaigners across the South East, challenging the government at every opportunity and raising the issue in the European Parliament, I have consistently used my position as an MEP to support the fight against this destructive industry. Furthermore, in response to any accusations of NIMBY-ism, I say we are working to stop this in everyone's backyard. The fight to create the energy we need from renewable and sustainable sources – wind, solar, wave and thermal ground pumps – continues, as does the fight against firms whose only interest is to profit from exploiting our natural resources, with no regard for the consequences.

Something in the Air

Another prime interest of mine is air pollution, most of which comes from the transport industry and energy operations. Toxic air is a global public health crisis; in the UK alone, it is linked with the premature deaths of almost 40,000 people every year.[24] Diesel is now recognised as a carcinogen by the World Health Organization (WHO), and polluted air has been shown to have links to asthma, respiratory diseases, heart disease, cancer, erectile dysfunction, dementia and a reduction in cognitive intelligence. Worldwide, the WHO estimates that seven million deaths are linked to exposure to polluted air, making it the planet's largest single environmental health risk.[25] The very young, the elderly and people with respiratory problems are the most vulnerable.

My first air pollution leaflet, *Air Pollution – The Invisible Killer*, was published in July 2011; since then, I have worked hard to bring public attention to the issue. I have also worked on legislation in the European Parliament to help ease the crisis, despite such actions often being opposed by Conservative MEPs. On the one hand, we have political inaction and denial, personified by the UK government. On the other, we have a mounting pile of scientific papers exposing the true and devastating health effects of the crisis.

It is only thanks to EU laws, which Greens helped craft, and the excellent work of the environmental lawyers at ClientEarth that the UK government has been dragged through the courts on no fewer than three occasions over its toxic air failures. These cases have helped increase awareness of both EU legal limits on air pollution and the government's repeated breaches of them. The government was judged by the courts to be at fault all three times.[26] Despite this, ministers are still failing to meaningfully tackle the problem. It seems the EU will be left with no choice but to impose huge fines on Britain, which would be a double whammy for the public. Soon, we may have to not only breathe the filthy stuff but also pay the fines levied against the government for failing to take action.

In my South East constituency, there are clean air groups in many of the worst-affected towns and cities, such as Brighton, Eastbourne,

Portsmouth, Southampton, Canterbury and Winchester. I have met with and worked alongside many of them, looking at the measures necessary to mitigate, monitor and minimise air pollution in their communities. That work goes on, while Greens in parliament are working on legislation to reduce air pollution emissions.

Figure 5. Keith Taylor joins an air quality protest in Portsmouth.

She'll Drive the Big Car

The other committee on which I sit is transport and tourism, where I have also worked to reduce the climate impacts of transport and championed sustainable mobility. Given that, in the UK, the majority of CO_2 emissions (34%) comes from the transport sector, and emissions have risen in the last decade, it is clear that there needs to be increased domestic focus on addressing the problem.[27] But this isn't just a UK problem; across the EU, transport accounts for almost a quarter of all CO_2 emissions. Within the sector, road transport and aviation are by far the biggest emitters, accounting for more than 85% of all greenhouse gas emissions from transport.[28]

The UK government is failing to recognise the role it could play here. Ministers' obsession with road building and their ridiculous decision to back Heathrow expansion – in spite of all the evidence regarding its climate impact – are just two examples of the disconnection between cause and effect in policy. That is why, at the European Parliament, I have been working for pan-EU solutions to the problem. It is not just the UK that needs a sustainable transport strategy. Building more roads and runways is a failing infrastructure programme pursued by too many European governments. This policy will always be doomed to fail, even on its own terms. Inducing traffic and congestion and encouraging growth in personal vehicle ownership is the wrong road to be heading down. But encouraging people to move away from personal vehicle ownership and towards integrated, sustainable public transport options relies on these alternatives being accessible and affordable. That is why one of the highlights of my final term has been the work I have done on the EU's Accessibility Act. I was the rapporteur, charged with drafting and reporting the committee's views on the transport aspects of the proposals to the rest of the European Parliament.

Working with disability federations and campaigners, we identified that the built environment, human-made space, was critical in ensuring that people with limited mobility were able to access sustainable public transport options. I argued to make it mandatory for all new infrastructure to be accessible to all people. It should not have been a big ask, but it was. After lobbying my colleagues and asking my supporters and constituents to rally their representatives to support my proposals, a large majority of MEPs in the parliament voted in favour of my plans.[29] EU ministers are still finalising the law, but I am hopeful for a positive outcome that will make a world of difference to the 80 million Europeans with mobility problems.

My parliamentary work includes drafting legislation, writing opinion reports and acting as group 'shadow' rapporteur, working to develop policies alongside shadows from across the political spectrum. The issues I've dealt with are many and varied. The vital EU laws I recall having a significant influence on, however, include the Clean Vehicles Directive, Passenger Rights, Alternative Fuel

Infrastructure, Maritime Spatial Planning, Port Reception Facilities, Road Safety, and Training for Seafarers. In my constituency, I have worked to support campaigns against airport expansion and new road building as well as promoted, shared and spoken in support of sustainable mobility solutions. As a Green, and with a constituency that is served by the failing private rail provider Govia Thameslink Railway (responsible for Southern Rail), I have also campaigned to bring railways back into public ownership and to drive investment in our public transport services.

Diamond Dogs

To me, animal welfare is a vital issue. Compassion for animals is deep within the Greens' DNA. That is why I have been honoured to serve as the animals spokesperson for the Green Party of England and Wales since 2016, while also serving as the vice chair of the European Parliament's animal welfare intergroup since 2014. One of the issues that will always stay with me is our fight against the cruel and scientifically illiterate culling of badgers in England and Wales. Had it not been for a member of my team scrutinising in great detail the 'review' of the cull announced by the government in 2017, we might never have exposed the fact that this extremely limited 'review' was nothing but a cover for the real announcement: that the unnecessary cull was going to be rolled out even more widely.[30]

The long-fought battle to end EU subsidies for bullfighting in Spain will also be pretty hard to forget. I recall first celebrating victory in October 2015, when the European Parliament voted to end all agricultural subsidies to land being used to rear bulls for bullfighting.[31] The vote represented what should have been the final nail in the coffin of a cruel and bloodthirsty spectacle. However, the European Commission, under pressure from the industry and the Spanish government, circumvented our amendment on a technicality. We did not give up, though. In May 2018 we once again voted through an amendment calling for an end to the controversial subsidy for bullfighting.[32] The amendment is watertight; no technicality will stop us this time. The end is nigh for bullfighting.

Other issues on which I have worked include: putting an end to the cage age for Europe's chickens and, more recently, rabbits; strengthening the safeguards for farmed animals and working to end factory farming; fighting for stricter controls on abattoirs; and working to improve zoo animal welfare across Europe. I have also campaigned for improvements in kitten and puppy welfare, including pushing for a ban on the third-party sale of dogs and cats that fuels the demand for illegally and cruelly farmed pets. Thankfully, the UK government has taken note of the campaign: in August 2018 it announced welcome plans to introduce such a ban, known to campaigners as Lucy's Law.[33]

The other major issue I have devoted my time to is live animal exports. It is a barbaric and entirely unnecessary trade. In my constituency alone, we have witnessed the cruelty first-hand, whether it is the horrifying tragedy of the death, by execution and drowning, of 45 sheep in Ramsgate, Kent, in September 2012, or the far-too-routine images of dehydrated and distressed animals packed onto boats with too little regard for their welfare. I have been working and campaigning to ban this for the best part of the last decade.[34] With the support of more than a million citizens across the EU, who have pledged to back the Stop the Trucks campaign, I have wholeheartedly backed cross-party efforts to effectively ban live animals from ever being transported from British shores.[35] Despite calls from Greens, activists and campaigners, the UK government has consistently refused to back these proposals.

The free movement of trade, which is one of the factors making an outright, EU-wide live exports ban difficult, is enshrined in the rules of the single market. Pro-Brexit politicians, who have previously expressed little concern over the issue, have tried to exploit this fact as a means of stoking anti-EU sentiment in Britain. The whole truth, as I have long argued, is a little more complicated. But the British media preference for removing any nuance from the EU debate has made live exports a complicated issue for pro-EU animal welfare campaigners.

The rules that both classify animals for export as goods and protect their free movement govern not just the EU single market but also membership of the World Trade Organization (WTO), the organisation that would oversee UK trade post-Brexit if the government insists on yanking Britain out of the single market.[36] It is likely because of this that the Brexit charlatans, now government ministers, who sold dedicated animal advocates the lie that leaving the EU would mean the UK would ban live exports have quietly backtracked on that promise.[37] It is my firm belief that by working together across the EU we are best placed to fundamentally alter in the short term and overhaul in the long term the live exports trade. I do not want national borders to limit the number of animals I can help.

Figure 6. Keith Taylor joins live export campaigners in Ramsgate, Kent.

Helping animals has often, perhaps unexpectedly, intertwined with my efforts to mitigate the very worst effects of climate change. Animal agriculture is an industry that continues to emit a lot of greenhouse gases; there has been little meaningful reduction in the sector's emissions over the last decade. A landmark UN report found that livestock farming accounts for 18% of global greenhouse gas emissions.[38] In comparison to growing protein crops for humans, meat production also relies on a disproportionate amount of water and huge tracts of land to grow feed. I proudly promote and campaign for more awareness of the benefits of plant-based diets. My hard work, if I do say so myself, was rewarded in 2017, when the Royal Society for the Prevention of Cruelty to Animals (RSPCA) handed me an Honours Award in recognition of my services to European animal welfare. I have long worked with the RSPCA on a host of issues, and receiving this award was one of my proudest moments as an animal advocate.

Peace on Earth

Like all Greens, I am a committed nuclear disarmament campaigner, a proponent of peace and a staunch defender of the fundamental rights of all people across the world. Since 2010 I have been a member of the European Parliament's Delegation for relations with Palestine. I visited Egypt, Syria and Gaza in 2011. It was a formative trip. I saw for myself the privations of Gazans, the hardships caused by blockades and the damage wrought by Israeli Defence Force (IDF) attacks. I come to these issue as a humanitarian, not coloured by blind ideology. What I am, however, is a firm believer that international law applies equally to everyone in the Middle East. Following my visit, I was faced with the reality that the policies pursued by the Israeli government are deliberately oppressive towards Palestine and Palestinians, from the West Bank to Gaza. Major IDF attacks on Palestine in 2008–9, and again in 2014, caused degrees of death and destruction that dwarfed any losses suffered by the IDF.[39]

I attended several meetings of the Russell Tribunal, which analysed the legal aspects of the conflict.[40] The independent tribunal heard from academics and top legal experts. It concluded that the State of Israel had violated international law and practised apartheid. It also criticised the US, UN and EU for failing to act to uphold international law. I have argued in the European Parliament that the EU can and should use its influence more effectively to help bring about an end to the conflict, using trade sanctions as a tool if necessary. I have found no majority to support my calls. Clearly, we need a change in the political will across Europe, but it seems we are moving in the wrong direction. The withdrawal of US funding from the United Nations Relief and Works Agency for Palestine Refugees in the Near East (UNRWA), which is the UN's Palestinian aid agency, and the provocative relocation of the US embassy to Jerusalem, the shared capital of Israel and Palestine, are worrying developments.[41] So is the lack of interest shown by presidents Benjamin Netanyahu and Mahmoud Abbas in working towards a peaceful settlement. There is a hill to climb, and until its summit is scaled, it is the Palestinian people that will, disproportionately, suffer.

A Small Plot of Land

Three things are uncontroversially true: (1) we only have one planet; (2) the pervasive neoliberal economic paradigm demands ever more growth; and (3) growth consumes ever more of our natural resources. Consequently, it should be obvious that either neoliberalism must burn or our planet surely will. Tinkering around the edges of the system will not solve the inexorable economic, social and environmental challenges we face. As Bob Dylan succinctly put it: 'Money doesn't talk, it swears.'

As a member of the Committee on Environment, Public Health and Food Safety, I have seen the neoliberal abuse of our planet characterised by the growth in industrial agriculture. Giant agribusinesses are continually developing genetically modified organisms (GMOs) and pesticides designed to increase farmers' reliance upon them while delivering no crop yield benefits that couldn't be achieved by a more sustainable approach to farming. Most importantly, they destroy biodiversity and rare and vital habitats across the world. Industrial agriculture is by no means the only culprit: the market is tirelessly developing new ways to profit at the planet's expense. But it is the one that has stuck with me from my work in the European Parliament.

As a group, Green MEPs in the parliament have been vigorous and successful in challenging the widespread use of 'probably carcinogenic' glyphosate-containing weed-killers and the fast-tracking of GMOs, and victorious in ending the use of bee-killing pesticides across Europe. A particular personal highlight, however, was our 2016 victory against the multinational corporations that were pushing the EU to increase the sugar limits on baby foods to 30% (the WHO recommendation was 5%). I led this campaign and felt both relieved and delighted when the parliament voted to reject the industry's proposals.[42]

Silly Boy Blue

In the continuing aftermath of the banking crash of 2008, which was born out of traders' greed and politicians' acquiescence to it, the newly elected Conservative-led coalition government embarked on a programme of brutal austerity. We saw budgets to government departments slashed and swingeing cuts to local authorities. The cuts continue to bite almost a decade later: by the time you read this, the number of councils facing bankruptcy may have reached double figures in England.[43] This means, in practice, that they will cease to provide statutory social care and health and child services. All this in the sixth-largest economy on the planet. How the British government responded to the crash is not the European Parliament's business, but as an elected representative of millions of people, it is mine. I care about what happens to my constituents.

Welfare cuts and the disastrous rollout of Universal Credit – with poor administration leading to devastatingly long payment delays and heinous penalties, dished out for minor transgressions – squeezed the unemployed or those on low incomes: those least responsible for the banking crash.

One of the most upsetting aspects of this was the dramatic rise in foodbank usage. Foodbanks barely existed in the UK prior to

2010.[44] I commissioned a series of reports to analyse the crisis in the South East of England. Between 2013 and 2017, foodbank use grew by 20% in the South East.[45] As wages stayed low, even working families were forced to seek support. I know. I visited many food banks and met the people for whom they became a lifeline. Even nurses in full-time jobs are struggling to stretch their falling incomes to cover increasing accommodation, travel, clothes and living costs. After seeing the crisis up close, I called on the government to seek emergency help from the EU's solidarity fund. The government refused. Concluding that they simply do not care about the people left destitute by their policies is inescapable.

Stay

Regrettably, this chapter must end with an issue that I am sure will be no less of a farce whenever it is you come to read these pages: Brexit. The origins of this lie in a decision made by one of Britain's worst-ever prime ministers, David Cameron, to offer a referendum on EU membership in order to face down the hard right in his own party and UKIP's electoral threat from the even further right. He thought it would provide an electorally beneficial distraction while being sure the country would vote to stay anyway. How wrong he was.

I campaigned long and hard across the South East for a Remain vote, along with many people from other parties. The issue should, in my view, have transcended party politics. The result was a shock, but perhaps not as much of a shock as the reality of the government's 'no deal' Brexit briefings; the government is dragging us, as I write, towards a future far starker than even the so-called fearmongering Remain campaigners could have predicted during the campaign.[46] I have never pretended the EU was perfect; in fact, Greens have advanced many ideas to improve it. But to leave an institution that has preserved European peace since its inception, and that has been the basis for the trade, social and environmental protections that Britons have enjoyed for over 40 years, is reckless.

Figure 7. Keith Taylor and Caroline Lucas launch the 'Greens for a Better Europe' EU referendum campaign on Brighton Beach.

The Leave campaign was built on lies and broke the law.[47] But, for me, one of the things that stung the most was the charge, by Leave campaigners, that EU supporters were backing an anti-democratic system. The hypocrisy in proclaiming the primacy of UK democracy while slamming the 'democratic deficit' in the EU was too much to bear. In the UK, the first-past-the-post electoral system can deliver to a party supported by just over a quarter of eligible voters a legislative majority in the House of Commons, while our second chamber remains stuffed with unelected peers and religious leaders. The real democratic deficit is much closer to home. It is time to revitalise our democracy and ensure that every vote cast really counts. We can learn much from Europe, where the proportional representation electoral system delivers MEPs who truly reflect the diversity of the communities they represent.

The future of Brexit may be clearer or rosier when you read this than it is now, but I doubt it. That's why, you will no doubt understand, I back the Green Party of England and Wales's call for a People's Vote on the final terms of any Brexit deal.[48] There is nothing undemocratic in giving the people the final say on the final deal. I may have already been proven right or wrong, hopefully, by now, but I believe a 'no deal' Brexit is where Britain is heading. The little-considered Irish border issue will be the Conservative government's undoing, I suspect. With the government reliant on support from the Democratic Unionist Party (DUP), who insist there should be no alignment of Northern Ireland and the EU, and the Irish government's understandable refusal to accept the fixed border that the DUP's position necessitates, there is little light at the end of the tunnel, unless the government embraces a full single market and customs union membership. The negotiations have demonstrated the unity of the remaining 27 EU countries, who will no doubt side with Ireland on the issue. In fact, Michel Barnier, the EU's chief Brexit negotiator, has confirmed to me that the transition period and a post-Brexit deal hinges on the UK coming up with an Irish border solution that is acceptable to EU member states.[49] All roads lead to no deal.

Brilliant Adventure

For me, Brexit will mean I leave a couple of months earlier than planned. Having served my party and voters for 20 years, I'd already decided to retire from Parliament at the end of the current term anyway. As I leave, I step into an uncertain future, but I am buoyed by the support of family and friends. Especially Lizzie, my partner for 26 years and my wife for the last four. She has been my rock, a constant source of advice, fun and a much-needed reality check on some of my wilder aspirations.

I have been lucky that both of my children have had children of their own. I am now a proud grandfather to four grandchildren: two boys in Brighton and two girls in Ireland. I really have no firm plans for the next instalment of my life's adventure, but whatever course it takes, I will still be the same chap with the same sense of justice. That same ambition to make things better will be hard to shake too.

I don't know where I'm going from here, but I promise it won't be boring.

– **David Bowie**

Endnotes

1   Environment Department, *Brighton Station Site Brief: Supplementary Planning Guidance* (Brighton & Hove: Brighton & Hove City Council, 1998), p. 7.

2   Colin Rallings and Michael Thrasher, *Local Elections Handbook 1999* [ebook] (Plymouth: Local Government Chronicle Elections Centre, University of Plymouth: 1999), p. 55; https://bit.ly/2QELe0K (accessed 31 August 2018).

3   *The Argus*, 'Inquiry ordered into closure of home for autistic children', 12 July 2000; https://bit.ly/2FpThNQ (accessed 31 August 2018).

4   *The Argus*, 'Autistic kids' centre is saved', 12 January 2001; https://bit.ly/2qN8QFd (accessed 31 August 2018).

5   See the *Local Government Act 2000*; https://bit.ly/2RSTHxy.

6   *BBC News*, 'Sedgefield votes no to elected mayor', 19 October 2001; https://bbc.in/2DkJaai (accessed 31 August 2018).

7   *The Argus*, 'City out of title race', 30 October 2002; https://bit.ly/2q-MaIOj (accessed 31 August 2018).

8   *Brighton & Hove Independent*, 'Warren Morgan: the evolution of Brighton and Hove', 7 January 2017; https://bit.ly/2K3rW2y (accessed 31 August 2018).

9   *BBC News*, 'Anti-war rally makes its mark', 19 February 2003; https://bbc.in/2RWlKMr (accessed 31 August 2018).

10 Caroline Lucas, 'Obituary: Mike Woodin', *Guardian*, 14 July 2004; https://bit.ly/2RS8Xuw (accessed 31 August 2018).

11 Matthew Tempest, 'Greens name new figurehead', *Guardian*, 6 August 2004; https://bit.ly/2qOfRWb (accessed 31 August 2018).

12 See electoralcalculus.co.uk. *Election Data 2001;* https://bit.ly/2QHrnOs (accessed 31 August 2018).

13 See electoralcalculus.co.uk. *Election Data 2005*; https://bit.ly/2zewkYi (accessed 31 August 2018).

14 Peter Walker, 'Green party celebrates as Caroline Lucas becomes its first MP', *Guardian*, 7 May 2010; https://bit.ly/2B9TOiP (accessed 31 August 2018).

15 European Parliament (Liaison Office in the United Kingdom), 'The voting system'; https://bit.ly/2Th0gvq (accessed 31 August 2018).

16 *The Telegraph*, 'European elections 2009: South East region', 4 June 2009; https://bit.ly/2QI2Pov (accessed 31 August 2018).

17 WWF, *Living Planet Report 2016* (Gland, Switzerland: WWF), p. 12.

18 UNFCCC, *Paris Agreement – Status of Ratification* (n.d.); https://bit.ly/2yRc1CN (accessed 31 August 2018).

19 UNFCCC, *Nationally Determined Contributions (NDCs)* (n.d.); https://bit.ly/2vw7XCU (accessed 31 August 2018).

20 European Commission, *2030 Climate & Energy Framework* (n.d.); https://bit.ly/2tvvYHG (accessed 31 August 2018).

21 John Worden *et al*, 'Reduced biomass burning emissions reconcile conflicting estimates of the post-2006 atmospheric methane budget', *Nature Communications*, Vol. 8, No. 2227, 2017.

22 Michael Marshall, 'How fracking caused earthquakes in the UK', *New Scientist*, 2 November 2011; https://bit.ly/2sKzL7p (accessed 31 August 2018).

23 Damian Carrington, 'Buried UK government report finds fracking increases air pollution', *Guardian*, 2 August 2018; https://bit.ly/2Aw8x9v (accessed 31 August 2018).

24 COMEAP, *Associations of Long-term Average Concentrations of Nitrogen Dioxide with Mortality* (London: Public Health England, 2018).

25 World Health Organization, *7 Million Premature Deaths Annually Linked to Air Pollution*, News Release (2014); https://bit.ly/1jpGo4S (accessed 31 August 2018).

26 ClientEarth, *UK Government Loses Third Air Pollution Case as Judge Rules Air Pollution Plans 'Unlawful'*, News (21 February 2018); https://bit.ly/2HzuxQ5 (accessed 31 August 2018).

27 Department for Business, Energy and Industrial Strategy, *2017 UK Greenhouse Gas Emissions, Provisional Figures* (London: Her Majesty's Government, 2018).

28 European Commission, *Transport Emissions* (n.d.); https://bit. ly/2oVQnFJ (accessed 31 August 2018).

29 Keith Taylor MEP, *Greens Celebrate as MEPs Back Crucial Amendments To European Accessibility Legislation* (14 September 2017); https://bit. ly/2qO4EFm (accessed 31 August 2018).

30 Keith Taylor MEP, *Green MEP Fury at Gove Broken Promises as Badger Cull Expands across South East* (8 March 2018); https://bit.ly/2QF6eEt (accessed 31 August 2018).

31 Keith Taylor MEP, *Bullfighting Will Be a 'Failing Business', Says Green MEP as EU Ends Subsidies* (28 October 2015); https://bit.ly/2qMEy5n (accessed 31 August 2018).

32 Keith Taylor MEP, *MEPs Vote to End EU Bullfighting Subsidies as Greens' Animal Spokesperson Handed Animal Welfare Award* (31 May 2018); https://bit.ly/2QFPltv (accessed 31 August 2018).

33 Department for Environment, Food and Rural Affairs, *Government Backs Ban on Third Party Sales of Puppies and Kittens*, News Story (22 August 2018); https://bit.ly/2MGSvyy (accessed 31 August 2018).

34 Compassion in World Farming, *Disaster at Ramsgate as 45 Sheep Die* (12 September 2012); https://bit.ly/2OITye8 (accessed 31 August 2018).

35 Eurogroup for Animals, *Over 1 Million European Citizens Call to #stopthetrucks* (20 June 2017); https://bit.ly/2sRuoTH (accessed 31 August 2018).

36 Keith Taylor MEP, *Animals and Brexit* (Brussels: Office of Keith Taylor MEP, 2018), pp. 31–2.

37 Keith Taylor MEP, *Green MEP: Brexit White Paper Drops Live Exports Ban, Worrying for UK Animal Welfare* (13 July 2018); https://bit. ly/2K5qkpd (accessed 31 August 2018).

38 Ibid.

39 Max Fisher, 'This chart shows every person killed in the Israel–Palestine conflict since 2000', *Vox*, 14 July 2014; https://bit.ly/2rAGBcj (accessed 31 August 2018).

40 See russelltribunalonpalestine.com. *About*; https://bit.ly/2Dn7QPx (accessed 31 August 2018).

41 *The Associated Press*, 'UNRWA chief: Trump cut budget to punish Palestinians for protesting Jerusalem recognition', *Haaretz*, 24 August 2018; https://bit.ly/2RTVfYc (accessed 31 August 2018).

42 Baby Milk Action, *European Parliament Votes for Big Reductions in Sugar in Baby Foods and Prohibitions on Labelling at Too Early an Age*, Press Release (20 January 2016); https://bit.ly/2TdZoYp (accessed 31 August 2018).

43 Benjamin Kentish, 'Local councils at risk of bankruptcy due to government "complacency", MPs warn', *Independent*, 4 July 2018; https://ind.pn/2IRbpfO (accessed 31 August 2018).

44 Full Fact, *How Many People Use Food Banks?* (28 April 2017); https://bit.ly/2qSA9wm (accessed 31 August 2018).

45 Samir Jeraj, *Escalating Hunger in the South East* (London: Office of Keith Taylor MEP, 2018), p. 2.

46 Ian Dunt, 'Sweaty and nervous, Raab fumbles his Brexit no-deal announcement', *Politics.co.uk*, 23 August 2018; https://bit.ly/2OX-O2VG (accessed 31 August 2018).

47 Emma Graham-Harrison, 'Vote Leave broke electoral law and British democracy is shaken', *Guardian*, 17 July 2018; https://bit.ly/2QuZtp6 (accessed 31 August 2018).

48 Green Party of England and Wales, *Green Party Calls for People's Poll to Reverse 'Calamitous Brexit'* (3 March 2018); https://bit.ly/2Ba0vkX (accessed 31 August 2018).

49 Keith Taylor MEP, *Green MEP Meets with EU Chief Brexit Negotiator to Talk Good Friday Agreement on 20th Anniversary* (10 April 2018); https://bit.ly/2PXNHq0 (accessed 31 August 2018).

Part III

The UK's Green MEPs: perspectives from friends

Chapter 6

Greens and campaigners: a natural affinity

Natalie Bennett

The Green Party of England and Wales, like other green parties around the world, has a close relationship with nongovernmental organisations (NGOs), campaigning groups and charities. This is unsurprising, given that the party grew out of the new social movements of the 1960s[1] and has always seen electoral politics and nonelectoral campaigning, including nonviolent direct action, as an essential part of its activities. The philosophical basis of the party says:

> We do not believe that there is only one way to change society, or that we have all the answers. We seek to be part of a wider green movement that works for these principles through a variety of means. We generally support those who use reasonable and non-violent forms of direct action to further just aims.[2]

It is naturally far closer to NGOs and campaigning groups than the Labour Party, which has its philosophical basis in the workplace and workers' rights, and exudes discomfort (which still continues) when confronting and opposing populist views on immigration and benefits. Even further away are the Liberal Democrats, who, particularly since the departure of many of their more left-wing activists following the 2010 coalition government, have been determinedly clinging to the middle ground, unlikely to take a stand – certainly not a physical one. I remember the words of a senior Liberal Democrat in Sheffield when I invited him to join me in backing protesters slow-walking in front of arborists, who had unnecessarily felled a healthy street tree as police were trying to end the action: 'No. You Greens are dangerous!' I didn't see him for the rest of the day.

The natural affinity between campaigners and the Green Party has been particularly evident in the anti-fracking movement, one of the key environmental struggles of the past few years. As the Dutch city of Utrecht has begun tearing out its gas infrastructure in preparation for a post-fossil fuel world, the UK government has been trying (and thus far failing) to set up a new gas industry in England (Scotland and Wales having used devolved powers to block it). In 2013 Caroline Lucas, by then an MP in nearby Brighton, was arrested and charged (and subsequently found not guilty) over a protest at the Balcombe site, where the anti-fracking movement had coalesced as a national force. For over a year, along with various NGOs, the party has led the green Mondays campaign at the Preston New Road anti-fracking camp in Lancashire, which MEP Keith Taylor visited.[3] He has also been at the forefront of the successful fight to stop oil drilling at Leith Hill in Sussex.

In addition, Greens have been at the fore in campaigning in both the UK and Brussels on refugee issues. We have clearly stood out in opposing Fortress Europe and the UK's 'hostile environment'. I'm proud of the defence of migration I was able to deliver in the second leaders' debate in the 2015 general election.[4]

How first-past-the-post gets in the way at Westminster

The natural closeness between Greens and campaigners hasn't always played out in Westminster electoral politics: certainly not before 2010, when Greens proved they could be a parliamentary party despite the lack of democratic representation provided by the first-past-the-post electoral system, but even since then. It's been a source of great frustration that major NGOs often fail to include Greens in their conclusions when assessing manifestos, playing into the classic BBC narrative of the Greens being a 'minor party'.

Spots at hustings events organised by NGOs and charities for Westminster elections have often had to be fought for, and all too often have not been won – again, leaving voters with the message that Greens are not to be taken seriously. In 2015 some NGOs, at least informally, came up with a new excuse for leaving us out: if they invited the Greens, they'd have to invite UKIP too, and they didn't want to do that. This is despite the fact that inviting us would have shown up the weaknesses and lack of ambition in the manifestos of both Labour and the Liberal Democrats on a range of issues. I proved as much in a hustings I did back in 2010, when a moderate women's group invited me as the chair of Green Party Women. Traditionally at such events, Labour and the Tories go first, then the Liberal Democrats, then us, and then any 'others'. On this occasion I'd had a busy day, and on a packed Tube I hadn't had the chance to write the usual back-of-the-envelope key point summary for my initial statement. I wasn't worried, though, as I expected the usual order to give me plenty of time to play catch-up.

However, the chair, with a mischievous glint in her eye, said she'd decided to go alphabetically. So, there I was, up first. Luckily, I was speaking on the political subject closest of all to my own heart; by the time I'd finished running through stable ongoing funding for women's refuges and rape crisis centres, universal basic income, three years' paid parental leave, just treatment of female asylum seekers and decriminalisation of abortion, there was a clear feeling in the room of 'well, the others aren't going to match that'. It's something NGOs might like to ponder as a way of pushing other parties further.

But in Westminster politics, by and large, with the notable exception of clear air campaigners (about which more later), the possibilities that Greens offer to shift the Overton window (the range of ideas seen as mainstream in public discourse) haven't been used nearly as much as they should have been. That bias and the difficulties in reaching and working with campaigning organisations it creates have been amplified by what the special rapporteur on the rights to freedom of peaceful assembly and of association has identified as a series of measures that, combined, have effected a 'closing of space for civil society'. These measures include the Transparency in Lobbying, Non-Party Campaigning and Trade Union Administration Act (generally known as the Lobbying Act) as well as the broad definition of 'domestic extremist' and the much-criticised (particularly by the Green Party) Prevent strategy.[5]

Brussels: far more democratic

Brussels has always operated very differently. In a far more democratic political system, with election by means of proportional representation; with an expectation of negotiation and genuine interest in expertise, rather than in political point scoring; and with the Greens/EFA group having been, in slightly varying forms, a force for decades, campaigning groups have regarded the UK's Green MEPs as a significant and important movement. They've been a natural go-to. This has played out in two significant ways. Firstly, on the broad campaigning level, groups seeking to shift the political debate on issues from the treatment of refugees to the banning of dangerous pesticides know that the Greens will be stronger, firmer and more likely to go further than other parties. They are prepared to put themselves on the line in campaigns, particularly when these involve opposition to major multinational companies and vested interests, such as those of the financial sector.

Secondly, the UK's Green MEPs have played major roles in many aspects of the serious, detailed, day-to-day work of committees that impact how political decisions are put into effect. As Nick Dearden of Global Justice Now,[6] previously of War on Want, Amnesty International and the Jubilee Debt Campaign, said:

England's Green MEPs have been among the highest profile and most effective MEPs, so far as civil society is concerned. Some individuals from other parties have used the position as a platform to proclaim policies and campaign, but the Greens have also taken the day-to-day work of regulation and operation very seriously, as other haven't. To create change, that's really important. Our Green MEPs have punched well above their weight.[7]

One reason why campaigners have found Green MEPs to be natural allies for campaigns (particularly the more radical groups: those calling for a system change away from the neoliberal, globalised economic structures that play into the interests of the few, not the many) is that the Green political philosophy, the complete critical ideology, makes for a comfortable meeting of minds. As the philosophical basis says:

> Conventional political and economic policies are destroying the very foundations of the wellbeing of humans and other animals. Our culture is in the grip of a value system and a way of understanding the world which is fundamentally flawed.[8]

No other party takes such a radical position, demanding change in the same ways as some campaigning groups do.

Speaking particularly of the time at the start of negotiations for the proposed Transatlantic Trade and Investment Partnership (TTIP), Dearden said:

> At this time no other political force in the parliament was awake to the damage being done by globalisation and so-called 'free trade'. As soon as you said 'trade deal' other groups uncritically applauded, but when the Green Group hears the term they are immediately on their guard. The Greens have long been critical of free trade and globalisation. They started out with a concern for the environment but that led them to a broader understanding of the social and broader impacts, for example on the food system. Other groups didn't have a really thought-out analysis of neoliberalism. We quickly developed a strong relationship based on shared analysis.[9]

The UK's Green MEPs continued their principled, strong opposition to TTIP throughout the negotiation process. All three MEPs collectively wrote a letter, published in the *Guardian* in 2015:

> The next few days will see a TTIP charm offensive...The Centre for Economic Policy Research estimates that the EU's combined GDP will be boosted by 0.5% in the ten years after TTIP's implementation. Even if such projections are correct, what is lacking is a guarantee that any benefits would be evenly distributed, or benefit the poorest. When 92% of those involved in consultations have been corporate lobbyists, citizens are right to suspect that TTIP will benefit corporations at the expense of democracy...There are many reasons to oppose this deal, but be aware of the pro-TTIP hype while we continue to keep up the pressure to have it dropped.[10]

Campaigners also noted that Green MEPs were prepared to be brave and tackle issues on which others might privately agree but decline to take the flak for speaking out publicly. Dearden said: 'In Brussels and after, Caroline Lucas was always prepared to speak out on Palestinian issues, and at a time when most people were not prepared to.' Back in 2007, to pick just one moment, then MEP Caroline Lucas went to Palestine to meet with its leader, Mahmoud Abbas, and call for the restoration of EU funding to the Palestinian Authority.[11]

What has 'working with the UK's Green MEPs' meant in practice for campaigners?

(1) *Delivering detail*
One useful – and very broadly welcomed – example of Greens' day-to-day work of passing directives and delivering on the detailed implementation of them is Caroline Lucas's leadership on the EU Timber Regulation (EUTR).[12] In the early 2000s the EU was looking towards a voluntary scheme in which companies would disclose the source of timber being used for a wide variety of products in the

EU, particularly packaging, for instance, through the Forest Stewardship Council. However, according to Tony Long, founder of the World Wide Fund for Nature's (WWF) European Policy Office in 1989 (and its director until he retired in 2015, when it had a staff of 45), it became obvious that a voluntary scheme wouldn't create a level playing field for companies seeking to meet environmental obligations.

Caroline Lucas became the rapporteur on the dossier proposing a regulation, and Long worked closely with her during the lengthy development process. He recalled how she organised an initial meeting that he regards as a model for how such regulation can be constructed in consultation with industry and NGOs:

> Something like 70 companies turned up, including really big ones like Ikea, B&Q and Kingfisher, as well as campaigners. It was an example of how the whole value chain of producers, importers and consumers could come together around a common position. It gave Caroline everything she needed to come forward with a rather bold proposal that was then passed into law.[13]

Long suggested this was an early example of what's come to be known in political science circles studying Brussels as 'transversal lobbying'.[14] Caroline's work continued, he noted, in developing the detailed regulation that allows this new regulation to be implemented – ensuring that timber coming into the EU can be recorded at the port of entry (the definition of which is not necessarily a simple process), and monitoring how it is traced and followed throughout.

Long regards the whole process of the EUTR as a blueprint for how the EU can work on environmental issues with practical input from campaigners and industry to produce an effective, workable plan of action. Since the Lisbon Treaty, he said, the implementation process for new legislation has been far more under the control of the Commission: 'In most cases the NGOs don't get a say, and it is all conducted off the record – a far less transparent process.'[15]

Furthermore, Long points out that, on different issues, the WWF has worked equally well with individuals from other parties: namely Labour and the Liberal Democrats, but also on occasion the Tories. He cited Linda McAvan, Chris Davis and Julie Girling in particular, who picked up and ran with issues about which they had passions and concerns, often not especially related to party ideology. The only real difference between this perspective and that of Global Justice Now is that the latter is focused on changing our economic, social and political systems, rather than working within them.

(2) *Making changes in Brussels that deliver locally*

Simon Birkett of Clean Air in London provides an enthusiastic, detailed account of the UK's Green MEPs' role (with Jean Lambert taking the lead first, followed by Keith Taylor) in taking local, specific-issue campaigns to Brussels and providing a tool with which campaigners can put pressure on Westminster. Birkett's campaigning work on this particular issue began in 2006, when he saw a gap being created as Friends of the Earth International shifted from focusing on air pollution to the Climate Change Act, just as it was becoming obvious that pollution levels were not falling the way they should have been (for reasons subsequently exposed by 'dieselgate'). He wrote to the European Commissioner for the Environment about the National Emissions Ceiling Directive but received a call from staffers saying he'd be better off focusing on the Air Quality Directive. Birkett reflected: 'That showed something that most people haven't understood, that the European Commission is generally more accessible to campaigners than Secretaries of State.'[16]

Birkett recalled how, later, he, Jean and Liberal Democrat Claude Moraes met with European Commissioner Janez Potočnik and his air quality expert:

> Just the five of us. The Commissioner noted that it was really pleasant to be meeting people lobbying for tighter laws rather than weakening. He then came to London and asked me to set up a meeting to talk with the key people, NGOs and all of the parties (except the Tories, who declined to participate). I

used to direct message him if there was something I thought important and sometimes he'd respond…[17] Before the Olympics in 2012, Clean Air in London wrote a formal complaint to Commissioner Potočnik about London's non-compliance with NO_2 limits – which was followed up by the Commission.[18]

This was while Boris was spraying glue in front of air pollution monitors and cutting the figures for PM10s by up to 40%, but only in a tiny area. Birkett called it 'public health fraud on an industrial scale'.

The EU further increased the pressure on London with the Year of Air in 2013, during which the National Emissions Ceilings Directive was also being revised: 'Commissioner Potočnik was really clear that we needed certainty and tightening of the rules – not revisiting the Air Quality Directive but enforcing it, with the aim of compliance throughout Europe by 2020.'[19] Later, Birkett suggested to Keith Taylor that he introduce diffusion-tube testing, which he did, focusing on schools in South East England.[20] 'I was happy to write the foreword for his report on the subject,' said Birkett. 'We need more people like Keith Taylor in the European Parliament.'[21]

He elaborated:

> I greatly valued everything that the Green MEPs and their teams have done. I've worked particularly with Keith and Jean and I really trust them and appreciate their efforts. Keith particularly hasn't hesitated in retweeting some of my more controversial tweets. He copies in senior WHO and UN people, and that makes these people take an extra look. Campaigns against air pollution would not have been as successful as they have been without the Green MEPs. It's a pity there aren't a lot more Greens.[22]

Simon Birkett has continued this work on air quality far beyond his home borough of Kensington and Chelsea. He's currently in the steering group for UN Environment, helping to produce its sixth report on the state of the environment, covering air, land and biota. There are 25 state representatives in this group and 10 from NGOs.

'I've got as much right to veto as the US State Department,' he explains. It's clear that concern about air pollution in choked central London has led to far broader and bigger issues being addressed.

(3) *Taking campaigns to Brussels*

Nick Dearden of Global Justice Now reflects on when he was working with War on Want as part of its Western Sahara campaign, which went to Brussels because the EU was looking to do a deal with Morocco on fishing rights that covered Sahrawi waters. This is one example of the Greens providing an organisation with a foothold on which to begin to engage with the Brussels system as well as an issue to put on the agenda.

He explains:

> The Greens really were a big voice – initially no-one else was interested. And for us as campaigners it was crucial to have friendly people explaining how the European Parliament worked and what role it could play.[23]

The MEPs and their staff helped campaigns to navigate the often confusing and opaque system of getting formal questions asked, statements agreed on, formal scrutiny processes instituted and opportunities for votes created, he says.

When activists visited Brussels, Dearden also found that the UK's Green MEPs 'spoke at exactly the right level' in meetings with them. That wasn't always the case with others, he said. Some were so enmeshed in the finer details that they couldn't provide a comprehensible picture of issues and actions:

> There is some truth to the claim that the European institutions can live in their own little bubble, with MEPs becoming more like bureaucrats than elected representatives…I've also seen some MEPs be very combative and rude.[24]

But the Greens haven't treated business like the Western Sahara campaign as one-off events. The engagement between NGOs working on this issue and representatives of the Sahrawi community has continued, and individual MEPs from a range of parties have since followed the Green lead. For example, in February 2018 MEPs from a range of political groupings joined Keith Taylor and Jean Lambert in asking a question about the impact of the EU–Morocco Euro-Mediterranean Aviation Agreement on Western Sahara.[25]

(4) *Using the title of MEP and the special access it provides to deepen and amplify the message*

A further role that MEPs play, which has developed over the years, is broadcasting the work campaigners are doing in Brussels and adding to its legitimacy. Especially since the development of social media, MEPs have had an opportunity to share both knowledge on the workings of the European Parliament and information they've been able to gather because of their role. Dearden points to Molly Scott Cato as being one of the first MEPs to go into the controlled reading rooms (as Caroline Lucas was in Westminster) in order to bring out what information was allowed about the TTIP proposals. She then wrote blogs, made videos and used social media to expose what she'd found. Scott Cato provided the *Guardian* with a colourful account of the experience, which was probably more politically useful than any detailed exposé of the clauses of the proposed treaty:

> Before I had the right to see such 'top secret' documents, which are restricted from the gaze of most EU citizens, I was required to sign a document of some 14 pages, reminding me that 'EU institutions are a valuable target' and of the dangers of espionage. Crucially, I had to agree not to share any of the contents with those I represent. The delightful parliamentary staff required me to leave even the smallest of my personal items in a locked cupboard, as they informed me how tiny cameras can be these days. Like a scene from a *James Bond* film, they then took me through the security door into a room with secure cabinets from which the documents were retrieved. I was not at any point left alone.[26]

Dearden says that simply having elected members of parliament on their side has also provided a big boost to campaigners in their work. All too often they feel like they are swimming against the tide and don't hear, particularly in the mainstream media, the perspectives they are promoting: 'It gives our own people, staff, volunteers and members, a lift and a boost to see MEPs supporting what they are saying. It adds respectability to the narrative.'

The 2016 referendum

The Green Party, on occasion, worked with the official Remain campaign in the 2016 Brexit referendum, particularly in the final weeks, when it was becoming clear that there was a real risk of the UK voting Leave. That meant working primarily with the national leadership, for it was very much perceived as a national campaign, and MEPs had almost no role in that Cameron-led effort.

Figure 1. (left) Caroline Lucas, Keith Taylor and Natalie Bennett campaigning at Sussex University on the day of the 2014 European election. **Figure 2. (right)** Easter 2013: Keith Taylor and Natalie Bennett (then leader of the Green Party of England and Wales) at a demonstration against nuclear weapons at Atomic Weapons Establishment (AWE) Aldermaston.

The Green Party focused most of its efforts, however, on the 'Greens for a Better Europe' campaign, which sought to present a positive case celebrating the free movement of people, the protection of hard-won workers' rights, the conservation of the environment and the championing of human rights. This was something the official campaign had neither the inclination nor the capacity to do, comprised overwhelmingly as it was of politicians from Labour, the Tories and even the Liberal Democrats, who had spent decades blaming the EU for much of the current state of Britain, including on matters for which the EU bore no conceivable responsibility.

The campaign, armed with limited financial and practical resources (this vote came just weeks after the important local council elections in May), took some advice from the Scottish Green Party, drawn from the latter's experience of the independence referendum. The campaign chose to focus on two primary audiences: natural Green voters (who, experience would show, were the strongest of any party affiliation in backing Remain), who were encouraged to vote and engage with campaigning for Remain; and the so-called Lexiteers, left-wing voters and activists who could be persuaded that acknowledging the faults of the EU in its current form did not have to mean discarding the whole concept of working together with the peoples of Europe. Green MEPs had a prominent role in Greens for a Better Europe and often coordinated with campaigners, particularly environmental ones, in that effort. 'For Global Justice Now, the Green MEPs' views on Brexit were very close to ours, particularly on migration and economic justice,' Dearden says.[27]

The MEPs joined in organising the campaign to highlight how European institutions, particularly the parliament, could be used to tackle corporate multinational interests by empowering the civil society voices that oppose them, in a manner that would be extraordinarily difficult, or impossible, to achieve at Westminster. As the vote approached, Molly Scott Cato could point to her work on the highly critical report on the New Alliance for Food Security and Nutrition in Africa, which was supported by 577 MEPs, with only 24 against and 69 abstentions.[28] It drew heavily on the work of an extensive league of NGOs and campaigners that had been scathing about the alliance.[29]

A piece by Scott Cato in *The Ecologist* covered all of these issues and drew heavily on her personal expertise from Brussels. She said:

Greens have never believed or said the EU is perfect. Many of the criticisms levelled against it will continue to energise our political campaigns if we remain a member. And of course, as an MEP, I have direct experience of its shortcomings. But leaving the EU would be the ultimate acceptance of defeat and failure of confidence. Walking away from our own continent will not solve its many problems. Facing them in a spirit of cooperation will ensure we tackle them together in solidarity.[30]

The result of the referendum in 2016 was a blow to both civil society and, of course, Green MEPs and the Green Party as a whole. Tony Long said that he felt Britain had been let down by parts of the environmental movement, particularly some of the largest mass membership organisations, such as the WWF, the Royal Society for the Protection of Birds (RSPB) and the National Trust, which were all more concerned about the risk of losing members than standing up for the environmental protections the EU has provided. (He noted Friends of the Earth International was an honourable exception to this.) He did, however, acknowledge that they probably could not have changed the result.

Looking forward: what next?

If Brexit goes through and there are no UK Green MEPs in the future, campaigners anticipate significant damage to their work. Global Justice Now is, of course, part of international and European networks of campaigners who will continue to work with Green and other MEPs from the 27 other EU states; but, as Dearden says, 'they'll be nowhere near as close as our MEPs.'[31] He also notes that on many of the issues about which his organisation has been most concerned, Westminster, more than in other policy areas, works 'like a dictatorship, through the Queen's prerogative. There is no democracy at all, with a strong desire to keep debate or discussion out of the public sphere.'[32]

Meanwhile, Simon Birkett is readying himself for the possibility of Brexit, working with Green peer Jenny Jones on a new Clean Air Act, provision for which was included in the 2017 Labour Party manifesto. However, Labour's proposal, he says, is source- and solution-specific and only half-a-dozen pages; the bill he has drawn up with Jenny is 25 pages and guarantees 'clean air as a right'.

We need to make Westminster work more like Brussels

When I told LBC radio just before the 2016 referendum vote that Brussels was more democratic than Westminster, it produced a rare outbreak of coverage in the right-wing, populist *Express* newspaper, with my claim being labelled 'bizarre'.[33] But that's clearly the view of many campaigners who've worked across both jurisdictions, as some of the comments above have illustrated.

If Brexit does go ahead, one important, possible way in which some of its worst effects may be reduced will be by drawing on the experience of Green (and other) MEPs and the campaign groups they have worked with to try to transfer some of the successes of Brussels across the Channel. It won't be easy, for, as Norwegian sociologist and political scientist Stein Ringen has outlined, Britain has not had an effective democratic government since the 1970s. The huge centrifugal force of increasing centralisation has left Britain's political centre without balance. By contrast, the regional, state and city governments are powerful on the Continent, and in dealing directly with Brussels they are able to negotiate, thus allowing space for civil society to have effective political influence.[34]

It's only a statement of the blindingly obvious to say Britain needs to use the proportional electoral system of Brussels for electing MPs in Westminster. As the campaigners for Make Votes Matter say, we have to see the number of seats match the number of votes. (The Electoral Reform Society points out that in the 2017 election 68% of the votes didn't count.[35]) Many NGOs – publicly when they can, privately when they feel they can't – look forward, with hope and expectation, to a future with a fair voting system and the consequent shift away from see-saw politics that sees each new government seeking to undo the actions of its predecessors. As Nick Dearden emphasises:

> Global Justice Now has always been in favour of a more pluralistic approach to left-wing politics. It is important that campaigns don't just have Labour Party voices and perspectives but also SNP, Plaid and Green. We need to make sure there is not a stranglehold of opinion on the left.[36]

When that happens, I say determinedly, MEPs who've worked in Brussels, with its relatively consensual, co-operative culture of negotiation (rather than point scoring), could play an important role in showing their Westminster colleagues how it can be done. Campaigners can bring the Brussels experience home and tell MPs this is how it can, and should, be done.

Endnotes

1   Robert Rohrschneider, 'Impact of social movements on European Party Systems', *The Annals of the American Academy of Political and Social Science*, Vol. 528, Citizens, Protest, and Democracy, July 1993, pp. 157–70.

2   The Green Party of England and Wales, *Philosophical Basis of the Green Party*; https://bit.ly/2K9KAGj (accessed 7 September 2018).

3   Tim Gavell, 'Call for review as fracking policing costs rocket', *Blackpool Gazette*, 21 November 2017; https://bit.ly/2PYEu0G (accessed 8 September 2018).

4   *Sky News*, 'Natalie Bennett tells her story of being an immigrant', Video, 16 April 2015; https://bit.ly/2DH9cFJ (accessed 7 September 2018).

5   United Nations Human Rights (Office of the High Commissioner), *Statement by the United Nations Special Rapporteur on the Rights to Freedom of Peaceful Assembly and of Association at the Conclusion of His Visit to the United Kingdom*, Press Release (London: OHCHR, 21 April 2016); https://bit.ly/2zTQxSI (accessed 7 September 2018).

6   Global Justice Now was formerly known as the World Development Movement.

7   Interview conducted by Natalie Bennett with Nick Dearden on 4 September 2018.

8   The Green Party of England and Wales, *Philosophical Basis of the Green Party*.

9   Ibid.

10   Jean Lambert MEP, Keith Taylor MEP and Molly Scott Cato MEP, 'Beware the TTIP charm offensive', *Guardian*, 17 March 2015; https://bit.ly/2zZc0tB (accessed 7 September 2018).

11   The Green Party of England and Wales, *Green MEP in Palestine to Meet President Abbas*, Press Release (27 April 2007); https://bit.ly/2FontsE (accessed 8 September 2018).

12   EU Forest Law Enforcement, Governance and Trade (FLEGT), *The EU Timber Regulation*; www.euflegt.efi.int/eutr (accessed 25 October 2018).

13   Interview conducted by Natalie Bennett with Tony Long on 4 September 2018.

14   'European lobbying: the new coalitions', *Euractiv*, 17 July 2007; https://bit.ly/2QIYdyx (accessed 7 September 2018).

15   Ibid.

16   Interview conducted by Natalie Bennett with Simon Birkett on 10 August 2018.

17   Ibid.

18   Ibid.

19   Ibid.

20   Keith Taylor MEP, *Polluted Playgrounds: Toxic Air Near Schools in South East England*, Report (The Greens/EFA and The Green Party of England and Wales, 2014); https://bit.ly/2Q0Frp5.

21   Birkett, op. cit.

22   Ibid.

23   Dearden, op. cit.

24   Ibid.

25   European Parliament, *Subject: EU-Morocco Aviation Agreement and Western Sahara*, Parliamentary Questions (8 February 2018); https://bit.ly/2Fs5WQu (accessed 7 September 2018).

26 Molly Scott Cato MEP, 'I've seen the secrets of TTIP, and it is built for corporations not citizens', *Guardian*, 4 February 2015; https://bit.ly/2RRWyqC (accessed 7 September 2018).

27 Dearden, op. cit.

28 Molly Scott Cato MEP, *MEPs Support Green-led Critique of Corporate-hijacked Africa Agriculture Initiative* (7 June 2016); https://bit.ly/2BcAXUe (accessed 8 September 2018).

29 CNCR *et al*, 'Letter addressed to the Government of Senegal, G7 members state, and the African Union', *farmlandgrab*, 11 June 2018; https://bit.ly/2Q06S2h (accessed 8 September 2018).

30 Molly Scott Cato MEP, 'Small is beautiful but big matters too', *The Ecologist*, 20 June 2016; https://bit.ly/2OMwUle (accessed 8 September 2018).

31 Dearden, op. cit.

32 Ibid.

33 Cyrus Engineer, 'Green Party leader claims the EU is MORE democratic than Britain', *Express*, 15 June 2016; https://bit.ly/2zgDMlP (accessed 8 September 2018).

34 Stein Ringen, *Nation of Devils: Democratic Leadership and the Problem of Obedience* (New Haven: Yale University Press, 2013), p. 198.

35 Jess Garland and Chris Terry, *The 2017 General Election: Volatile Voting, Random Results* (London: Electoral Reform Society, 2017); https://bit.ly/2S3en6j (accessed 25 October 2018).

36 Dearden, op. cit.

Chapter 7

Powerhouse parliamentarians: how Greens made friends and influenced policy

Samir Jeraj

In 20 years of parliamentary life across four MEPs, Greens have made an impact on every part of EU policy. It is no easy task to condense this into a single chapter, and there are many different ways to think about how to measure impact or recognise achievement. There are the votes, meetings and casework that make up the bread and butter of any representative, although this is something former staffers said was a real strength of UK MEPs, and the Greens in particular. Each MEP produced dozens of reports shaping discussion on myriad topics. Some of these were on issues in constituencies, such as Keith Taylor's report on food banks in the South East or Molly Scott Cato's report on housing in the southwest. Others went beyond this and sought to address the underlying economic model in Europe, such as the Green New Deal report, written by a group that included Caroline Lucas, or to get important subjects on the agenda, such as Jean Lambert's refugees and the environment report. All set out a path for 'green recovery' from the recession.

Inside and outside of the parliament, Green MEPs were leading on issues that other parties have only just begun to recognise, and on which they are still far behind. Back in the early 2000s Jean Lambert reported on her work to tackle air pollution from diesel cars. Caroline Lucas produced a report for the EU Parliament on trade relations with China in 2005, just as its economic might was becoming clear. Also, Greens continue to be the leading voices for action on climate change. Erica Hope, a former staffer, commented that there are a handful of 'powerhouse MEPs' in the parliament, who disproportionately come from the Green Group. She added that the UK's Green MEPs always commanded respect across the parliament for the quality of their work, their approach to parliamentary process, and the experts and staffers they brought with them.

Green MEPs also had a huge impact on the development of UK politics, and this is particularly true for the Green Party of England and Wales. Without the profile of being an MEP, Caroline Lucas would have faced an even greater struggle against the UK's antiquated electoral system to become the UK's first Green MP.

Victor Anderson, an academic and researcher who has worked with Green MEPs, feels this experience of the EU Parliament also had an impact on the effectiveness and experience of Greens. As he explains:

> I think one of the things that's been achieved through having MEPs is that there are people there with experience of a very complicated structure, because you've not only got the very complicated political issues themselves, you've got the different political groups, and you've got the different countries, and so people put in that situation learn something which they can then pass on to the rest of the party and kind of educate the Green Party, so I would put that pretty high up in what they've achieved.[1]

The offices of the MEPs provided a training ground for a generation of political operatives and staffers. Former Green MEP staffers hold important roles in the UK Parliament, central government and NGOs. They have even found their way into other political parties. In one memorable exchange, Shadow Chancellor John McDonnell, when asked about how his new press officer had previously been a staffer for Keith Taylor, replied: 'I can only assume the Green Party must have given him a very good reference.'[2]

Erica Hope, a researcher from 2005 to 2009 for MEP Caroline Lucas, remembers how future councillor Alex Phillips (then a stagiaire) almost single-handedly canvassed the necessary majority of votes from MEPs for a written declaration (the EU Parliament equivalent of an early day motion) on supermarket power. This campaign involved enlisting fellow staffers from the offices of MEPs, dressing up as fruit and carting around produce in Strasbourg.

Beyond the Green Party, these MEPs played leading roles in cross-party and cross-community campaigns in the UK for peace, against nuclear weapons, for an independent Scotland and for remaining in the EU. Caroline Lucas served on the board of the Stop the War Coalition in 2003 as Britain slid into a war in Iraq, the legacy of which we are still dealing with.

As MEPs, they got to forge international links and relationships in order to stand up for oppressed groups, human rights and a progressive international politics. The Green Party's long-standing support of and relationship with Kurdish groups comes from work done by Jean Lambert and Caroline Lucas to support their autonomy and human rights. More recently, Jean Lambert has been a leading voice in supporting human rights in Burma – particularly for the Rohingya. The UK's Green MEPs have consistently supported a free and independent Palestine, investigations into human rights abuses across the world, and action on arms sales to oppressive regimes.

As I said at the start, it is difficult to fully grasp those 20 years of work in a few thousand words. I've decided to look at what these MEPs accomplished by choosing five particular achievements and discussing them in depth: how they happened, why they happened and what the impact has been.

Exposing how car companies fiddled their pollution figures

In September 2015 Volkswagen, one of the corporate giants of car manufacturing, was revealed to have fixed their pollution data on diesel cars. For years VW had been installing 'defeat devices' to manipulate their figures, in direct violation of an EU law passed in

2007, contributing to the EU's 400,000 premature deaths and the €330–940 billion per year cost of air pollution.[3,4]

In the three years since what has been termed 'dieselgate', the scandal has spread to BMW and Daimler, car companies have recalled millions of vehicles, investigations have been launched in the US and Europe, and legal action has been lodged by states and investors. In the UK, the government has faced court action for failing to hand over evidence pertinent to the dieselgate investigations – one of a string of cases it has lost for failing to address poor air quality.[5]

Bas Eickhout, a Dutch MEP from GroenLinks, said 'Greens have been at the front of this',[6] mentioning the roles played by Caroline Lucas up to 2010 and Keith Taylor thereafter. Of Keith Taylor, Eickhout said: 'He has been working on air quality continuously.'[7]

Within the EU Parliament, Greens fought for tougher standards and better testing in 2007, but they faced strong opposition from the governments of EU member states. The proposed testing regime was particularly important, as how cars perform in a laboratory is often a poor indicator of how they actually perform on the road. The EU Commission was given the role of developing some new tests, but these were still under discussion when dieselgate hit in 2015. It later turned out that one of the manufacturers' tricks was developing software that would enable a car to know it was being laboratory tested and adjust itself accordingly.

According to Eickhout, 'not so much happened at the political level when the scandal broke'.[8] In response to the scandal, Green MEPs pressed for an inquiry into dieselgate. 'We thought "this shall not pass"', said Eickhout,[9] and in December 2015 the inquiry was established.[10] He argued that it was the persistence of Greens such as Keith Taylor that kept the inquiry on the agenda: this 'had been a continuous fight', according to Eickhout.[11] The Greens argued that it was an issue of both environmental protection and consumer protection,[12] as EU citizens had often been encouraged to buy diesel cars as a 'cleaner' option when the manufacturers knew they were not.[13] It was also a tax issue. Greens commissioned research showing EU states had lost over €8 billion in taxes because of emissions fixing.[14]

In the UK, this equated to €2.2 billion in lost taxes in 2016 alone, and around €8 billion over the previous six years.[15]

In April 2018 this led to new legislation allowing the EU to 'monitor national authorities, to conduct its own market surveillance, to organise EU-wide recall procedures and to impose penalties on fraudulent manufacturers'.[16] In practice, this means powerful car companies are less able to subvert environmental rules by influencing their national governments.[17,18] It also led, along with scandals such as the Luxembourg Leaks (LuxLeaks) and the Facebook–Cambridge Analytica data scandal, to new protections for whistleblowers.[19] However, the industry still managed to delay implementation and water down standards, which shows that this is still a continuous struggle. Some cities are now taking legal action against the EU Commission to defend these tougher standards.[20] The Commission itself is also taking a tougher, less-trusting attitude towards car manufacturers: it has started a cartel case against car manufacturers in Germany, something that would have been unimaginable five years ago.

Eickhout believes the better-performing Euro 6-standard cars show the standards were not 'too tough', as the industry once claimed. However, the issue now is what happens to the old, dirty cars. Eickhout thinks manufacturers will likely dump their dirty cars into the second-hand markets of Eastern Europe, moving and intensifying the air quality problems there. While the EU sets the standards, it is down to national governments to implement them. As the UK continues to struggle with its air quality issues, the lessons from dieselgate and the challenges of improving standards are becoming ever more relevant.

A sweet victory over Big Sugar

One of the greatest public health challenges facing us now and in the coming decades is obesity, a significant cause of which is too much sugar in our diet. We know that sugar makes us fat, raises our risk of diabetes and heart disease, and rots our teeth, yet we consume more and more of it. The EU Commission's own research found that between a third and a half of women, and between a half and two-thirds of men, are overweight across EU member states.[21] Over six in ten adults in England are overweight or obese, and a third of children aged five have tooth decay.[22]

One of the reasons why is the power of the sugar industry. A review of research on sugar and health found a disturbing pattern of manipulation of research and researchers in order to downplay sugar's role in heart disease and cancer over a period of decades.[23,24] In 1996 the World Health Organization (WHO) took action against conflicts of interest so that the industry would find it more challenging to influence decision makers. It is no easy task to take on Big Sugar, but the Greens did it – and they won. In 2016 MEPs rejected a proposal from the EU Commission to allow large amounts of sugar in some types of baby food, something that would have had a dramatic effect on infants' health. The 393 to 305 vote against was led by Keith Taylor MEP.

The battle over what babies can and should be fed has been fought in Europe for over 30 years. Various proposals from the industry have been beaten back by parliamentarians seeking to bring Europe into line with World Health Assembly guidance on the quality of food and the age group to which it should be marketed.[25]

What we feed babies and infants is an extremely emotive and sensitive topic. There are immense pressures on mothers with babies but no systems in place to support them. For Patti Rundall of Baby Milk Action, it's about improving the quality of baby food and ensuring the WHO guidance on marketing is in place, not about questioning the difficult choices mothers make. In 2016 the EU Commission proposed a new food for specific groups act to MEPs. The new regulations would allow 'cereal-based' baby food to contain 30% sugar. Just one year earlier, in 2015, the WHO cut the recommended amount of sugar in a healthy diet from 10% to 5%, one-sixth of what was being proposed for baby food.

The European Parliament's Committee on the Environment, Public Health and Food Safety (known as the ENVI committee) caught sight of these proposals first. Keith Taylor drafted and tabled an objection to the Commission's proposals. The aim of the objection was to bring the draft laws into line with WHO and World Health Assembly recommendations. In his speech to the committee, Taylor told fellow ENVI members that the introduction of foods with such a high sugar content – especially so early – was likely to contribute to the rising levels of childhood obesity.

The committee voted by 35 votes to 28 to endorse the objections and put them to the 751 MEPs in Parliament a week later. Before and during this time, Taylor's team was putting together papers and briefings, and liaising with other parliamentarians and interest groups. When the vote came to the floor, Taylor was the rapporteur for the Greens and set out the case for his amendment. If it passed, the legislation would be sent back to the EU Commission for a redraft. The main points were: rejecting the sugar proposals, acting to tackle unscrupulous marketing, and lobbying for tougher rules on genetically modified (GM) foods. Obesity was one of two key arguments, the other being the Convention on the Rights of the Child. The Convention placed a duty on all EU member states and the Commission to promote the rights of children, including their health. MEPs rejected the EU Commission's sugar proposals but also voted down Taylor's proposals on marketing and the stricter regulation of GM foods.[26]

The EU Commission went away, revised the legislation and came back with a new version that was passed by parliamentarians in July 2016.[27] However, the sugar aspects were not part of this, and they are the subject of further discussion. In response to the original amendments on sugar and marketing, the Commission went back and asked for further research to be conducted by the European Food Standards agency on the 'complementary feeding' of infants in order to update their opinion. The Commission also asked for further research on processed cereal-based and other baby foods to inform future legislation on processed cereal-based foods.[28] Patti Rundall highlights the importance of MEPs being vigilant as this long process happens: 'If parliament doesn't stay onside and keep on and make sure that their wishes are carried out, then it may mean not very much.'[29] Nevertheless, Rundall still feels it is 'amazing' that it got through. 'They were brave and that was good,' she said.

These battles over protection and regulation against corporate power and interests are going to continue within Europe, and they are likely to become more intense in post-Brexit Britain. Baby Milk Action is currently campaigning against attempts to trade US products and undermine WHO guidance, and to get the EU to take an even stronger stance against marketing.

Making polluters pay

One of the great positives of the EU is being able to co-operate on cross-border issues such as climate change. Without it, nations face the challenge of cleaning up their polluting industries while trusting that competing industries in other states will do the same. Globally, emissions trading continues to be an important, if much criticised, policy, aimed at reducing CO_2 by effectively creating a market for it and incentivising companies to reduce their impact on climate change.

In the early 2000s, under the framework established by the Kyoto Protocol, Europe created its own emissions-trading scheme (ETS). Policymakers sought to create a European market for carbon reduction, but one important industry was left out: aviation. Air transport had been left out of the Kyoto Protocol specifically on the agreement that it should establish its own ETS, which had not happened by 2006.[30] From the 1990s to the early 2000s the rapid growth of aviation saw its emissions nearly double; but the power of the industry was such that it was a two-year battle before it became part of Europe's efforts to tackle climate change.

In 2006, then South East MEP Caroline Lucas tabled a report during a debate in the EU Parliament on the ETS. Lucas had produced an initiative report, which, if adopted, would become the opinion of the parliament. Erica Hope, then a researcher in the MEP's office, remembered this as a big opportunity to end the strange position of aviation being outside the existing ETS. They brought in experts, academics and NGOs to talk about options for bringing the aviation industry's emissions under control. 'Our strongest idea was a separate ETS,'[31] explained Hope; this would avoid inflating the overall emissions ceiling and make the aviation industry focus on reducing its emissions rather than subsuming them into other industries. She added that there were voices within both the Green Party and the NGOs which were early critics of trading schemes and pushed for greater taxes instead. The decision was to make the best of the system already in place: a recognition of the need to get the proposals through Parliament.

The final document called for a specific aviation ETS, instead of air transport being included in the Kyoto Protocol. Under the proposed system, airlines would be subject to an emissions cap and would have to pay if they exceeded this; they would not be able to receive free or discounted permits to pollute.[32] The report was contentious to say the least. The EU Parliament's committees on transport and the environment were split, with the former opposing and the latter supporting the move. But when it came to the vote in Parliament, the MEPs supported Caroline's call for aviation to get its own trading scheme.

The next stage was a further report from an official parliamentary rapporteur, Peter Liese (a centre-right MEP from Germany). The Liese report took over a year to make its way through the system. Liese was more radical than either the centre-right group of MEPs or the German government of the time were prepared to be.[33] His report called for 75% of allowances to be free from the start of the scheme (in 2011), and for this to be reduced to zero by 2013. In effect, aviation would have to start paying early and rapidly increase payments. It also called for a cap on emissions of 90% of 2004–6 levels from the start of the scheme.[34]

Finally, in late 2008, MEPs, the EU Council of Ministers and the EU Commission came to a compromise. The final scheme would apply to internal EU flights from 2011 and all flights from 2012. The emissions cap was watered down to 97% of 2004–6 levels by 2012, and 95% by 2013; costs were reduced for airlines; and member governments were not required to spend the revenue on low-emission transport (but they did have to report on how they used it).[35] Throughout this complicated process, Caroline Lucas was pressing for stronger policies. One of the most important of these was pushing for all flights coming into or leaving the EU to be included in the scheme as early as possible, which the EU Commission managed to hold off on until 2012.[36]

How Green MEPs took on the bankers

Since the financial crisis and subsequent recession, there has been a renewed focus on the power of finance and of bankers. Following the collapse of banks due to widespread fraud and manipulation, governments stepped in to bail them out and restore the flow of credit. The policy orthodoxy was turned upside down, banks were brought into public ownership, public borrowing and spending soared, and the government intervened in markets in a way unheard of since the 1930s.

The political right quickly moved to blame government overspending, social security protections and migrants for the recession, ignoring the real cause of the crisis. The power of finance had grown in Europe since the 1980s, underpinned by deregulation, privatisation and globalisation. Eventually, that edifice came crashing down. Greens opposed the neoliberal policies that brought about the crash and were determined to take action to address its causes: the power and regulation of finance. Then MEP Caroline Lucas was a leading voice in support of the Green New Deal, a recovery package for the economy that would see the government taxing the financial industry and spending money on the green infrastructure, such as renewable energy and public transport, necessary to move the economy towards a sustainable future.[37]

In 2011 a long-awaited financial transaction tax was introduced to curb speculation on financial markets.[38,39] The UK government was one of the holdouts, taking legal action to try to protect corporate interests in the City of London but ultimately losing the case.[40] In 2013 the European Greens successfully proposed an EU-wide cap on bankers' bonuses, one of the ongoing sources of public out-rage towards corporate leaders, who were taking home multimil-lion pound bonuses while presiding over the practices that led to the financial crisis.[41] Philippe Lamberts, the Green MEP who led on the banker bonus cap, was labelled the 'number one enemy' of the City.[42]

Against this background, Molly Scott Cato, newly elected in 2014, got to work on issues around tax justice and green finance. She was the first Green MEP from the UK to be part of the Committee on Economic and Monetary Affairs (ECON). Within the EU Parlia-ment, the Greens pressed hard on tax transparency. They proposed and won a vote that required companies to report the taxes they pay to each country, so they can be held accountable for moving money between states and declaring their profits not where they are made but where they can pay the least tax.[43] Greens also used their power in the parliament to tackle the shadowy world of money laundering. In 2015 they successfully proposed a new central register of corporate owner-ship, which makes it much more difficult for money launderers to hide behind shell companies and organisations registered to empty build-ings or PO Boxes.[44] Following the revelations of the Paradise Papers and the Panama Papers, in 2018 a new version of the anti-money laun-dering directive made this information on corporate ownership public and extended regulation to digital currencies.[45]

Molly Scott Cato highlighted the impact of tax havens and Britain's tax regulations in a set of reports. These found their way into the parliament's position on tax and had an influence on the EU Commission. 'The report we commissioned into tax avoidance by IKEA led Vestager to launch an investigation. The pressure we put on to shift decision making from unanimity to QMV [qual-ified majority voting] has influenced Moscovici and turned up in Juncker's state of the union speech,' she said, before adding: 'We have been very public in our criticism of the way the tax-haven blacklist works, and this has had some impact, although the system is still absurd.'[46]

František Nejedlý, a tax justice campaigner and Green staffer, explained some of the further work they have done:

In January 2017 we have published a report highlighting the diverse nature of intermediaries that have been involved in tax scandals (namely the Panama Papers, the Bahamas Leaks and the Offshore Leaks). Our pressure in this case leads to a proposal made by Commission Autumn 2017 to oblige intermediaries to disclose to tax authorities information on [the] potentially aggressive tax planning schemes they help their clients to set up. The proposal has been approved during the spring this year. The financial authorities will be also obliged to share the information automatically.[47]

One of the changes brought in by Greens on ECON was through the Prospectus Directive, adopted in 2017. This required banks and other financial institutions to include warnings in their prospectuses for selling bonds and similar products to smaller investors that the latter could be 'bailed in' and lose their money. According to David Kemp, an advisor to the Green Group, the purpose of such warnings is to ensure small investors don't get caught up in bail-ins when these investments fail. 'Lots of European banks have gone to customers and sold them bonds, and when things go wrong it's the customers who pay,' he explained.[48] Greens want bail-ins, but not ones that disproportionately fall on small investors; this is similar to allowing costs to be passed on to taxpayers.

In terms of sustainable and green finance, Scott Cato worked as part of the Green Group in the parliament to put this at the top of the EU Commission's agenda. Some of the legislative proposals have found support in the parliament, and even within the financial industry itself. Sven Giegold, a German MEP, noted that the financial industry in the UK was more engaged than the UK government with issues of green finance, as they saw a 'green revolution' in finance as an opportunity. Scott Cato worked to ensure this interest did not end up as some form of 'greenwash' by establishing strong standards. She was even able to get representatives from the industry to engage.

Banking structural reform was another key area of work, which started before Molly Scott Cato was elected but was still a live issue in the European Parliament in 2015.[49] This was the EU's version of Vickers's reforms in the UK. In short, it was seeking to split retail and much riskier investment banking. Ultimately, according to David Kemp, the EU Commission proposal was relatively weak: it allowed regulators to require parts of investment banking to be separated from retail banking if they felt it had got out of hand, but it did not require this. However, even that was unacceptable, and the reforms died because of 'ferocious resistance' from French and Italian governments. The national champion banks of both countries are based on the universal banking model of retail and investment banking together. In the UK, this model had already failed and as such the approach was more mature. According to Kemp, 'Greens led the resistance to the centre-right attempts to completely neuter the legislation'.[50] MEPs ended up voting on two texts: one drafted by the Greens and backed by left-wingers, and one drafted by a centre-right MEP. When it came to voting, the latter didn't have enough votes; in practice, this meant nothing further happened on the reforms.

Green MEPs have responded to the financial crisis by seeking to address its immediate cause: a deregulated system that supported speculation and rewarded extreme risks that were ultimately paid for by taxpayers. Although relatively new to the ECON committee, Molly Scott Cato has played a leading role in improving tax transparency and on the longer term project of green finance, something which has influenced the thinking of the Commission and of financial institutions.

The long fight for migrants' rights

European politics has become dominated by questions of national identity, a reaction to the crisis of financial capitalism in 2008 and questions over immigration and the integration of migrants within and outside of the EU. In 2007 then UK Labour Party Prime Minister Gordon Brown borrowed a line from the far-right British National Party and called for 'British Jobs for British Workers'.[51] In 2015 Labour's Ed Miliband made 'immigration controls' the fourth of his six key policy pledges, ahead of promises on housing and for young people.[52] Subsequently, Labour under Jeremy Corbyn's leadership has sent mixed messages at best, strengthening rhetoric on refugee rights but still flirting with the 'British Jobs for British Workers' narrative.

Since the start of the current 'migrant crisis', EU states have enacted ever more punitive laws to make it more dangerous and difficult for people fleeing war, poverty and persecution to come to Europe to live. During the UK's EU referendum, a poster showing hundreds of refugees was one of the tactics the Leave campaign used to play on racial anxieties about difference.

Against a tide of vicious anti-migrant, anti-refugee and anti-Muslim rhetoric, policy, action and even terrorism, the Greens have been a voice for migrants' rights. Within that sphere, Jean Lambert gained a reputation for effectively steering policy. Judith Sargentini, an MEP with GroenLinks, described Lambert's work as an effective blend of 'principled and practical politics', underpinned by a clear idea of coming debates and how they connect with the Green vision.[53]

In practice, it means she has been able to negotiate with the larger groups in Parliament and make practical arguments that lead to real differences in the lives of refugees and migrants. Her approach is to look at issues for documented and undocumented migrants, refugees and asylum seekers, using her role on the employment committee to do so. With this, Lambert has been able to move beyond the 'good immigrant, bad immigrant' narrative and focus on practical politics. Judith Sargentini remembers her work on ensuring unaccompanied children could choose to go to a country where they had relatives, rather than being taken into institutional care wherever they happened to end up.

'I always found Jean Lambert very receptive and helpful...not just taking everything we said, [but] having a strong political nous,' says Richard Williams, former EU representative for the European Council on Refugees and Exiles, now consultant on refugee policy.[54] 'She is really respected within the parliament for her expertise on these issues and her willingness to talk to other parties and find common ground.' This expertise, according to Torsten Moritz from the Churches' Commission for Migrants in Europe, can be seen in the fact that Lambert has been asked to author a number of reports on the issues of asylum and migration. Moritz feels the Greens have 'punched above their weight'[55] under Jean Lambert's leadership on these issues. He describes her as a 'power broker', before adding that this may not be a term she would choose for herself. Moritz commends Lambert's ability to build bridges with other MEPs, working to achieve practical improvements guided by principled politics.

The Dublin Regulation, which dominated European asylum policy for over two decades, was just two years old when Jean Lambert and Caroline Lucas were first elected in 1999. A year later EU member states agreed to establish a Common European Asylum System (CEAS), implementing the regulation's principles. As rapporteur on the regulation that set up the European Asylum Support Office (EASO), Lambert has been a driving force behind the CEAS.

She was also one of the MEPs behind the *Beyond Dublin* report in 2015. This set out the Greens' critique of how Dublin was failing and provided options for reform. The report noted that arrangements under Dublin allowed for huge variation in the conditions under which asylum seekers were living. These depended on whatever state they happened to get to first; Greece's treatment and accommodation of asylum seekers was judged to breach human rights in 2011. The Green-backed report also argued that Dublin was unsuccessful on its own terms, failing to prevent people from submitting multiple applications to multiple states, delaying decisions on cases, and being so opaque that its cost could not be analysed by the EU Commission. All of this means that asylum seekers are being forced in large numbers to live dangerous lives, putting themselves at risk of serious harm for the chance to live a safe and decent life.

A year later, the same group of MEPs set out the Green alternative to Dublin, calling for a radically humane approach:

- a system based on a fair allocation of asylum seekers across EU member states, based on objective criteria and binding for all member states;
- a system built around asylum seekers' existing ties to and preferences for a certain member state;

- a system based on incentives for asylum seekers to stay in 'their' member state, rather than on coercive measures against their onward movement to another member state;
- an integrated EU asylum system to improve harmonisation and implementation of EU asylum legislation, including substantial integration measures;
- the positive mutual recognition of asylum decisions, so that beneficiaries of international protection can move between member states one year after their recognition as refugees; and
- the development of the current EASO into a fully fledged EU asylum agency, tasked with ensuring the functioning of the preference-based allocation system and the EU asylum system in general.

According to Richard Williams: 'The Greens had a strong influence on the overall European Parliament position.'[56] When changes to the Dublin system were debated in the European Parliament, its final position adopted key parts of this paper on human rights and on the choice of where people are settled, earning praise from the European Council on Refugees and Exiles. 'Greens, more than other parties, tend to remember that asylum seekers, refugees and migrants are people, and treat them as such,' Williams added.[57]

Conclusion

The UK's Green MEPs have achieved a huge amount in their 20 years in the European Parliament. What we have explored here is just a small sample, chosen to illustrate the depth, breadth and skill brought by Jean, Caroline, Keith and Molly to the parliament. They show how parliamentarians should use their power, vision and leadership to contribute to policymaking and putting green politics and values into practice. The issues of industry and economic power, regulation, and human rights are going to become a much greater part of the UK political debate as its representatives try to tackle these questions independently of Europe. None of the issues explored in this essay will go away, and the ever-growing threat of climate change demands green political action.

Having Green MEPs transformed the Green Party of England and Wales, giving the party a platform that the UK's Victorian electoral system had denied it. This in turn helped Caroline Lucas to successfully overcome this system and become the first Green Party MP in the UK. The MEPs were also able to engage experts to develop policy, to forge links with NGOs and civil society, and to train and employ a set of staff who have added further expertise inside the party and beyond.

Outside of Europe, these opportunities to develop and influence policy, and to grow the leadership skills and talent in the Green Party, will have to come from within the UK. That means taking leadership of councils, winning seats on proportionally elected assemblies (such as the Scottish Parliament and those of London, Northern Ireland and Wales), electing more MPs and gaining further representation in the House of Lords.

Endnotes

1   Interview with Victor Anderson by Joanna Eckersley on 3 September 2018.

2   Joseph Watts, 'Shadow chancellor John McDonnell under fire for employing Momentum and Plane Stupid activist,' *Evening Standard*, 23 February 2016; https://bit.ly/2QgOkeF (accessed 19 October 2018).

3   European Parliament, *Vehicle Emission Tests: Beyond the VW Case*, At a Glance: Plenary (1 October 2015); https://bit.ly/1RjSbP6 (accessed 19 October 2018).

4   Martin Banks, 'Dieselgate: commission must step up to the plate, say Greens,' *The Parliament Magazine*, 8 September 2017; https://bit.ly/2wN6WrL (accessed 19 October 2018).

5   Green Party of England and Wales, *Greens Welcomes New Legal Action Against UK over Dieselgate*, Press Release (8 December 2016); https://bit.ly/2qUZrv9 (accessed 19 October 2018).

6   Interview with Samir Jeraj on 18 September 2018.

7   Ibid.

8   Ibid.

9   Ibid.

10   European Parliament, *Dieselgate: Parliament Sets Up Inquiry Committee*, Press Release (17 December 2015); https://bit.ly/2ziJOTc (accessed 19 October 2018).

11   Interview with Samir Jeraj on 18 September 2018.

12   Green Party of England and Wales, *Dieselgate: Greens Welcome EU Step in the Right Direction*, Press Release (4 April 2017); https://bit.ly/2OU59r0 (accessed 19 October 2018).

13   Adam Forrest, 'The death of diesel: has the one-time wonder fuel become the new asbestos?', *Guardian*, 13 April 2017; https://bit.ly/2obqWxH (accessed 19 October 2018).

14   Molly Scott Cato MEP, *Greens Say False CO₂ Emission Ratings for Cars Have Cost UK €8bn in Lost Tax Revenue*, Press Release (9 March 2018); https://bit.ly/2AhwK03 (accessed 19 October 2018).

15   Molly Scott Cato MEP, *Loss of Revenues in Passenger Car Taxation Due to Incorrect CO₂ Values in 11 EU States*, Report (Green/EFA Group, 10 March 2018); https://bit.ly/2FzPpKd (accessed 19 October 2018).

16   Keith Taylor MEP, *Dieselgate: 'Some Real Victories in New EU Rules but UK Consumers Could Lose Out,' Green MEP*, Press Release (20 April 2018); https://bit.ly/2S1UGLV(accessed 19 October 2018).

17   Green/EFA Group, *New Rules Will Ensure Greater Transparency in Car Industry*, Press Release (19 April 2018); https://bit.ly/2FauwQb.

18   'Transport ministry pushed to block environmental organisations from taking legal action against diesel cars', *Clean Energy Wire*, 28 February 2018; https://bit.ly/2DOfgMM (accessed 19 October 2018).

19   Georgi Gotev, 'EU move to protect whistleblowers gets praise from MEPs, NGOs', *Euractive*, 24 April 2018; https://bit.ly/2BknU3g (accessed 19 October 2018).

20   Dominique Pialot, 'European cities take Commission to court over air quality in landmark case', *Euractive*, 18 May 2018; https://bit.ly/2Jp-Kr3g (accessed 19 October 2018).

21   'Overweight and obesity – BMI statistics', *Eurostat*, 24 September 2018; https://bit.ly/2ORJTSA (accessed 19 October 2018).

22 Denis Campbell, 'Sugar and Britain's obesity crisis: the key questions answered', *Guardian*, 23 October 2015; https://bit.ly/2A6TXSu (accessed 19 October 2018).

23 Amanda Holpuch, 'Sugar lobby paid scientists to blur sugar's role in heart disease – report', *Guardian*, 12 September 2016; https://bit.ly/2czXNLn.

24 Hilary Brueck, 'New evidence shows the sugar industry suppressed studies linking sugar to heart disease and cancer', *Business Insider,* 21 November 2017; https://read.bi/2FAtJh1 (accessed 19 October 2018).

25 World Health Organisation, *Infant and Young Child Nutrition*, Resolutions and Decisions WHA49.15 (1996); https://bit.ly/2S1RrUL (accessed 19 October 2018).

26 European Parliament, *Objection to a Delegated Act: Specific Compositional and Information Requirements for Processed Cereal-Based Food and Baby Food*, Report P8_TA(2016)0015; https://bit.ly/2qRVLdQ (accessed 19 October 2018).

27 European Commission, *Foods for Specific Groups: The New Regulation on Food for Specific Groups*, Webpage; https://bit.ly/2OU9cmU (accessed 19 October 2018).

28 Baby Milk Action, *Update on Sugar in Baby Foods: JRC Report Published*, Press Release (24 March 2017); https://bit.ly/2QbwedL (accessed 19 October 2018).

29 Interview with Samir Jeraj on 30 August 2018.

30 Hans Kundnani and David Gow, 'Airlines ready for a dogfight over EU's plan for cleaner, greener skies', *Guardian,* 4 July 2006; https://bit.ly/2PIlpAA (accessed 19 October 2018).

31 Interview with Samir Jeraj on 21 September 2018.

32 Stephen Castle, 'MEPs vote for tough action to curb pollution by airlines', *The Independent,* 5 July 2006; https://ind.pn/2PJkArn (accessed 19 October 2018).

33 Corporate Europe Observatory, *Climate Crash in Strasbourg: An Industry in Denial*, Report (December 2008); https://bit.ly/2S3VDTT (accessed 19 October 2018).

34 'MEPs fight for stricter terms for aviation in ETS', *Transport and Environment,* 14 May 2008; https://bit.ly/2Dz19dq (accessed 19 October 2018).

35 'First EU aviation deal confirmed – but is it a milestone or a missed opportunity?', *Transport and Environment,* 22 July 2008; https://bit.ly/2QZxg9W (accessed 19 October 2018).

36 'Commission goes ahead with plans to cut aviation pollution', *Euractive,* 21 December 2006; https://bit.ly/2DxOuY5 (accessed 19 October 2018).

37 *The Green New Deal Group*; www.greennewdealgroup.org (accessed 19 October 2018).

38 Jill Treanor, 'MEPs back Robin Hood tax on banks', *Guardian,* 8 March 2011; https://bit.ly/2TyUfui (accessed 19 October 2018).

39 Keith Taylor MEP, *UK's Green MEPs Welcome Strengthening of Proposed EU Financial Transaction Tax,* Press Release (23 May 2012); https://bit.ly/2QYQ9tu (accessed 19 October 2018).

40 Green Party of England and Wales, *Financial Transaction Tax: Greens Welcome Europe's Move to Rein In Casino Banking,* Press Release (30 April 2014); https://bit.ly/2qUZZBl (accessed 19 October 2018).

41 Jean Lambert MEP, *City MEP Welcomes EU Cap on Bankers' Bonuses,* Press Release (n.d.); https://bit.ly/2qUbk4u (accessed 19 October 2018).

42 Interview with Samir Jeraj on 14 September 2018.

43 Greens/EFA Group, *Corporate Tax Transparency,* Press Release (7 May 2015); https://bit.ly/2S1Wp3W (accessed 19 October 2018).

44 Greens/EFA Group, *EU Money Laundering Rules,* Press Release (20 May 2015); https://bit.ly/2TrwvIk (accessed 19 October 2018).

45 Greens/EFA Group, *New Legislation Will Be Tough on Financial Crime, Thanks to Greens/EFA Group,* Press Release (19 April 2018); https://bit.ly/2K6XfJv (accessed 19 October 2018).

46 Email to Samir Jeraj on 17 September 2018.

47 Ibid.

48 Interview with Samir Jeraj on 14 September 2018.

49 European Parliament, *Banking Structural Reform* (20 October 2018); https://bit.ly/2S1LSFR.

50 Interview with Samir Jeraj on 14 September 2018.

51 Deborah Summers, 'Gordon Brown's "British jobs" pledge has caused controversy before', *Guardian,* 30 January 2009; https://bit.ly/2PB6EPZ (accessed 19 October 2018).

52 'Why the Ed Stone continues to haunt Labour', *The New Statesman*, 25 October 2016; https://bit.ly/2S5Jazo (accessed 19 October 2018).
53 Interview with Samir Jeraj on 28 August 2018.
54 Interview with Samir Jeraj on 26 August 2018.
55 Interview with Samir Jeraj on 29 August 2018.
56 Interview with Samir Jeraj on 26 August 2018.
57 Ibid.

Part IV

Brexit and beyond: solidarity for the future

Chapter 8

Stronger In? The logic of pan-European co-operation in the era of Trump and climate change

Molly Scott Cato

Introduction

This chapter is not about Brexit. However, it implicitly addresses the real question that should have been asked during the 2016 referendum: which powers should be exercised at which level of government? In a world that is becoming increasingly interconnected, this question – an inherently Green question – needs to be made explicit as a first step towards addressing the crises that are undermining faith in democratic politics. If, as a nation, we are dissatisfied with the way the EU is working, the logical consequence is to influence it to be more effective in future, not to leave it. That's like voting to leave your county council because you feel dissatisfied with ongoing problems in your local health service. To walk away from the centre of power is simply to diminish one's power and one's national standing. My own view is that walking away from the EU, which is the only body in the world with the willpower and market size to challenge global corporations, is tantamount to accepting corporate domination for the twenty-first century.

In this chapter, I make the case that, as Greens, in spite of our political penchant for the local and our liberal approach to government in general, we should learn to love the EU, and we should celebrate the way we have successfully colonised it and exercised influence that far exceeds the size of our electoral support. I will also explain how British influence has had a powerful impact on both the shape of European institutions and the policies that emerge from them. These two arguments imply that as a Brit and a Green you would be entirely misguided to walk away from this platform of power that has served you so well.

Figure 1. Molly's campaign speech (alongside Caroline Lucas) during the 2017 general election.

So, this chapter is about power: about how power works within the EU and between its member states, and about how Greens have been immensely successful at shaping both the institutions and the policies of the EU. It is precisely because of EU legislation's power to constrain the worst excesses of wealthy and powerful individuals and corporations that it has come under attack from the far-right and from authoritarians like Trump, Putin and Erdoğan. For this reason, I believe we need to read Brexit as part of a geopolitical power struggle to wrest global leadership away from the EU and to simultaneously weaken the liberal and democratic values that Europe represents in the world.

The metropolitan elite

In spite of the acres of copy and hours of discussion about Brexit, there has been relatively little by way of a power analysis. Given that the winning slogan of the EU referendum campaign was 'take back control', this is surprising. To understand Brexit, it is necessary to understand who was taking back control from whom.

The big lie of the Brexit campaign was that it was somehow a rebellion by a people's army against the bureaucrats of Brussels and their paymasters, the liberal elite. As Hitler and Goebbels knew and stated publicly, the way to get away with a whopping lie is to make it so huge as to defy all credibility. The larger the lie, the easier it is to sell it. As an intellectual, I find this hard to fathom – as, I expect, do you – but I have witnessed it with my own eyes in recent years. We only have to think about the £350 million claim emblazoned on the Brexit bus.

Here is how it might work. While you know that human beings are fallible, it seems improbable that they would damage their credibility so utterly as to publicly state something that is wildly and provably untrue. Hence, the bigger the lie, the harder it is to identify it as such. More importantly, once you have believed a big lie, it is extremely difficult to backtrack. To accept that Brexit was just an enormous scam to make the wealthy wealthier, when you believed it was your chance to stick it to the metropolitan elite, would damage your sense of self so utterly that it is safer to hang on to the lie and write off all evidence to the contrary as 'fake news'. The very invention of the term fake news and the non-concept of 'alternative facts' helps to turn the bedrock of shared and provable understanding into quicksand, which is easily exploited by the cheats and liars who abound in modern political life.

But let's just look at the evidence. Although many MPs later climbed on the bandwagon, the House of Commons Library briefing still notes that it was Team Molly MEP that first raised the issue of the Brexit impact studies.[1] We actually had letters going back and forth about this for a while before Steve (in my Bristol office) thought of the Enid Blyton-ish label '50 secret studies' and it suddenly took off. In a feat of misdirection that would have made a Soviet leader proud, Brexit ministers refused to reveal the outcome of the studies they had conducted in 'excruciating detail', before later telling the House of Commons that they did not, in fact, exist. In a rare display of parliamentary footwork, Hilary Benn's backbench Brexit committee used an archaic procedure called a 'humble address' to force the government to release the studies to the members of the Department for Exiting the European Union (DExEU) scrutiny committee he chaired, who then leaked them to the public.

Before discussing their content, let's just pause to consider the fact that, while you cannot put up a bus shelter without undertaking a public consideration of the impact, the government is still proposing to go ahead with the biggest political change since WWII without allowing the public to know the likely impacts. The data when it did come out was shocking: any route out of the EU will inflict significant damage on the UK economy. According to *Financial Times* analysis: 'GDP would be 2 per cent lower in 15 years time than would have otherwise been the case under the Norway model, 5 per cent lower under the Canada model, and 8 per cent lower under the [World Trade Organization] model.'[2] Ironically, the impact of these studies was limited by the nature of their publication – through a leak – which allowed ministers to downplay their significance; this was exactly what the government had intended. In terms of the big lie, the takeaway is that the poorest will lose the most – especially in regions like the northeast, where the 'people's army' fought hardest for Brexit.

In the sense that politicians tend to be better educated and better paid than the average person, democratic politics has always been a battle between elites; but the elites who have spawned Brexit are in a different class altogether. I have profiled some of the key figures on a website called *Bad Boys of Brexit*, after Arron Banks's self-congratulatory book of the same title. (I have the dubious privilege of being his MEP, as well as Jacob Rees-Mogg's.) When we study the key players, what becomes immediately clear is that their central cry is for freedom, but not freedom à la *Braveheart*, with a sense of liberty and equality attached. What they are after is freedom from the irritating restrictions that democracy brings, where their economic activity is curtailed by 'red tape', much of it arising from the EU, which limits their 'business opportunities'.

One of these key players is hereditary peer Matt Ridley, or the 5th Viscount Ridley of Blagdon Hall, Northumberland. Like Owen Paterson and many other leading Leave campaigners, Ridley is a vociferous opponent of action on climate change and a keen advocate of the continued use of fossil fuels. He has frequently tried to cast doubt on the science of global warming. He is on the Academic Advisory Council of Nigel Lawson's climate sceptic Global Warming Policy Foundation and has used his seat in the House of Lords to oppose the development of renewable wind energy. By chance, Ridley also enjoys a substantial income from two open-cast coal mines[3] on his large estate in Northumbria, which are owned by his family trust: together, these are estimated to contain coal worth £336 million. Ridley is a big supporter of fracking. He has also claimed that red tape is stifling science in the EU, giving as one example the EU ban on neonicotinoid pesticides, known to be harmful to bees and now banned as a result of Green campaigning in the European Parliament. Flying in the face of all scientific evidence, Ridley claims that the ban will harm bees.[4]

The architects of Brexit also want to be 'free' to spend all their own money, leaving the payment of tax to the little people. Jacob Rees-Mogg has built his fortune offshore, co-founding Somerset Capital Management, which is managed via subsidiaries in the tax havens of the Cayman Islands and Singapore.[5] Rees-Mogg has defended the use of tax havens, saying: 'I do not believe people have any obligation to pay more tax than the law requires.'[6] His name was one of those to emerge in the Paradise Papers scandal in late 2017, when leaked documents showed he once held more than

50,000 shares in a company based in the British Virgin Islands, Lloyd George Management, and had made C$680,000 (£520,000) when it was bought by Canada's Bank of Montreal in 2011.[7] Both tax dodgers and hedge fund managers view EU attempts to prevent their anti-social activities (of which more later) as a hostile attack on their 'freedom'.

Figure 2. Molly has championed political reform, including introducing a fair and proportional voting system as is the case for European elections.

While many of us were shocked and grieved after losing the EU referendum, those who had driven the campaign to leave the EU (many of whom had been planning this moment for 30 years) rapidly began organising to gain the maximum advantage for themselves and their causes. Following the central principle of disaster capitalism – never waste a good crisis – they began lobbying to install those who shared their extreme Brexit stance into key positions of influence. They also began establishing and building organisations that would lobby government to ensure Brexit was not wasted as an opportunity to push forward the next stage of the global reign of free markets. We have profiled these organisations on a website called *The Brexit Syndicate*.

Beyond self-serving Brits and the global 'citizens of nowhere' oligarchs, there is also a strong geopolitical aspect to Brexit, which will strengthen the hand of new authoritarians against the flourishing democracies that make up the EU. The role of Putin in the Brexit referendum – and his alliance with Trump – becomes clear once you see the struggle against the EU as a geopolitical struggle over who will control the world in the twenty-first century. This is a battle for the soul of our democracies against authoritarian leaders and the nightmare of oligarchy. Brexit is an elite project that undermines the rights and livelihoods of the poor. We can see this directly in the impact studies, but, more fundamentally, the attack on democracy that Brexit represents will prevent democratic politicians from protecting citizens from the overweening power of the global elite.

Think local, act global

There was a relatively small but determined – and entirely principled – group of Green Party members who campaigned for Brexit during the referendum campaign, under the name Green Leaves. I have always had some sympathy with their objection to the sheer size and remoteness of the European institutions, since I share their romantic love for the local, as many Greens do. What changed my mind, and I think many other Greens have followed a similar path, is that we cannot run away from globalisation and so must find a way to tame the process and harness its benefits for the citizens of the world at large. To do this requires more power than a single national government can muster.

The clue lies in the description of the companies that dominate the global capitalist economy: multinational corporations. They benefit from their ability to straddle many national economies and to exploit the spaces between them to accentuate their power. The person who has done more than any other politician to restrict this power and to force these corporations to heel is EU competition commissioner Margrethe Vestager, my political pin-up, who I have

called the White Knight of the global tech-wars. She has launched
a series of investigations into tax avoidance and anti-competitive
practice by the corporations that dominate the global economy.
In June 2018 the European Commission imposed a record fine
of €4.3 billion on Google for abusing its dominant position in
the market and for forcing smartphone manufacturers that use
its Android operating system to have Google apps pre-installed.[8]
This followed a number of fines for illegal tax avoidance, the most
famous of which resulted from a secret deal between the Irish government and Apple culminating in an effective tax rate of around
0.005%. Vestager demanded Apple repay the lost taxes, which were
worth an eye-watering €13 billion.[9] As the *Guardian* journalist
Tim Adams noted, the sheer presence of Margrethe Vestager, who
was the inspiration for the TV character Birgitte Nyborg in the
programme *Borgen*, is the most compelling argument in favour of
the EU.[10]

Another major victory against the power of global corporations,
this time requiring opposition to the Commission, was the defeat of
the Anti-Counterfeiting Trade Agreement (ACTA) in 2012. ACTA
was negotiated by the EU, the US and a small group of other states
supported by industry lobby groups behind closed doors, without
the involvement of national parliamentarians or representatives of
civil society. It would have enhanced the power of corporations to
enforce their right to intellectual property or knowledge, including
in areas such as patents for medicines, which are protected against
the profit motive. This was the first time the European Parliament
had used its power under the Lisbon Treaty to reject trade treaties,
and it laid the groundwork for the battle against the Transatlantic
Trade and Investment Partnership (TTIP) that is now moribund.

Another area where national action can never succeed, and
where concerted, global action is urgently required, is that of climate change. The EU has shown global leadership on policies to
tackle climate change, especially since the Paris Agreement reached
on our continent in December 2015. This has led to policies to
reduce CO_2 emissions directly via targets and investments as well as
indirectly via a reshaped Emissions Trading Scheme. While none of

this action is fast enough or strong enough for Greens, we use the Paris Agreement, sometimes daily, to justify stronger climate action. The sustainable finance agenda is one important outcome I discuss in a later section. With Trump pulling out of the Paris process, it is more important than ever that the EU shows global leadership, and Greens are proposing that we introduce a border adjustment mechanism – effectively a tax on goods from countries that do not meet Paris climate standards in production. This will allow us to use the purchasing power of 500 million wealthy global citizens to put upward pressure on other production markets.

My own major area of work as an MEP has been tackling corporate and personal tax avoidance. I was well placed when the Lux-Leaks scandal broke in November 2014: the first in a series of scandals, which later included the higher profile Panama Papers and then the Paradise Papers, that we have used as political pressure for much stronger action against tax dodging. Some of this work is arcane, but it ranges from requiring much greater transparency and sharing of information between tax authorities, to proposals and legal protection for whistleblowers, to preventing any European funding from going to companies that have offshore branches in tax havens.

Tackling tax avoidance is a classic example of a global issue that cannot be handled by one member state alone. Worse, corporations are deliberately playing states off against each other as they persuade politicians to give them sweetheart deals to their selfish, short-term benefit, while, in the long run, all national treasuries are drained of the resources they need to provide the public services on which we all depend. LuxLeaks revealed Luxembourg to be offering just such specially tailored deals, while the arrangement between the Government of Ireland and Apple was found to be illegal under fair competition rules.

Corporations also use the free flow of capital to transfer their profits from one country to another to ensure the lowest corporate tax rate on their profits. This is partly through having special deals but also through arranging elaborate 'transfer pricing' systems, where they charge themselves vastly overinflated prices for internal trades, especially for intellectual property, which is notoriously difficult to cost accurately. To avoid this profit shifting, the EU has proposed a one-stop-shop taxation system, know as the Common Consolidated Corporate Tax Base. This would mean companies paying tax according to an agreed formula, and paying once across the whole EU, with money then being allocated to member states based on turnover, value generated, number of employees and so on. This is the Holy Grail to end corporate tax avoidance and, although it is being blocked by a number of states, including the UK, it is clear that only such a system of multinational co-operation can force the multinational corporations to pay the tax they rightfully owe.

As with the competition agenda, on the question of tax justice we have benefitted from the commitment and strategic insight of an excellent commissioner in the person of Pierre Moscovici, former French Minister of the Economy, Finance and Industry. My work on tax has made it clear to me that we can propose radical and progressive measures by agreement between Parliament and Commission; it is usually the member states in the Council that block them. I note this just to indicate how, at least from a Green perspective, more European integration on policymaking has strengthened our political agenda rather than weakening it.

Take back control?

When considering the relative power of the UK and EU in our historic relationship, we should start by noting that the UK has the sweetest deal – or the most selfish, depending on your perspective – of any EU member state. We have maintained our own currency, and the huge sovereignty and seigniorage advantages that come with that, but we have also operated as the dominant financial centre for much of the eurozone: a classic example of us having our cake and eating it that will not outlast Brexit. We have enjoyed the benefits of freedom of movement while standing outside the passport-free Schengen area. In addition, we have negotiated the largest rebate[11] – based on the argument that we have fewer farmers than other countries, and thus a disproportionately large contribution to the common agricultural budget – while continuing to benefit disproportionately from many of the EU budgets, especially the research budgets, of which Horizon 2020[12] is the latest incarnation.

It is in the area of law and policy that the 'take back control' mantra seems so absurd, as UK lawyers and diplomats have played such a central role in shaping the EU institutions. This is demonstrated by the irony that, when Theresa May made the decision to invoke Article 50 of the Lisbon Treaty, she was availing herself of a piece of law drafted by the British diplomat John Kerr.

As well as shaping the actual treaty law that frames the operation of the EU, British politicians have been hugely influential in all three arms of the institutions. During the 2014–19 term, our commissioner, Jonathan Hill, was given the powerful brief covering financial markets, which enabled him to keep an eye on the interests of the City. Given that we continued to stand aside from the EU's own euro currency, this was pretty extraordinary. Hill resigned the day after his puppetmaster, David Cameron, and we lost this powerful position, although our current commissioner, Julian King, continues to hold the brief for the Security Union, including protection against terrorism, cybercrime and disinformation.

When it comes to the European Parliament, I, together with my British colleagues, am hugely advantaged in that business is conducted in English, so when we speak most members are listening to us without translation. Until June 2016 we were regarded with great respect, and our reputation for negotiation and policymaking was strong. This is reflected in the powerful positions held by British MEPs: we have held the chairs of some of the most powerful committees. In the previous term, Sharon Bowles (Liberal Democrat) was chair of the economics and monetary policy committee, while Vicky Ford (Conservative) was chair of the committee that oversees the single market, until she resigned to become a Westminster MP in June 2017. Claude Moraes (Labour) continues as chair of the civil liberties committee. My colleague Richard Corbett (Labour) has recently steered through a revision to the rules of operation of the European Parliament, while my colleague Richard Ashworth (Conservative) recently did the same for the parliament's budget rules. In every aspect of the law, policy and process of operation of the EU, British politicians have been central. It is not *their* Union, as so much of the Brexit propaganda implies: it is *our* Union.

However, all this talk of internal markets and monetary policy might sound a long way from central green concerns. So, what should we make of the suggestion that the EU has been obsessed with untrammelled economic growth and serving the interests of a capitalist economy? Here, I think the critique has some merit. Most of the politicians I have encountered during my life as an MEP seem to consider 'jobs-and-growth' to be a compound noun. In spite of really positive initiatives, such as the End of Life Vehicles Directive (which makes producers responsible for the disposal of their goods) and the Circular Economy Package, Greens are a lone voice in calling for a halt to the lunacy of exponential growth on a finite planet.

Of course, Europe is not alone in that misguided quest, but the rules governing the economy are much tighter on our continent than elsewhere, and Greens can claim much credit for that. The major achievement for Greens in the legislative process has been to colonise the single market: rather than allowing it to be merely a platform for business to trade with lower costs and higher profits, we have made it a vehicle to raise the social and environmental standards of production and for consumers. This has turned the EU – the world's largest market, with 500 million of the richest consumers in the world – into a force for good. I have seen this happen again and again. Here are a few examples.

To start, we can consider the new law to exclude conflict minerals from EU markets; this is an example I know well because its driving force is Judith Sargentini, a Green MEP from the Netherlands, who sits next to me in the parliament. You have probably heard of blood diamonds: gemstones exported from conflict regions (such as Angola) that fuel the supply of arms that feed ongoing conflicts. In 2014 the European Parliament strongly supported Judith's report on conflict minerals, which called for binding transparency rules for all firms in the mineral supply chain. This pushed the Commission into issuing a draft law in favour of mandatory supply chain transparency. Note also that this is the way to get around the lack of an official power for the European Parliament to initiate legislation.

From 1 January 2021 the new law – the Conflict Minerals Regulation[13] – will come into force across the EU. It requires that EU importers of 3TG metals (tin, tungsten, tantalum and gold) meet international responsible sourcing standards, set by the Organisation for Economic Co-operation and Development (OECD). The law is weaker and comes into force later than we would have liked, but it does mean that in just over two years' time EU manufacturers of electronic goods using these four metals will have to monitor their supply chain to ensure they only import these minerals and metals from responsible and conflict-free sources. It is an important limit on trade that drives conflict, and one that was initiated and negotiated by a Green MEP.

Greens have also been instrumental in ensuring stronger regulation of the internet. Throughout the battle for the internet, Greens have taken the side of freedom against attempts by cyber corps to use it as an enclosed, profit-driven space that they control. A typical focus for conflict is over so-called net neutrality, which means that all individuals and companies have equal access to and equivalent service on the World Wide Web. Corporations and larger companies have argued that they should have the right to pay for faster channels, so the strict equality that currently governs cyberspace would be replaced by the principle of some being more equal than others. Without net neutrality, smaller companies might have to use the equivalent of B-roads or pay a toll to use motorways through the internet superhighway. While the US has abandoned free and equal access to the internet, this is an ongoing battle in the EU, with Greens leading the charge for freedom.

Another Green MEP colleague, Jan Philipp Albrecht (of Germany's Alliance 90/The Greens), was responsible for guiding the General Data Protection Regulation (GDPR),[14] which came into force in May 2018, through the EU's policymaking institutions. It is an important step towards ending the Wild West of data communications and putting us back in control of our personal data.

The unreadable small print we sign up to without reading and the data scraping that has made fortunes for data companies – as well as allowing them to microtarget us with advertising – are a thing of the past, and internet giants are now required to have our informed consent before they store or use our data. As Jan Philipp put it when the law came into force:

> Take my house as an example: under the GDPR, it can be legitimate to use my street address for direct marketing mail, as long as I can expect it and can exercise my right to object. However, what I say inside my house to my wife or child is no one's business. The same applies to business communication, including machine-to-machine communication.[15]

This is another example of Greens developing EU regulation that then becomes the global gold standard. Facebook CEO Mark Zuckerberg acknowledged this in a backhanded compliment to Jan Philipp when he gave testimony before EU Parliament representatives including the German MEP. He acknowledged: 'A lot of the philosophy that is encoded in regulation like GDPR is really how we've thought about a lot of this stuff for a long time.'[16]

While the governance of the internet can sometimes seem like a techy backwater, nothing could be further from the truth. The future will be digitised, and hence it is vital that the gains for high standards and consumer protection made in the world of physical goods are reproduced in cyberspace. It was the Greens who first saw the importance of this, and we have led on regulating the digital world.

My final example concerns a relatively new but rapidly developing area of policymaking where the Commission is taking a strong lead: sustainable finance. This agenda builds on the advances made by the divestment movement – where universities or public bodies shift their money from fossil fuel assets to sustainable sectors like renewables – and enhanced company reporting, so that we know much more about what the companies who have our pension savings are doing with them. The sustainable finance agenda is similar to this work but much, much deeper, wider and is legally enforceable. Because the EU is a financial regulator, the European Supervisory Authorities (yes, they are known as ESAs!) can determine which assets are considered viable when determining whether banks are solvent or whether pension funds will be able to afford to pay out. So, if we as regulators take the initiative to legislate that coal mines or intensive farms will not be viable assets after, say, 2030, we will ensure an orderly transition away from these assets and towards the assets of the future, such as wind farms and organic farms. This is the promise of the sustainable finance agenda: to use finance as a lever on the whole economy. Sustainable finance may be in its early stages, but it helps us to create the · incentives to ensure that future investment is compatible with the Paris Agreement and eventually with a whole raft of environmental, social and governance standards.

Most of what I am describing here is perhaps news to you, which brings us to an important question: why has the UK media failed to report on important legislation? They can't have it both ways: if European law is so powerful that many British people were convinced we had lost our sovereignty, then why did we not hear more about these laws as they were being negotiated? I believe we must lay this failing squarely at the door of British media outlets and journalists. It is no surprise that tabloids and fake quality papers like *The Times* and *The Telegraph*, whose owners are largely offshore billionaires, might object to the way the EU seeks to enforce laws on taxes and regulate their businesses. But what about the BBC? As a public-service broadcaster, why has it not performed its vital duty to inform electors about the European legislative process? Why do we not have a programme called *Yesterday in the European Parliament*?

Without this vital information, voters are unable to accurately assess the contribution that EU law is making to their lives, and they lack the knowledge to challenge false narratives around the size of UK influence in developing that law, including the achievements of British and other Greens. This failure to report on European lawmaking has fed the anti-EU narrative that gave rise to

Brexit and also undermined the position of the Green Party in the UK.

Conclusion: you don't know what you've got till it's gone

I explained earlier that I have changed my mind and learned to love the EU because I recognise that we cannot resist globalisation and we need to enhance the power of citizens in the globalised economy. This must mean stronger democratic platforms, at both a European and a global level, so that twenty-first-century politicians can work together to reinforce the power of citizens vis-à-vis multinational corporations. With Trump and other authoritarians in the ascendancy, Europe needs to protect high standards for citizens and the environment. Greens have done this effectively by exerting progressive influence on the rules of the single market and by using the power of our market to create a global race to the top on our standards.

Figure 3. Molly at the Irish insurance meeting in Brussels, October 2018. The Green Party has more women in senior positions than any other political party.

We are already seeing that, as the power over environmental policy begins to shift from the EU to the UK, we are losing important laws that strengthen environmental protection: most importantly the Precautionary Principle, which exists as a fundamental guiding principle in EU treaty law and was not preserved during the debate over the withdrawal bill. Similarly, the principle that those who produce pollution must pay the cost of remedial action to clean up after themselves has not been transferred into UK law. And the environmental watchdog offered by environment secretary Michael Gove fell far short of the expectations of environmentalists by not offering any power to issue legal proceedings against the government should the latter fail to adhere to its own environmental laws, which is something we have had available in the European Court of Justice as EU members.[17]

These are just a few key legal protections that will be lost if Brexit goes ahead. As I hope I have made clear, Greens in the European Parliament have managed to colonise the single market and use it as a tool for progressive improvement across a huge range of areas, from financial regulation and fighting tax avoidance to improving human rights in the supply chain and banning harmful chemicals. Outside of the EU, we will lose not only the benefit of this work but also the opportunity to send our own politicians to influence the agenda of a powerful institution and force for good in this world.

European politics can feel like a vast stage compared to a local or national government. But now that the world is truly operating as one system, we need to have the courage to, as E F Schumacher put it, 'look at the world and see it whole'. With attacks on the rule of law and authoritarian leaders threatening hard-won democratic freedoms, it is more important than ever that Greens defend the global rules-based system of which the EU is a vital part and build up the strength of the UN and its vital institutions. While it will be a tragedy if Brexit does go ahead, I have confidence in the ability of my Green colleagues in the European Parliament to carry on this work with the courage, principles and intellect that has made them so successful thus far.

Endnotes

1   *Exiting the EU: Sectoral Assessments*, House of Commons Library Briefing Paper 08128 (London: House of Commons, 9 March 2018).

2   George Parker and Laura Hughes, 'What the UK's Brexit impact assessments say', *Financial Times*, 9 February 2018; https://on.ft.com/2rnKvWA (accessed 25 October 2018).

3   'Matt "King Coal" Ridley', *DeSmogUK*; https://bit.ly/2KWkc2N (accessed 25 October 2018).

4   Matt Ridley, 'Gove's ban on neonicotinoids will harm insects', *The Times*, 10 November 2017; https://bit.ly/2UeFpcN (accessed 25 October 2018).

5   Juliette Garside, Hilary Osborne and Ewen MacAskill, 'The Brexiters who put their money offshore', *Guardian*, 9 November 2017; https://bit.ly/2zvMsUl (accessed 25 October 2018).

6   Rajeev Syal and Martin Williams, 'Tory treasurer wants UK to become more like a tax haven', *Guardian*, 21 September 2012; https://bit.ly/2QhVlMP (accessed 25 October 2018).

7   Andrew Gregory, 'Tory Jacob Rees-Mogg pocketed $680,000 payment while working for offshore firm', *Mirror*, 9 November 2017; https://bit.ly/2Qcfjc3 (accessed 25 October 2018).

8   'Google hit with €4.3 billion fine from EU for abusing market', *New Scientist,* 18 July 2018; https://bit.ly/2G1wus5 (accessed 25 October 2018).

9   European Commission, 'State aid: Ireland gave illegal tax benefits to Apple worth up to €13 billion', Press Release, 30 August 2016; https://bit.ly/2bOwMln (accessed 25 October 2018).

10 Tim Adams, 'Margrethe Vestager: "We are doing this because people are angry"', *Guardian*, 17 September 2017; https://bit.ly/2ftmLet (accessed 25 October 2018).

11 Janosch Delcker, 'Oettinger wants to scrap all rebates in post-Brexit EU budget', *Politico*, 6 January 2017; https://politi.co/2EfQDsD (accessed 25 October 2018).

12 European Commission: Representation in the UK, 'Horizon 2020: three years in, UK tops league of participants', News Release, 31 January 2018; https://bit.ly/2KXeMEO (accessed 25 October).

13 European Commission, *Conflict Minerals Regulation* (8 June 2017); https://bit.ly/2mxGYRO.

14 Derek Scally, 'On May 25th GDPR comes into force for Europe's 500m citizens', *The Irish Times*, 19 May 2018; https://bit.ly/2KQaC03 (accessed 25 October 2018).

15 Jan Philipp Albrecht, 'The time for ePrivacy is now', *The Parliament Magazine*, 27 March 2018; https://bit.ly/2pJjcoI (accessed 25 October 2018).

16 Ryan Browne, 'Zuckerberg says Facebook has "always shared" the values of Europe's new data', *CNBC*, 24 May 2018; https://cnb.cx/2SuwJgx (accessed 25 October 2018).

17 Catherine Early, 'Brexit bill amendment on environmental protection' "not good enough"', *The Ecologist*, 15 June 2018; https://bit.ly/2ARwKny (accessed 25 October 2018).

Chapter 9

European Greens: a global vision?

Reinhard Bütikofer

Wish you were here: from Liverpool to the world

When the Global Greens organised their fourth Congress for the spring of 2017, it was a natural choice for the European Green Party (EGP), as the host, to invite them to Liverpool. Previous Global Greens Congresses had been held in Australia, South America and Africa, but finally the Global Green family came to Europe, where we have some of the oldest and most successful green parties in the world. Bringing together around 2,000 delegates from all corners of the globe, the Green Party of England and Wales (GPEW) and the EGP created a memorable event. We at the EGP were happy to team up with the GPEW because of its internationalist character, providing a bridge to the rest of the world.

Liverpool was an obvious choice for the location of the Congress because of what the city symbolises. One of the major topics of our conference was the contradictory character and the highly problematic consequences of globalisation. Where better to discuss this than in a city that at a certain point in its past had been the most important hub of an early phase of globalisation, and even played a major role in the ugly slave trade? We also discussed the development of internationally shared values, struggles, hopes and campaigns. What city could have been more appropriate for these discussions than one where, almost two generations ago, a cultural movement arose that brought together young people from all lands by providing a shared musical language through which they could express their identities and even their hopes for creating a better world?

Guests from more than 80 countries happily joined us in Liverpool, with many eager to meet Green leaders from across Britain who they had heard a lot about before. Many countries in continental Europe – including Belgium, Cyprus, Denmark, Finland, Germany, Greece, Hungary, Ireland, Latvia, Lithuania, Luxembourg, the Netherlands, Portugal, Spain, Sweden and Switzerland – have stronger green party representation than is the case in the House of Commons in terms of numbers. But because the British media, untrustworthy as it may be, is the biggest window through which the public in many countries has viewed what's going on in Europe, Caroline Lucas, the sole GPEW MP in the House of Commons, has arguably had a bigger impact in many worldwide media markets than all other European green leaders combined. Of course, another former leader of the GPEW, Natalie Bennett, originally hails from Australia, a country with its own strong green representation; that may be a coincidence, but it is not an uninteresting one, as it underscores the internationalist character of the UK Greens.

The UK Greens are one of the most senior founding forces of the European green family. The first green party in England was the PEOPLE Party, founded in 1973. In many parts of Europe it took another decade or more before green parties emerged. Today the UK Greens have almost 50,000 members – the GPEW has more than 39,000 members[1] and the Scottish Greens[2] and the Green Party in Northern Ireland[3] have more than 8,500 between them – which makes them the second biggest EGP member, in terms of membership, behind only the German Greens, who have almost 70,000 members.

The unfair electoral system that governs elections for the House of Commons has, for a long time, held back the English, Welsh, Scottish and Northern Irish Greens, as has been discussed at length elsewhere in this book. Originally, this first-past-the-post system was also used in the UK for electing MEPs, and in the memorable year of 1989, when the GPEW won an astonishing 15% of the popular vote (meaning that 2.3 million people went Green), they were still shut out from representation in the European Parliament, returning not a single MEP. Ever since then, though, the application of pro-portional representation has made European Parliament elections a regular opportunity for the GPEW. In other words, being part of the EU gave Green voters around the UK a better chance of taking back control over who was to represent them than the time-honoured and deeply flawed British electoral system.

The English Channel has also undeniably, at times and on vari-ous issues, kept the green parties of England, Wales, Scotland and Northern Ireland apart from their continental cousins. I recall fun-damental disagreements between the GPEW and my own German Green Party over NATO's military interventions in the Balkans against the genocidal policies of Serbia's President Milošević. The UK Greens were also, for quite some time, among the softly euro-sceptic wing of the European green family, together with greens from Ireland, Denmark and Sweden at the time. However, many of the erstwhile divisions have unquestionably been overcome. And through that process of mutual alignment, the voices of green parties from the British Isles became louder and more discernible among European Greens. It is an irony of sorts that through Brexit, the integration of the UK into the EU will be undone at a moment when UK Greens and continental Greens are closer together than ever before.

Co-operation and allies: in the wake of Brexit

Brexit, whether we are fans of it or not, is going to have a disrupt-ing effect on the relationship between English, Welsh, Scottish and Northern Irish Greens and the rest of the European Greens. Not working together week after week in the European Parliament will deny both sides many shared experiences. Acting under different regulatory frameworks after Brexit, as I assume we will, at least to some degree, will result in differences in our agendas. There will also, of course, be some continuity. We will continue to meet twice a year at EGP Council meetings, for instance. We will hopefully continue to exchange experience and best practice examples with regards to campaigns that we run on either side of the Channel, be that on carbon divestment, humanitarian refugee policies or gender issues. But I do think that we will both – the UK Greens and the continental Greens – have to make sustained and conscientious efforts to make fresh investments in the relationship if we don't want the disruption to turn into a rupture. I see a parallel there with many public discussions about the future of good neighbourly relations between the EU and the UK after Brexit. There will be a lot of space for fertile co-operation in many areas, but this space will have to be filled proactively.

Brexit will hurt the EU and it will hurt the UK even more. Brexit will also hurt European Greens in several ways, and the UK Greens in particular, who have benefitted considerably from the fact that there is much better electoral justice for European elections than is the case under British electoral law, with its famous/infamous first-past-the-post principle, which disadvantages smaller parties. Election injustice will undoubtedly remain on the agenda of all progressive forces in the UK, but it might be a while before British voters are able to enjoy the benefits of proportional representation or a single transferable vote system in elections for the House of Commons. Until that day comes, it will be difficult to substitute for the voices of the three current GPEW MEPs (Jean Lambert, Molly Scott Cato and Keith Taylor). Three of the four most highly visible English Green parliamentarians have so far been European ones. Losing those three seats will mean not only losing three parliamentary fighters, but also losing three voices, three offices. It will reduce Green Party visibility in the UK overall. The visibility brought about by working in the European Parliament has always been an opportunity to remind the general public that British Greens are indeed much more than just one member of the House of Commons.

I also expect a negative effect from the discontinuation of day-to-day co-operation with other green representatives in the European

Parliament, as this will limit practical access to information, experience and new ideas from other countries. To sustain even a fraction of the traditional level of co-operation, which has always spanned an abundance of topics and issues, will be very difficult. Loss of contacts, of budget and of organisational power is unavoidable. This is a particularly bitter pill to swallow, as Greens are not able to rely on the organisational support of Union backers nor on big money from corporate donors to support their work. To put it in a possibly overly simplistic way, green ideas from the UK will lose hundreds of thousands of pounds of funding every year. In the post-Brexit world, it will obviously be more difficult to continue co-operation that has become pragmatic second nature. Working together on the promotion of renewables, or on 'greening finance', or on a new Africa policy, or on dealing with sensitive Chinese direct investment, or on defence issues – all of this will require additional effort in the future.

Finally, UK Greens will also be hurt by the fact that even though they will continue to be members of the European green family, they will find it much harder to demonstrate this, practically, to their own members, their voters and the general public. Brexit will also cost the rest of the European green family dearly, no question about it. At the level of the Greens/EFA group in the European Parliament, Brexit will deny us six of our (current) 52 members: the three GPEW MEPs, two members of the SNP and one member of Plaid Cymru. Of course, this loss of six people (and perhaps the May 2019 European elections might have seen a greater number of successful candidates joining our group) also means losing the competency with which they have enriched our common work. On so many issues, each of them stood not just for themselves or for a UK party, but for all of us, because they were our experts in important committees such as the Committee on Economic and Monetary Affairs, the Committee on Employment and Social Affairs and the Committee on Transport and Tourism.

It is obvious that the momentous change that Brexit will bring will force all of us – the EGP, the Green Group in the European Parliament and our British friends – to think anew. We have to strategise over the development of common answers in order to offset, as best we can, the negative impact for our party and parliamentary work.

When I ponder these questions, several aspects of such a future undertaking spring to mind. One dimension is the future co-operation of municipal entities and elected local officials. Another is bilateral relations between Green Party members of the House of Commons, the House of Lords and the Scottish Parliament, and national and regional Green parliamentarians from other European countries. A third consideration is looking at how to co-operate in the context of social, environmental, feminist, LGBT, human-rights-related and other international movements. A fourth dimension is that both sides should consider making a special effort in order to avoid losing sight of the general orientation, the priorities, the pre-occupations and the concerns that are developing on the other side of the Channel.

The EGP has increased its investment in transnational co-operation across green parties on the Continent. We may not have utilised the potential of this co-operation sufficiently, but the EGP's local councillor seminars have certainly enjoyed a lot of enthusiastic participation and have really helped to create bonds. The EGP should emphasise this line of work even more in the future, regardless of the effect of Brexit. Because the local level of democracy is the mother of all democracy – 'all politics is local!'– and because Greens in many European countries have strong roots in local politics, we have very good reasons to reinforce this line of our work. We will have to emphasise the participation of UK Greens in that realm in the future, making sure to use this mutually advantageous exchange to help create new bonds. We could make it a rule that local councillor seminars are regularly held in the UK, for example.

Regarding the future co-operation of national and regional Green parliamentarians, it would be best if this was to be organised around topically defined issues. Obviously, it would not be feasible to come up with a formal organisation for this sort of working together. It therefore requires a keen interest on all sides of such exchanges to identify promising topics again and again and again. This could be proactively supported by party leaders, as has been the case, for instance, in exchanges between the GPEW and the German Greens. Many green parties have international secretaries. It could be one of their future tasks to give regular attention to bilateral, or even pluri-lateral, exchanges between national and regional parliamentarians, or they could be supported in that regard by other party officials. The Green Group in the European Parliament could also contribute by making a point of regularly and systematically inviting UK Green participants to their important events and by freely sharing the results of their work. Green parties on the continent could contribute in their own way: by offering internships to young British Greens, for instance, or by sending interns.

Greens have come from a diverse array of civic movements, and to this day, green parties and green activists are involved in many such movements. Over the last three years, the EGP has made additional efforts to make our green involvement with movements such as the global divestment movement, World Cleanup Day, International Women's Day and Earth Day more visible by coordinating the efforts of national member parties. In 2018, for instance, Greens in more than 18 European countries made use of tools that were developed by the EGP to raise our voices on World Cleanup Day in September. With the growth of *tilt!*,[4] the online mobilising tool for green campaigns that the EGP developed, we will have an even greater opportunity to campaign together. The EGP will make an effort, and so should UK Greens, to co-operate closely on the multitude of campaigning opportunities that will undoubtedly arise.

Practical ways of co-operating should not be our only concern, though, in defining the future relationship between continental and UK Greens. We should positively strive to ensure that we involve each other in the development of our overall orientation. I believe it would be useful to agree on the organisation of an annual event in the UK, collectively planned, managed and financed by the EGP, the GPEW, the Scottish Greens and the Northern Irish Greens. This annual event could serve as a platform for topical, strategic and philosophical debates. It could seek to regularly include green thinkers from outside of Europe and progressive participants from outside of the green family. Such an event could help all European Greens by highlighting, in a very special way, the centrality of green thinking in solving the many and complex challenges that we are all facing. Perhaps such an event would not be as grandiose as the 2017 Liverpool Global Greens Congress, but it would certainly enhance the international outreach and political attraction of European Greens.

Paying attention: beyond the EU

Will all of this happen? That depends, as is so often the case, on the will of all sides to make it happen, and on the level of engagement in sustaining these dimensions of co-operation. Let's give it a good go.

The work that we will put into developing our partnership and good neighbourliness in spite of Brexit might, by the way, specifically benefit some of the EGP member parties that are already outside of the EU. Out of a total of 44 member parties, the EGP has 13 full members, associate members and candidate members in European countries that are not represented in the European Parliament: Albania, Andorra, Azerbaijan, Belarus, Georgia, Macedonia, Moldova, Norway, Switzerland, Turkey, Ukraine and Russia (two). Some EGP member parties outside of the EU are rather small, while others hold some power in their national context: our member parties in Norway, Switzerland, Macedonia and Georgia are represented in their national parliaments. But, in all honesty, we must concede that these parties may more than once have felt somewhat excluded when work within the EGP focused too much on EU-specific issues. The UK Greens will now join the ranks of our non-EU member parties. Playing a major role as they do – because of the international relevancy of the UK, but also because of the high number of members that the GPEW and the Scottish Green Party have – the balance within the EGP will shift somewhat. The EGP will have to adapt by paying more attention to Europe beyond the EU.

It will be imperative for the EGP and the Green Group in the European Parliament to reconsider the balance between the work that we do solely within the EU and between EU member parties, and the work that we do Europe-wide and internationally.

The Brexiteers' marvellous idea of creating a new Global Britain will probably prove to be delusional. However, in one way or another, Britain will have to re-engineer and reprioritise its international relations. It is also conceivable that in some way British Greens will look at reprioritising their own trans-border relations post-Brexit. Maybe in a Britain that moves away from the EU and looks to refurbish its relationships with other partners, it might become more important for the UK Greens to develop and to invest more in relationships with green allies elsewhere. Maybe they will come to the conclusion that some of their European efforts should be reformulated in favour of enhanced international efforts beyond Europe. None of the ideas for the future of the European green family that I have presented would be rendered obsolete if that happened. However, we should be open to new developments and opportunities, particularly when both resources and time are limited.

From the point of view of the EGP it is clear that future changes in the relationship with the UK Greens would not imply an abandonment of the latter's European calling. Instead of just playing defence and trying to hold on to what we have built thus far, the EGP should not hesitate to view the change that is going to occur as an encouragement to consider our international relations with new eyes, to look more eagerly beyond the EU and beyond even the continent of Europe, and to find new ways of building international bridges between actors that promote progressive green causes. In that way, ideally, a certain shift in the relationship between British and continental Greens could help both of us open up to the world and to all the allies we might find there.

'A magic dwells in each beginning', the German poet Hermann Hesse once wrote.[5] It is an often-quoted phrase in Germany, although personally I am not sure it is true: I could well do without the 'magic' of Brexit! However, our task is not to invent an ideal world but to make the existing one better. I have enjoyed doing just that together with many green friends from the UK: with Alyn, Amanda, Caroline, Claire, Ian, Jean, Jenny, Jill, Jonathan, Keith, Maggie, Molly, Natalie, Patrick, Ross, Siân, Steven, Tom and many others. And have no doubt, I am dead set on continuing to do that!

Endnotes

1   Lukas Audickas, *UK Political Party Membership Figures: August 2018*, Report (London: House of Commons Library, 3 September 2018); https://bit.ly/2QPV9Rm.
2   The Scottish Green Party, *Statement of Accounts for the Year Ended 31 December 2017*, Report (Electoral Commission, 2017); https://bit.ly/2R1k2cA.
3   Steven Agnew, 'Greens' growth has just begun', *Belfast Telegraph*, 31 March 2015; https://bit.ly/2QZPf08.
4   *tilt!*; https://www.tilt.green/.
5   Hermann Hesse, 'Steps' (Stufen), 1941. See also, Hermann Hesse, *Erste Gesmtausgabe Der Gedichte / Complete Poems* (Zürich: Fretz & Wasmuth, 1942).

INDEX

A

Aarhaus Convention 86
Abbas, Mahmoud 154, 170, 181
Accessibility Act 149
acid rain xiv
Acorn House Restaurant 92
Additional Member System (AMS) 66
    (Table 1)
Afghanistan 142
afrophobia 103
agriculture committee 85
air pollution xiv, 111, 143, 147–8,
    160, 172–4, 183, 186
Air Quality Directive 172–3
air quality xiv–xv, 88–9, 148, 172–3,
    186–7, 200
airport expansion 88–9, 150
Allies for Democracy 138
Alternative Fuel Infrastructure 149
Alternative Vote (AV) 71–2
Amnesty International 168
Anderson, Victor 86, 184, 199
Andor, Lazlo 92–3
animal welfare xvi, 122, 142, 150–1,
    153, 161
anti-discrimination 85
anti-fracking 145, 166
anti-racism 85, 103
Arcola Theatre 92
Association of Small Island States
    (AOSIS) 95

asylum xvi, 85, 98, 100–3, 106, 117,
    167, 196–8
    seekers xvi, 100–2, 106, 117, 167,
        196–8
austerity 5, 23–4, 27–30, 35, 48, 110,
    127, 155
Austria 4, 6, 16, 29, 35–6, 38, 40
Aznar, José María 103

B

B&Q 171
baby milk 162, 188, 190, 201
badger cull 161
Balcombe 145–6, 166
bandanas 115
Bangladesh 94–5, 97, 100, 112
banking crash 155
Barka 109
Barnier, Michel 158
Baroness of Moulescoomb see also
        Jones, Jenny 86
Bartley, Jonathan 75
bees 211
Behrend, Juan 83
Belfast South 63
Belgium 3, 5–6, 8–9, 11–12, 17, 19,
        29, 35–6, 38, 40, 44–5, 51, 61,
        64, 228
Bermingham, Gerry 54
Berry, Siân 89
Bhutan 94

biodiversity 143, 154
Birchfield, Vicki 69, 80
Birds Directive xiv
Birkett, Simon 89, 172–3, 179, 181
Black, Asian and Minority Ethnic
         (BAME) 66
Blackpool 146, 180
Blair, Tony 53, 63, 122, 131, 139
Bonzo Dog Doo-Dah Band 135
boundary changes 110
Bové, José 26
bovine spongiform encephalopathy
         (BSE) 123
Bowie, Angie 134
Bowie, David 133–5, 159
Boyle, Frankie 47, 76
Brearley, Mark 86
Brexit 88, 110–11, 113, 121, 128–9,
         151–2, 156–8, 161–2, 176–9,
         190, 205, 207, 209–13, 216,
         218, 222–5, 229–32, 234–5
Brides Without Borders 105
Brighton 126–7, 131, 136–41, 147,
         157–9, 166
    & Hove Council 136–40
    Argus 139
    Pavilion ix, 126–7, 131, 140–1
    Urban Design and
        · Development 136
Brussels 6, 14, 83, 88, 93, 95, 106,
         109, 111, 115, 117, 119, 121,
         127, 130, 161, 166, 168,
         170–2, 174–5, 177, 179–80,
         209, 222
Bulgaria 20–1, 23, 32, 36, 38, 40,
         107, 146
bullfighting 150–1, 161
Bundestag 16, 61
Bureau 83
Bursík, Martin 24
Bush, George 60

C
cage age 151

Calais 104
Callaghan, Jim 53
Calverts Press 92
Cambridge xvi, 187
Cameron, David 107, 156, 176, 217
Campaign Against Climate
         Change 92
campaign xvi, 8–10, 13, 16, 23, 25,
         30–1, 50, 57, 63, 73–7, 84–6,
         89, 92, 96, 116–17, 125–6,
         128–30, 138–9, 146, 149–53,
         155–7, 165–80, 185, 190, 193,
         196, 208–9, 211–13, 227, 230,
         233
Canada 47, 60, 64, 70, 79, 115, 210, 212
Canary Islands 101
Capacity Global 90–1
carbon emissions xiv–xv, 69, 87,
         90–4, 121, 143–4, 148, 153,
         160, 172–3, 186, 190–1, 214
CARE international 96
Casablanca 98
Cassola, Arnold 23, 31
CEDEFOP 91
Ceuta 101
Chan, Steve 70, 80
Change.org 73
Charter 88 85
Charter of Fundamental Rights 98
Chelsea 173
Chernobyl 12
Child, Rik 53, 87, 100, 107, 126, 136,
         155, 189, 201, 220
Chittagong Hill Tracts 97
circular economy 218
circular migration 105
civil liberties xvi, 99, 103, 217
civil society 26, 88, 97, 103, 168,
         177–9, 199, 214
Clean Air in London 89, 172–3
clean air initiatives 89
Clean Clothes Campaign 96
Clean Vehicles Directive 149
Clegg, Nick 71

ClientEarth 147, 160
Climate and Migration Coalition 106
climate change xiv, xvi, 12–13, 23,
        68–9, 89–92, 94–5, 105–6,
        111–12, 122, 144, 152, 172,
        184, 190, 199, 207, 211, 214
Climate Outreach and Information
        Network (COIN) 106
Climate Parliament 142–3
closed-list 66
coalition 5, 10, 16, 18–19, 22–5, 28,
        30, 34–5, 42, 58, 67, 69–70,
        106, 155, 166, 185
co-decision 101, 107
Cohn-Bendit, Daniel 26–8, 31–2
Commission Flagship Initiative 97
Commissioner for Regional Affairs 88
commissioners 91
Committee on Citizen's Freedoms
        and Rights, Justice and Home
        Affairs (LIBE) 85
Committee on Employment and
        Social Affairs (EMPL) 85
Committee on Environment, Public
        Health and Food Safety
        (ENVI) 142, 154
Committee on Industry, External
        Trade, Research and
        Energy 85
Committee on International
        Trade 123
Common European Asylum
        System 98, 100, 102, 197
Commonwealth 110
Compass 76
Conservative MEPs 95, 147
conservative 13, 24–5, 63, 73, 95,
        109, 137, 147, 155, 158, 217
Conservatives 30, 53–4, 56, 61–2,
        103, 136
Constitutional Affairs Committee 85,
        88
Consultative Committee on
        Constitutional Reform 53

consumers 130, 171, 200, 218
Coordination of Green and Radical
        Parties 9–11
Cornwall xiii
corporate 95, 115–16, 122, 124,
        129–30, 170, 177, 182, 185,
        190, 192–3, 201–2, 207,
        215–16, 231
    social responsibility 95
co-secretary general 83
Council of Europe 51
Crepaz, Markus 67, 69, 79–80
Croatia 5–6, 30, 36, 38, 40
cross-party group on children's
        rights 100
Crystal Palace 85, 111
Curtice, John 57, 79
customs union 158
Cyprus 4, 22, 36, 38, 40, 228
Czech Republic 22, 24, 32, 36, 38,
        40, 47, 103

D
Daily Express 107
Dalits 97
Davis, Chris 172
De Gucht Report 53
De Gucht, Karel 53
Dearden, Nick 168–70, 174–8, 180–2
death penalty 97
Delegation for Relations with the
        Countries of South Asia
        (DSAS) 94, 97
Delli, Karima 102
democracy 4, 20, 27, 32, 40, 44, 50,
        63–5, 67, 70–1, 74–9, 98, 126,
        138, 157, 162, 170, 178, 180,
        211, 213, 232
Democratic Unionist Party
        (DUP) 158
Denmark 9, 11–12, 28, 36, 38, 40, 46,
        51, 61, 64, 66, 228–9
deportation 99, 109
development committee 142

Dhaka 95
Die Grünen 40, 60–1
directly elected mayor 138
displacement 98, 106
Doctors of the World 100
Dover 116
Dr. Feelgood 133
Dublin Regulation 101, 197
Dunleavy, Patrick 56, 68, 72–3,
        79–80
Duverger, Maurice 54–5, 78
Duverger's Law 55
Dylan, Bob 154

E
early day motion 185
earthquakes 146, 160
eastern Europeans 103, 107
Eastwood Free Festival 134
ecosystem xvi
Edgar Broughton Band 135
election xvi, 5, 7–9, 11, 13–15, 17,
        19–20, 22–3, 25–8, 30–1, 34–7,
        44, 46–8, 51–3, 55–8, 60–4,
        67–8, 71–3, 79, 83–4, 86–7,
        98–9, 116–17, 119, 125–6, 131,
        140–1, 159–60, 166, 168, 176,
        179, 182, 208, 230
    wrong winner 64
Electoral Reform Society 65, 76, 179,
        182
electoral reform 65, 72, 74, 76–7, 179,
        182
electoral system 4, 7, 9–10, 18, 33–4,
        45–6, 49, 51–3, 55, 57, 59,
        64, 66, 68, 70–2, 74, 79,
        83–4, 110, 117, 126, 128,
        140, 157, 166, 179, 184, 199,
        228–9
Emsis, Indulis 21
En Marche 32
Energy Efficiency of Buildings
        Directive 91

England 12, 20, 30, 43, 59, 76, 83–4,
        110, 120, 140–2, 146, 150,
        155–7, 160, 162, 165–6, 168,
        173, 176, 180–1, 184, 188,
        199–200, 202, 227–9
English Channel 229
environment xv, xvii, 12, 31, 78, 85–6,
        89–90, 106, 111–12, 123, 128,
        130, 142–4, 149, 154, 159, 161,
        166, 169, 172–3, 176, 183, 188,
        191, 201–2, 222–3
Environment, Public Health and Food
        Safety Committee xv, xvii,
        12, 31, 78, 85–6, 89–90, 106,
        111–12, 123, 128, 130, 142–4,
        149, 154, 159, 161, 166, 169,
        172–3, 176, 183, 188, 191,
        201–2, 222–3
Environmental Impact Assessment
        Directive (EIA) 85
Environmental Law
        Foundation (ELF) 86
Equality and Human Rights
        Commission (EHRC) 103
Estonia 36, 38, 40
EU
    agencies 91
    ambassadors 97
    asylum agency (EASO) 198
    Commissioner for Trade 96
    Social Fund 87
    Sustainability Strategy 91
EU4U! 91, 111
EU–Morocco Euro-Mediterranean
        Aviation Agreement 175
Eurocommunists 120
Europe 2020 92, 112
European
    Agency for Safety and Health at
        Work (EU-OSHA) 91
    Capital of Culture 138
    Council on Refugees and
        Exiles 102, 196, 198

European *cont.*
Council 102, 112, 120, 196, 198
Court of Justice 51, 53, 223
Economic Community (EEC) 51
elections 17, 22, 25–6, 28, 31,
35–6, 46, 51, 79, 83, 117, 176
1989 elections 5, 12, 14, 15, 34,
44, 46, 48, 53, 58, 79, 83, 117
External Action Service (EEAS) 97
Federation of Green Parties 15
Federation of National
Organisations Working
with the Homeless
(FEANTSA) 109
Foundation for Living and Working
Conditions 91
Free Alliance 20, 93, 131
Green Coordination 11, 83–4
Green Party (EGP) 5, 11, 20, 28,
29, 32, 36–7 (Table 1), 58, 83,
227–8, 230–5,
Health Insurance Card (EHIC) 107
Network of Equality Bodies
(Equinet) 104
Network on Statelessness 99
Parliament xv, 3–4, 6–7, 10–12,
14–15, 20, 24, 26, 30–3, 35,
44–7, 49–55, 57–8, 72, 78–9,
83–5, 88–91, 94–6, 101, 103,
105–6, 111–12, 115–21,
124–5, 127–8, 131, 141–4,
146–7, 149–50, 153–5, 160,
162, 173–5, 181, 188, 195,
198–202, 211, 214, 217–19,
221, 223, 229–31, 233–5
Training Foundation 91
Eurostar 117
Express 179

F
Facebook 74, 187, 220, 225
Farage, Nigel 117
Financial Transaction Tax 88, 192, 202

Finland 4–5, 16–17, 25, 28, 35–6, 38,
40, 61, 66, 228
first-past-the-post (FPTP) 4, 9, 13,
49, 52, 54–6, 58–61, 63–73,
83, 110, 126, 140, 157, 166,
228, 230
Fischer, Joschka 26
Fleetwood Mac 133
foodbanks 155
Forest Stewardship Council 171
fracking 144–6, 160, 166, 180, 211
France 4–9, 11–13, 15, 17, 26–7,
31–6, 38, 40, 48, 54, 58–60,
104, 146
free movement 106–7, 109–10, 124,
151–2, 176
free trade 122–3, 169
Fukushima nuclear accident 27

G
Gahrton, Per 44, 46, 119
garment and textile industry 95
Gauche Plurielle 59
GDP 170, 210
gender identity 101
general election xvi, 8–9, 13, 30, 34,
47–8, 53, 58, 60–2, 68, 71–3,
140, 166, 182, 208
2015 general election 34, 60
(Figure 3), 61, 71–3, 166
Generalised Scheme of
Preferences 95
Germanwatch Global Climate Risk
Index 94
Germany 3, 5–9, 11, 15, 17, 19, 27, 29,
35–6, 38, 40, 44–5, 51, 54,
60–1, 64, 66, 146, 187, 191,
219, 228, 235
Gini coefficient 70
Girling, Julie 172
Global Justice Now 168, 172, 174,
177–8, 180–1
Global South 122

globalisation 26, 115–16, 122–5, 130–1, 169, 192, 213, 222, 227
glyphosate 155
GMOs 154–5
Good Systems Agreement 76
government participation 18, 24, 25, 35
grassroots 27, 31, 72–5, 87, 91
Great Gathering for Voting Reform 73–4
Greater London Authority 84, 86
Greece 3, 6, 14, 29, 31, 36, 38, 41, 47, 197, 228
green grid 86
Green Group 8, 15, 43, 83, 94, 102, 106, 119–20, 169, 184, 194, 231, 233, 235
green jobs 88–92, 94, 112
Green Jobs Initiative 92
Green Party of England and Wales 20, 30, 43, 59, 76, 83, 120, 140, 142, 150, 157, 162, 165, 176, 180–1, 184, 199–200, 202, 227
Green Party Women 167
Green Work: Employment and Skills – The Climate Change Challenge 91
Green–Alternative Europe Link (GRAEL) 11, 83
greenhouse gas emissions see carbon emissions
Greens–European Free Alliance 20, 93
GSP+ 95
Guardian 140, 170, 175, 214

H
Habitats Directive 124
Hamburg 90
Harper, Robin 84
Harvard University 96
Hassi, Satu 25

Hautala, Heidi 25
Heath, Ted 53
Heathrow 88, 149
Hellyer, Paul 115
Hesse, Hermann 235
High Court 138
Himalayas 94–5
Home Office 105, 110
Honourable Friend 127
Hoskyns, Catherine 51, 78
Hothouses 91, 111
House of Commons 46, 50, 52, 56, 59, 71, 76, 78–9, 126, 157, 210, 224, 228, 230, 232, 236
House of Lords 127, 199, 211, 232
Housing Benefit 108
Hübner, Danuta 88
human rights defenders 97
Hungary 5–6, 32, 36, 38, 41, 103, 228

I
I Must Work Harder? 109
ice&fire 105
Ikea 171, 193
ILO Convention on Domestic Workers 105
immigration 5, 23, 61, 85, 98, 102, 104, 106, 165, 195
implementing regulation 107
indigenous communities 97
intergroups
    animal welfare 142, 150
    anti-racism and diversity 103
    LGBTI rights 142
    youth 91
International Centre for Integrated Mountain Development (ICIMOD) 95
International Labour Organization (ILO) 105, 112
International Lesbian, Gay, Bisexual, Trans and Intersex Association (ILGA) 101

Iraq War 139
Ireland 6, 11, 20, 24, 29, 32, 36, 39, 41,
        43, 47, 51, 56, 59, 64, 66, 110,
        146, 158, 199, 215, 224, 228–9
Irish Peace Process 142
Islam 103
Islamophobia 103
Israel 66, 153–4, 161
Israeli Defence Force (IDF) 153
Italy 5, 9–10, 13, 17, 29, 32, 35–6, 39,
        41, 51, 66, 101

J
Jerusalem 154, 161
Johnson, Boris 88
Johnson, Darren 86
Joint European Support for
        Sustainable Investment in City
        Areas (JESSICA) 88
Joly, Eva 26
Jones, Jenny 86, 104, 112, 179
Jordan, Klina 49, 74, 77
Jubilee Debt Campaign 168
'just transition' 92–3

K
Kelly, Petra 7
Kensington 173
Kingfisher 171
Kinnock, Stephen 75
Knapp, Andrew 57
Kosovo 18
Kyoto Protocol 69, 79, 190–1

L
Labour 20, 22, 34, 52–54, 56, 62–3,
        74, 76–7, 84, 87, 90–1, 97,
        105, 109–10, 112, 117, 127,
        136–9, 165, 167, 172, 177,
        179–80, 195–6, 203, 217
    for FPTP 54
    government 20, 84, 109, 117
Lalonde, Brice 7–8, 15

lamb 122
Lambert, Jean xv, 20, 51, 57–8, 83,
        111–13, 119, 172, 175, 181,
        183, 185, 196–7, 202, 230
Lambert, John 51, 78
Lancashire 166
Latvia 24, 28–9, 37, 39, 41, 46, 228
Latvian Farmers' Union 21, 29
Lawrence, Dave 134
Lebanon 100
Leblang, David 70
left-libertarianism 9–11, 21, 44, 45
Les Verts 40, 47–8, 58–9
Lexiteers 177
LGBT xvi, 232
Liberal Democrats 13, 30, 53, 61–2,
        71, 76, 165, 167, 172, 177
Lijphart, Arend 67, 69–70, 79–80
Lisbon Treaty 171, 214, 217
Lithuania 37, 39, 228
live exports 151–2, 161
Livingstone, Ken 88–9
Lobbying Act 168
lobbying 75, 117, 144, 149, 168,
        171–2, 181, 189, 212
Local Government Association 142
London Assembly 86–7, 89, 104
London Borough of
        Westminster 109
London Green Fund (LGF) 88
London House 88
Long, Tony 22, 26, 28, 53, 57, 68–9,
        71, 74, 85, 88, 94, 117, 119,
        121, 127, 133, 142, 150–3,
        155–6, 160, 169, 171–2, 178,
        181, 185, 189, 192, 195, 215,
        218, 220, 228
Lucas, Caroline xv, 20, 30, 57–9, 71,
        84, 89, 115, 118, 123, 131–2,
        139–40, 157, 159–60, 166,
        170–1, 175–6, 183–6, 190,
        192, 197, 199, 208, 228
Lucy's Law 151

Luxembourg 6, 14–16, 19, 28, 32, 35, 37, 39, 41, 48, 51, 100, 187, 215, 228
   Presidency 100

M
Macron, Emmanuel 32
Make Votes Matter 50, 72, 74, 78, 179
   local groups 74–5
Maldives 94–5
Malmström, Cecilia 96
Malta 4, 22, 31, 37, 39, 41, 47, 64, 66, 101
marginal seat 63–4, 68
Maritime Spatial Planning 150
Mayall, John 133
McAvan, Linda 172
McCarthy, Mike 116
McDonnell, John 76, 184, 199
McKenna, Patricia 119
Melilla 101
Member of the European Parliament (MEP) Heart Group 142
Member State 14, 98, 101, 107, 197–8, 215–16
Michael Chapman 135
microcredit schemes 97
Migrants' Rights Network 104
migration 98, 103, 105–6, 130, 166, 177, 197
Milton Keynes 116
Mitterrand, François 7, 13, 18
Moraes, Claude 172, 217
Morgan, Andrew 46, 79, 96, 159
Morocco 106, 174–5, 181
multipartism 62, 69, 72
multiparty 49, 55–6, 63
Muslim 103, 196
My Skype Family 105
Myanmar 99

N
National Action Plans for employment and social inclusion 90
National Assembly 13, 18, 59
National Children's Homes (NCH) 137
National Emissions Ceilings Directive 173
National Union of Teachers (NUT) 92
nature corridors 86
neoliberalism 125, 154, 169
Nepal 94
Netanyahu, Benjamin 154
The Netherlands 4, 6, 9–12, 16, 19, 29, 31–2, 35, 41, 51, 61, 64, 122, 146, 218, 228
New Labour 117, 137, 139
new social movements 9, 165
New Zealand 60–1, 64, 66
Newquay xiii
nongovernmental organisations (NGOs) 22, 95, 101, 165–7, 171–4, 177, 179, 184, 191, 199
North Africa 101
North Atlantic Treaty Organization (NATO) 18–19, 229
Northern Irish Greens 228–9, 233
nuclear power 9, 13, 18–19, 28, 61, 126

O
O'Grady, Frances 92–93
open-list 66 (Table 1)
Orellana, Salomon 69, 79
'own-initiative' report (INI) 93
Oxfam 84, 117
Oxford 126
ozone layer 12

P
Page 3 128
Pakistan 94–5, 100, 106
Palestine 142, 153–4, 161, 170, 181, 185
Palmeira Project 137
Pankhurst, Helen 76
Pannella, Marco 9

Paris Agreement 143–4, 160, 214–15,
    221
Parkin, Sara 43, 84
parliamentary chamber 127
Parliamentary Reform, The Case for 128
Partis Socialiste 59
party system 18, 54, 57
party-list proportional
    representation 141
passenger rights 149
Peel, John 135
Pennsylvania 145
People's Vote 130, 157
personal, social, health and economic
    education (PSHE) 128
Peshawar 97
pesticides 154–5, 168, 211
Petitions Committee 85, 105, 142
photovoltaics xiv
Platform for International Cooperation
    on Undocumented Migrants
    (PICUM) 100
Poland 22, 37, 39, 42, 47, 103
policy advisor 84
policymaking 65–9, 70–1, 198, 216–20
polluter pays principle 143
polluting industries 190
pollution xiii–xiv, xvi, 111, 143–4,
    146–8, 160, 172–4, 183,
    185–6, 201–2, 223
pork 122
Port Reception Facilities 150
Portugal 3, 6, 11, 14, 37, 39, 42, 66, 228
post-materialism 22, 45
Potočnik, Janez 172–3
Powell, Enoch 52
Precautionary Principle 143, 223
Preston New Road 166
principal speaker 140
Privy Council 127
proportional representation (PR) 4, 7,
    14, 18, 20, 33, 49–58, 60–1,
    64–77, 79–80, 83, 141, 157,
    168, 229–30

Prosser, Christopher 55–6, 79
Public and Commercial Services
    Union (PCS) 92

Q
Qualification Directive 101
Question Time 128

R
rainforests xvi
Ramsgate 151–2, 161
Rana Plaza 95–6
rapporteur x, 93, 101, 107, 109, 121,
    149, 168, 171, 180, 189, 191,
    197
ready-made garment (RMG)
    sector 95
Receptions Conditions
    Directive 102
Redcurrent Films 91, 111
Rees, Merlyn 52, 211, 224
referendum xiii, 47, 71–2, 128, 138,
    156–7, 176–9, 196, 207, 209,
    212–13
*Refugees and the Environment:
    The Forgotten Element of
    Sustainability* 106
refugees xvi, 88, 100, 102, 106,
    112, 154, 168, 183, 196,
    198
Regulation 1408/71 (on the co-
    ordination of social security
    between Member States),
    revision of 106
regulation xiv–xv, 23, 101, 106–8,
    125, 169–71, 181, 189–90,
    192–3, 197–8, 201, 219–20,
    223, 225
Remain 95, 104, 116, 120, 129–30,
    136, 156, 176–8, 230
Renewable Energy Directive xiv
renewable energy xiv, 69, 143, 192
renewables 220, 231
Right Honourable Member 127

rights to freedom of peaceful
assembly 168, 180
Ringen, Stein 179, 182
road safety 150
road transport 148
Rohingya 99, 185
Romania 20–1, 23, 37, 39, 42, 107
Rosenmöller, Paul 19, 31
Royal College of Occupational
Therapists 92
Royal Society for the Prevention
of Cruelty to Animals
(RSPCA) 153
Royal Society for the Protection of
Birds (RSPB) xvii, 178
Ruskin Spear, Roger 135
Russell, Caroline 89, 153

S
Safe Passage 102
safe seat 63–5
Sahara 174–5, 181
Sahrawi 174–5
Sainsbury's 136
Sangatte 104
Scotland x, 20, 47, 56, 59, 66, 77, 110,
146, 166, 185, 229
Scott Cato, Molly 30, 59, 75, 175,
177, 181–3, 193–5, 200, 207,
230
Scottish Greens 47, 228, 233
Scottish National Party (SNP) 62, 73,
76, 127, 180, 231
Scottish Parliament 84, 199, 232
SDP–Liberal Alliance 34, 62
Seattle 115–16
Sedgefield 63, 159
sewage xiii
Sheen, Michael 76
Sheffield vii, 166
single market xv, 122, 151–2, 158,
217–18, 222–3

single transferable vote (STV) 20, 66,
230
skateboards 119
Skinner, Dennis 52
Slovakia 22, 37, 39, 42, 103
Slovenia 22, 37, 39, 42
Social Democratic and Labour Party 63
Social Democrats 13, 19, 28, 42, 63,
120
social justice xvi, 8
Social Mobility Commission 129
solar xiv, 146
Sousek, Joe 74
South Downs 145
South East 20, 74, 84, 89, 116–17,
141, 146–7, 156, 160–2, 173,
181, 183, 190
Southend 133, 135
Southern Rail 150
Soviet Union 83
Space Oddity 135
Spain 3, 6, 11, 14, 23, 32, 37, 39, 42,
146, 150, 228
special interests 69
Spiders from Mars 135
Sri Lanka 94, 97
St Peter's 136, 141
Status Quo 133
Stop the Trucks 151
Strana Zélèny 83
Strasbourg 50, 108, 124, 185, 201
Straw, Jack 53
student movement 9, 26
substitute 85
Sun 128
supplementary vote 56
supply-chain compliance 95–6,
218–19, 223
Surly Bird 135
Sussex 145, 166, 176
Sweden 4, 11, 16, 29, 35, 37, 39, 43,
61, 66, 228–9

Swedish Democrats 103

T
tactical voting 62–3
Tampere Conclusions 104
Taylor, Keith xv, 73, 76, 89, 126,
    133–4, 139, 145, 148, 152,
    157, 161–2, 166, 172–3,
    175–6, 181, 183–4, 186,
    188–9, 200, 202, 230
Tazreen fire 95
Temporary Agency Work
    Directive 92
Thames Gateway 'green' initiative 86–7
Thatcher, Margaret 12
The Nice 133
The True Cost 96
third pole 94
third-country nationals 98, 102, 104
Timber Regulation 170–1
Tory 110, 224
Totnes 75–6
trade unions 90, 92–3, 96
Trades Union Congress (TUC) 92
Training for Seafarers 150
transport committee 120, 142,
    148–50, 190–2, 231
Treaty of Amsterdam 98
Treaty of Rome 49–50, 53
treaty 18, 49–51, 53, 85, 98, 111, 122,
    171, 175, 214, 217, 223
Tunisia 100
Turkey 103, 234
turnout 17, 67, 72, 79
two-round system 34

U
UK Independence Party (UKIP) 30,
    61–2, 73, 76, 84, 103, 107,
    156, 167
Union of Greens and Farmers 21, 29,
    41

United Nations (UN)
    climate framework 106
    Development Programme
        (UNDP) 91
    migration forum conference 106
undocumented migrants 99–100,
    196
United States (US) 60, 64, 70, 145,
    153–4, 174, 186, 190, 214,
    219
universal credit 155
University of East London 86
Unlock Democracy 76
UNRWA 154, 161
Utrecht 166

V
Values Party (New Zealand) 60
Vējonis, Raimonds 29
Visegrád Group 103
voting reform 73–4
Voting Reform Team 74

W
Wales 12, 20, 30, 43, 56, 59, 66,
    76–7, 83, 110, 120, 140, 142,
    146, 150, 157, 162, 165–6,
    176, 180–1, 184, 199–200,
    202, 227–9
War on Want 168, 174
war 70, 139, 159, 168, 174, 185, 196
welfare state 68–9, 155
West Dorset 63–4
West, Pete 15, 30, 45, 48, 51, 54, 59,
    63–4, 136, 145, 153, 219
Westminster 59, 72, 109, 115, 125–6,
    128, 138, 166–7, 172, 175,
    177–80, 217
wildlife xiv, xvii, 143
Willey, Fred 52
Williams, Richard 102, 196, 198,
    224

Wilson, Harold 53
Winchester Town Hall 116–17
Winter, Owen 49, 74
Women Ambassadors 106
women's empowerment 97
Women's Equality Party 76
Woodin, Mike 140, 159
Working Time Directive 92, 108–9,
        113, 124
World Health Organization
        (WHO) 147, 155, 173,
        188–90, 201

World Trade Organization
        (WTO) 84, 131, 152, 210
World Wide Fund for Nature
        (WWF) xvii, 171–2, 178
Wright, Vincent 57

Y
Your Vote Counts 84

Z
Ziggy Stardust 135
zoo animal welfare 151

ACKNOWLEDGEMENTS

Making a book like this is harder than you might think. The editors would not have been able to do this without the hard work of all the writers and contributors. That goes without saying, but it is worth doing so nonetheless.

Special thanks must also go to the team at London Publishing Partnership: without Sam Clark and Richard Baggaley's guidance and expertise, you may not be holding this book in your hands today; and without Ellen White's masterful and diligent work, you definitely wouldn't be.

Natalie Bennett would like to thank Simon Birkett, Nick Dearden and Tony Long, who generously gave their time to share their memories of working with the Green MEPs; Danny Bates in Jean Lambert's office, for sharing contacts and ideas; and Molly Scott Cato, for her thoughts.

James Brady would like to thank his wife, Sarah; his daughter, Chloë; and his comrade Neil for their patience and support. He also extends his sincere thanks to Liam and the Green MEPs for having faith in his editorial energy and passion for books.

Reinhard Bütikofer would like to thank the GPEW for continuing to proudly fly the Green flag under much adversity, and his great team for their support with his chapter.

Samir Jeraj would like to thank Joanna Eckersley for her help in researching his chapter.

Klina Jordan and Owen Winter would like to thank Joe Sousek and Mary Southcott, whose joint report *The Many Not the Few: Proportional Representation and Labour in the 21st Century* provided key research for their chapter. They would also particularly like to thank the Joseph Rowntree Reform Trust as well as Mark and Marian Tucker for their support.

Tony Juniper would like to thank Maddie Juniper for assistance in research into the role of EU agreements in improving UK environmental quality.

Jean Lambert wishes to offer her warm thanks to her family, staff and the Greens/EFA group advisors for their support over the years, and to the many wonderful people she has worked with on specific issues.

Caroline Lucas would like to thank Matthew Butcher for his help with her chapter, and the constituents, campaigners and activists who have made her work in Brussels and Westminster possible.

Wolfgang Rüdig would like to thank the current and past staff of the European Green Party (EGP) in Brussels as well as representatives of green parties throughout Europe for their patience and willingness to answer numerous queries over many years.

Molly Scott Cato would like to take this opportunity to say a big thank-you to all the wonderful people who have worked with her since 2014. Although politicians are the ones out in public, everybody knows that they wouldn't achieve anything without their staff. Although she has written her chapter, she wants to make it clear that the work it is based on is a joint effort with her team, especially Andrew Bell, Steve Hynd and Tom Scott.

Keith Taylor would like to thank his wife and family as well as his loyal and dedicated staff.

Liam Ward would like to thank his friends and family, and in particular his partner, Emma, whose patience and support helped alleviate his almost constant fear that the book was never going to happen. Liam would also like to thank the Green MEPs for giving him the opportunity to edit his first book.